SOUREI

SOURED ON THE SYSTEM

Disaffected Men in 20th Century American Film

Robert T. Schultz

McFarland & Company, Inc., Publishers
Jefferson, North Carolina, and London

LIBRARY OF CONGRESS CATALOGUING-IN-PUBLICATION DATA

Schultz, Robert T.
   Soured on the system : disaffected men in 20th century
American film / Robert T. Schultz.
      p.   cm.
   Includes bibliographical references and index.

   ISBN 978-0-7864-6991-8
   softcover : acid free paper ∞

   1. Men in motion pictures.   2. Alienation (Social psychology)
in motion pictures.   3. Motion pictures — Social aspects — United
States — History — 20th century.   I. Title.
PN1995.9.M46S34   2012
791.43'65211— dc23   2012022636

BRITISH LIBRARY CATALOGUING DATA ARE AVAILABLE

On the cover: Ron Livingston (left), David Herman and Ajay Naidu
in the 1999 *Office Space* (© 20th Century–Fox/Photofest)

Manufactured in the United States of America

*McFarland & Company, Inc., Publishers
   Box 611, Jefferson, North Carolina 28640
   www.mcfarlandpub.com*

For Adeline:
A principled and independent spirit,
always conscious of "Mother Culture."

Table of Contents

Acknowledgments

    This book became an idea about 12 years ago, at the close of the twentieth century. I started jotting down ideas for an article that I eventually wrote but held on to for far too long. I was doing what I tell students in my writing courses authors do when we compose preliminary drafts: discover what we think by writing it and reading it so we can then rewrite, and rewrite and rewrite to communicate effectively to others what it is we believe we have to say, our contribution to what should be a civil but perhaps spirited conversation about ideas and evidence. Once I decided to let go of that article and it was accepted for publication, I began to conceptualize the book and write drafts of some of the chapters that appear here. During these early years I don't recall doing what I began to do about three years ago: talking, sometimes incessantly and at length, to friends, colleagues and family about what I began to refer to as representations of discontented and disaffected men in American films. I must first acknowledge, then, all those poor but patient souls who for brief moments surely felt trapped on my ship as I dwelled on and chased my leviathan as passionately — and perhaps as maniacally — as Captain Ahab did his whale and Gordon Gekko (Michael Douglas) his next illicit stock deal. I trapped them in kitchens and dining rooms and restaurants, libraries and offices and common areas adjoining offices, even public restrooms. They didn't seem to mind. But, of course, I was blinded by my enthusiasm. So, thanks to all of you who must remain nameless due to your sheer numbers.

    Two close friends deserve special thanks, however, for the many times they put up with me. Tari Renner and Alfonso Reynoso were sometimes literally trapped. I can't recall how many times Tari sat patiently in booths or at tables in restaurants and listened to me compare Batman and characters like him to heroes in American westerns who are in society but not of it. Al had it even worse. On annual canoe trips in the boundary waters between the United States and Canada, he listened to me around campfires, on portages, and in a canoe on the water. Two people looking for moose, nesting bald eagles, otters and other wildlife are supposed to be quiet. When one person in the canoe talks about Tyler Durden and Bartleby the scrivener, the other no doubt sometimes wonders why he signed on for the trip. I apologize to Al for too often breaking our much-coveted silence.

A couple of colleagues at Illinois Wesleyan University and some anonymous peer reviewers for McFarland and *The Journal of Popular Culture* read drafts that were organized differently from the material finally incorporated into this manuscript. I thank the reviewers for their comments and their recommendations to publish what they read. Colleagues Chuck Springwood and April Schultz read early drafts of some of the chapters. Additional thanks, Chuck, for being one of the many people who listened to me talk about these films on numerous occasions. April read drafts of the introduction, the two chapters on the 1940s and 1950s, and the conclusion. Her suggestions were insightful and much appreciated. Two friends, David W. Noble (also an intellectual mentor) and Bill Mittlefeldt, suggested that some of the characters I discuss lack cultural alternatives and that fact limits the characters' potential actions. Their insights caused me to expand my analysis of a number of films.

I first wrote about the films *It's a Wonderful Life* (1946) and *Johnny Guitar* (1954) 22 years ago in relation to a different thesis. The article, "Celluloid History: Postwar Society in Postwar Popular Culture," appeared in the spring 1990 volume 31 of *American Studies*. Portions of that article appear in sections of chapters 1 and 2. More recently, I analyze the short story "Bartleby, the Scrivener" and the novel (1996) and the film (1999) versions of *Fight Club* in "White Guys Who Prefer Not To: From Passive Resistance ('Bartleby') to Terrorist Acts (*Fight Club*)." The article appears in the June 2011 volume 44 of *The Journal of Popular Culture*. Material from the article appears in the introduction and chapter 4. I thank these journals for permission to reuse the material in the revised versions herein.

Researchers depend on librarians' knowledge and skills. That fact rang true for me during the years I worked on the manuscript. The Ames Library faculty and staff at Illinois Wesleyan have secured for me crucial materials at great speed. I worked most closely with University Archivist and Special Collections Librarian Meg Miner. She taught me how to get what I needed, and at times when I had to go through the same process to acquire something else but forgot how to do it, she patiently taught me again. Invisibly and rapidly Circulation Services Manager Tony Heaton located electronic copies of numerous materials even when I wasn't able to provide him with all of the information he needed. I would click a button and the document would appear shortly thereafter. University Librarian Karen Schmidt met with me, talked on the phone with me, contacted lawyers for me and exchanged email messages with me regarding copyright information and issues. Thanks to you all for your efficiency and your professionalism.

Some of my colleagues helped me in a variety of ways. The Illinois Wesleyan Faculty Development Committee and Provost Jonathan Green provided me with time and financial support when I needed it. I thank my colleagues on the committee for the time and Jonathan for the movie stills that illustrate the book. Colleague, friend and Associate Dean of Faculty Irv Epstein called me one year and said he thought this project sounded interesting and suggested I propose to present a faculty colloquium. I said "no." He called again a year later and I said "yes." Irv's enthusiasm about and support for the project was one of a few things that happened at that time to give me the incentive to work like a fiend to complete the book. Thanks, Irv. The work you've done during your years as Associate Dean is much appreciated.

Finally, I want to thank those who mean the most to me: April, Adeline, Willy and Scout. They have watched many movies with me, including some of those I analyze in these pages. Movies viewed in our home — like politics, religion and everything else — are often topics of lively discussion and even intense debate. I wouldn't want it any other way. April and Adeline participate with me in the discussion and the debate. Willy sleeps on the floor and sometimes asks me, by placing his long nose in the palm of my hand, to scratch him on the head. Scout watches some scenes and barks at the screen, but for the most part she just tries to get me to throw her a ball. Now that this project is finished, I promise to do more of that.

Preface

Soured on the System is a study of cultural representations of discontented and disaffected middle-class men in American film from the end of World War II to the turn of the twenty-first century. Although the book focuses on the postwar years, the introduction reveals the historical and cultural roots of a significant theme in American culture that gets scant attention in film studies or in American culture studies generally. Much has been written concerning the changing norms associated with masculinity and gender relations, but writers have placed little emphasis on the historical roots, development and persistence of a significant source of male discontent and disaffection within changing historical contexts. Despite significant cultural and historical change in a dynamic corporate capitalist American society, men's discontent and disaffection are often depicted as being rooted in mundane, uncreative labor over which they have little control. Moreover, combined with the nature of work and one's lack of control over what he does and how he does it, disaffected men in the late twentieth century are often represented as questioning and rejecting the cultural assumption that one should be content spending his life doing such labor in exchange for monetary compensation that enables him to consume material goods. While excellent books examine cultural representations of the historical struggles of blue-collar men on the big screen and in American culture generally, studies devoted to manifestations of discontented and disaffected middle-class and upper–middle-class men tend to focus on race and gender issues, especially since the 1970s. By focusing on the cultural terrain of film, *Soured on the System* analyzes cultural representations of men's discontent and disaffection in relation to mundane, repetitive white-collar work in an increasingly organized society and to the cultural assumption that happiness and contentment are to be discovered through consumption.

1

While the chapters are devoted to an analysis of postwar films, the introduction focuses on early twentieth-century short films and silent and "talkie" features, and on late nineteenth and early twentieth-century American literary texts, some of which predate the development of motion picture technology, and many of which were adapted into short and feature movies. Cultural representations of discontented and disaffected men first appeared in these literary texts. The dramatic social and economic changes of the late nineteenth and early twentieth centuries were accompanied by a growth in literacy and publishing, and many of those literary texts feature white middle-class protagonists and other characters whose experiences resonated with those of readers and with early twentieth-century moviegoers. The discussion of these early literary and film texts therefore sets the stage for the analysis of postwar films in the chapters that follow the introduction. Although film content changes dramatically throughout the twentieth century and the films studied here reflect those changes, striking consistency is evident regarding the general sources of men's discontent and disaffection. The analysis of cultural representations of discontented and disaffected men over an extended period of time reveals the nature of that consistency while also emphasizing the shifting historical contexts that at times cause men's discontent and disaffection to be manifested in diverse ways. The consistency, however, is apparent in characters' lack of agency and control in an increasingly organized society where authority becomes embedded in private corporate, as well as government, institutions.

The introduction sets the stage, but each of the four chapters that follow contains an in-depth analysis of selected popular and historically significant films that reveal the persistence of the book's major theme but also its adaptation to new historical circumstances. The analysis of each film is situated within the changing historical contexts of the second half of the twentieth century, the years when the films were produced, released and originally viewed by Americans sitting in theaters across the country. Chapter one situates the analysis of *It's a Wonderful Life* (1946) and *The Man in the Gray Flannel Suit* (1955) within the changing social and economic context of the early postwar years. These were years when corporations wielded increased influence over people's lives and in society generally, when social critics lamented men's declining autonomy and authority in an increasingly organized society, and when prominent politicians emphasized that men needed to adjust to the changes and instructed women to make the American home a refuge where men would be rejuvenated after experiencing the anxieties associated with daily life in modern corporate bureaucracies. Chapter two continues the analysis of films in these years of significant structural and social change, but more emphasis is placed on the political context of the postwar red scare known as McCarthyism and the constraints placed on filmmakers as a result of that political environment. The analysis of *Force of Evil* (1948) and *Johnny Guitar* (1954) makes it clear that filmmakers whose work critiqued declining individual autonomy and increasing corporate influence had to veil their critiques in the gangster and western genres to avoid having their names added to the Hollywood blacklists. Chapter three analyzes four films released in the turbulent years of the late 1960s and early 1970s: *The Graduate* (1967), *Easy Rider* (1969), *Joe* (1970) and *Dirty Harry* (1971). Each of these films contains characters that respond very differently to the realities of unfulfilling work, declining autonomy, and increased materialism in the postwar corporate order, and the film narratives are influenced in part by historical developments such as the Vietnam War, the emergence of the counterculture, the successes of the civil rights movement, the women's movement, and the increased creative liberty filmmakers experienced when the movie rating system replaced the Motion Picture Production Code. Some of these films contain elements of the violence and militancy associated with discontented and disaffected men evident in the late twentieth-century films discussed in chapter four. Although a variety of films produced in the 1980s and 1990s are discussed in this final chapter, the analysis is devoted to the popular films *American Beauty* (1999), *Office Space* (1999) and *Fight Club* (1999). The three college-educated, discontented and disaffected protagonists in these films are somehow awakened to the reality of their mind-numbing and unfulfilling work and act to change their situations, and two of the characters critique the idea that the ability to consume material goods is just and satisfying compensation for spending one's life engaged in such work.

I decided to write a book on cultural representations of predominantly white, middle-class men in the twentieth century, with a particular emphasis on the second half of the century, for three major reasons. First, when early film producers sought to expand their market from the ethnic, working-class neighborhoods where their film shorts were shown in nickelodeons, they targeted an expanding white middle-class audience in order to gain respectability for their industry and to increase profits. Producers catered to that market as they shifted production from New York to California and theater palaces were constructed in urban areas from coast to coast. Although many early feature films had working-class themes, the expanding white middle class represented the most lucrative market. Consequently, the aspirations, anxieties and experiences of the expanding middle class became significant and pervasive themes in American films. Second, some authors I discuss in the introduction have written excellent studies on representations of working-class men and working-class families in American film. Others have written numerous works on race, class and gender issues during relatively short historical periods and in specific decades. I saw there was a place for a book on cultural representations of predominantly middle-class men with a primary focus on the five decades when the middle class expanded more rapidly and more broadly than at any time in American history. These were decades when more Americans achieved middle-class status and stability, but when, ironically, men are often depicted as being significantly discontented and disaffected during the half century of the country's greatest growth and prosperity. Third, studies of men and representations of men tend to focus on what we can learn about the nature of manhood and masculinity during years of significant social change, such as the turbulent 1960s and early 1970s. *Soured on the System* is based on a different premise: what we can learn about the sources of men's discontent and disaffection as they are represented in the medium of popular film during years of turbulent change *and* relative stability. The long-term focus reveals significant continuity with the theme of declining independence and agency that emerged in the late nineteenth century and intensified in the increasingly organized and centralized corporate-capitalist society of the postwar years.

Introduction

The Roots and Early Cultural Representations of Discontented and Disaffected Men, 1853–1945

As the United States expanded both geographically and economically in the nineteenth century, the demand for lawyers increased as more property changed hands and as more business deals were made. These lawyers needed scriveners to make multiple copies of the legal documents generated for each business transaction. In 1853 a quiet young man named Bartleby secured a position as a scrivener with one of those lawyers and dutifully and meticulously copied without complaint until one day he refused, informing his employer he "preferred not" to copy any longer. He first refused to check his copies with the lawyer. He then refused to copy another word. He remained in the office building day and night, preferring not to leave when the lawyer told him he must. Eventually and against his will, he was removed from the building and placed in an asylum, where he preferred not to eat and died of starvation, preferring not to continue his bleak existence. More than a century later in 1967, a recent college graduate named Benjamin Braddock was adrift in a culture that prescribed he should do something with himself: go to graduate school to study a subject that would then define him, think about "plastics," get a meaningless white-collar job and exist much like his upper–middle-class parents and their friends — drinking cocktails, smoking cigarettes, and basking in American materialism. Rather than make a decision that would commit him to such an unappealing fate, he lounged around his parents' house all summer, floated in the pool, started smoking, had an extended and excruciatingly meaningless and unfulfilling affair with a married alcoholic woman the same age as his parents (a friend of the family), fell in love with the woman's daughter, rescued her from a wedding she did not want to go through with, and rode off with her in the back seat of a bus and into an ambiguous future. About thirty years after Benjamin's ordeal, a nameless college graduate had a well-paying job, one from which he received no satisfaction and that was arguably immoral: he spent his days crunching numbers to decide if it would be cheaper for his company to let some people die in defective cars rather than recall and repair the entire line of vehicles. He tried to find happiness through conspicuous consumption and by joining therapy groups for terminally ill patients, even though he was not one himself. But unlimited consumption and trying to connect with dying people could not fill the void in his meaningless, empty life. It was out of character for him to take control of his life and move it in a new direction, so he developed an assertive and aggressive alternative personality, organized other discontented and disaffected men into clubs where they beat each other to a pulp, and then transformed the clubs into terrorist cells where the men began to carry out a secret project to destroy the society from which they were disaffected and to obliterate the historical memory of it so it could never again be resurrected.

Bartleby, Benjamin and the nameless college graduate are not real men, of course. They are three of a multitude of fictional characters that exist in the present as well as the past, cultural representations of discontented and disaffected American men from the mid–nineteenth century to the end of the twentieth.[1] *Soured on the System* is a study of such cultural representations of discontented and disaffected predominantly white, middle-class men in twentieth-century American films. When Dustin Hoffman portrayed the Benjamin Braddock character in the now classic sixties film *The Graduate* (1967), and when Ed Norton played author Chuck Palahniuk's narrator in the 1999 film version of Palahniuk's novel *Fight Club* (1996), they did so under historical circumstances much different from those that existed when Herman Melville created the Bartleby character. Despite 150 years of dramatic historical change, however, cultural representations of discontented and disaffected men often share some common themes, although they also diverge in ways rooted in the more particular historical situations out of which the cultural representations were created.

The purpose of this book is to analyze how predominantly white, middle-class men are represented in a central artifact of twentieth-century American culture, major motion pictures, with a concentration on the late 1940s through the end of the twentieth century. For it was in the post–

World War II years that social and cultural critics and important American politicians commented on what they realized had become a dominant reality of American life: men's declining agency in the modern corporate order, where business leaders, their managers, and seemingly abstract historical and economic forces curtailed men's control over their lives at work and in society generally.

Some circumstances that significantly curtail or deny the agency of men at work and elsewhere in society, and men's frustration with those circumstances, predate the invention of motion pictures and the creation of the movie industry. The roots of the themes that I define and argue are central to understanding the sources of men's discontent and disaffection in postwar American culture are evident in literary and film texts much earlier: in literature published in the late nineteenth century, in early short films produced during the first years of the motion picture industry, and in the silent and sound ("talkies") feature films of the 1920s and 1930s.[2] The continuity between these early cultural texts and films produced since the end of the war is associated with men's agency in society, or lack of it, with their ability to act to control their own lives and, in many cases, to influence society in an increasingly corporate and bureaucratic world. In various late nineteenth- and early twentieth-century cultural texts men's agency is depicted as being on the decline, and that decline is associated predominantly with the reorganization of social and economic life that accompanied the corporate reconstruction of American capitalism. That transformation began in the mid–nineteenth century and intensified in the early twentieth. Following the war, social commentators and politicians recognized the transformation as being complete, although commentators critiqued the change while mainstream politicians tended to accept it as the new reality of American life.

In American films produced before the mid–1930s, men are often represented as facing significant, even insurmountable barriers within the social and economic system. This is the case in many short and feature films produced in the 1900s, 1910s, and 1920s, movies often adapted from and influenced by naturalist and realist literary texts that place characters within the context of seemingly abstract natural and historical forces beyond their control. During the Depression decade of the 1930s, however, and influenced by the diverse calls for reform and the actual reforms that occurred in those years, films are more likely to feature protagonists who wield significant influence over events and circumstances even when they face seemingly insurmountable barriers. In such films men do not have to

accept their fate within the system; they can influence the system themselves, and they rely on rhetoric associated with D⸻⸻⸻⸻ ⸻d earlier
Progressive-e⸻ ⸻concen-
trated econom⸻ ⸻ich Pro-
gressive-era r⸻ ⸻entieth-
century rhetor⸻ ⸻oducers
who struggled ⸻orations
and corrupt p⸻ ⸻rhetoric
is more appare⸻ ⸻l to the
integration of ⸻ral to a
film like Frank
    In the lat⸻ ⸻iticians
abandoned suc⸻ ⸻repre-
sented by Illinoi⸻ ⸻didate
Adlai Stevenso⸻ ⸻d but
acknowledged a ⸻uch as
William H. Wh⸻ ⸻sman.
In an address to ⸻ege in
1955, Stevenson ⸻⸻⸻⸻⸻ American women to create sanctuaries in their
homes, to make the American home a refuge for men whose independence
and agency Stevenson asserted was significantly diminished in the organized
corporate bureaucratic society that the United States had become, a system
Paul Goodman assailed for not wanting "real men," and one Stevenson
talked about as creating a social and psychological "crisis" for American
men while choosing not to name the source of the crisis directly as Goodman and other social critics did.[4]

    Unsurprisingly, in major motion pictures produced in the postwar
years, such as *The Man in the Gray Flannel Suit* (1956), men are depicted
as negotiating their way within the organized system at work and within
the new frontier of American consumer culture. Men were expected to be
complacent employees and active consumers in the organized system now
represented as an inevitable reality. We will see, however, that even in the
oppressive political climate of the late 1940s and the 1950s, the years of
Hollywood blacklists and politically opportunistic anti-communist politicians such as Joe McCarthy and Richard Nixon, some filmmakers created
movies that not only critiqued aspects of that system and men's lack of
agency in it, but also questioned the seemingly inevitable nature of an
organized system that demanded individual employees and independent
businessmen (and women) become easily replaceable cogs in the wheels of

the postwar corporate order. When male and sometimes female characters confront and oppose that system directly in films of the forties and fifties, their opposition is veiled in the gangster and western genres, while men in traditional dramas tend to negotiate their way gingerly through the system in order to avoid making waves so they can keep their jobs and, therefore, the security they provide for their families.

In many cases, men's discontent and disaffection are depicted as being associated with a mundane existence devoid of fulfilling, meaningful work in a suffocating business culture and, more broadly and increasingly in the second half of the twentieth century, in an expanding consumer culture that values purchasing things over creatively producing them.[5] A significant dimension of many characters' situations, then, is the monotonous, sometimes dehumanizing, and even immoral nature of their work and their lack of control over what they do and how they do it. The characters have agency; they act. But how they act, their resistance or accommodation to accepted social practices and the cultural values associated with those practices, is shaped dramatically by their experiences at work and in relation to the nature of work and to the realities of social and economic life as they are represented in the films. The characters are not entirely stuck in their social situations, but their choices and actions are often limited, even severely restricted, because they exist in situations not of their own making and depend on others for their security because their security is tied to their jobs. They consequently must live and act in those situations unless they resist the dominant agency and power of others and rebel against the confining and sometimes suffocating and degrading nature of their situations.

The characters that represent American men in the films I discuss in the following chapters have relationships with other characters — fellow workers, women, minorities and children, for example — and their relationships with these characters sometimes compound the men's anxieties and get them to express their frustrations in divergent ways. But the central thing that influences their anxieties and frustrations and the discontent and disaffection that result from those anxieties and frustrations is their relationship to the industrial and, in the late twentieth century, increasingly postindustrial society that shapes their opportunities, their work routines, even their personal and social relationships, as well as the cultural assumptions they either internalize or resist to various degrees and in diverse ways. The more family ties the characters have, the less likely they are to resist the authority of others and, in some cases, to rebel against society itself.

Like the movies they create, filmmakers are situated in history, and the content and themes of their cultural creations are shaped but not determined by the historical circumstances within which they create. This historicity is especially true of major motion pictures, whose producers and directors seek wide distribution of their artistic but commercial products. For films to be popular with general audiences, they must resonate in various ways with the realities of moviegoers' lives: with their social situations and relationships, with the values they hold, and with the desires and anxieties they often share. For this reason major motion pictures marketed to general audiences provide a revealing and important, albeit singular, cultural window through which to view and understand discontented and disaffected men in American culture.[6]

Beyond Manhood and White Masculinity

My historical focus in *Soured on the System* results in part from what I see as the primarily conceptual nature of cultural studies of American men. In many of these studies, men's agency is subordinated to the actions of anthropomorphized concepts that seemingly determine historical processes and outcomes. These studies focus on the concepts of American manhood and white masculinity, and the concepts rather than real men or actors in roles that represent real men become the major characters in the authors' narratives. Whether an author uses the term masculinity or manhood, she or he basically refers to the same thing: the norms that men are socialized to internalize and act on in their everyday lives. According to these authors, the norms are associated with being inner-directed, individualistic, self-made, in control, principled, a loyal comrade to other men, and even homophobic.[7] In Michael Kimmel's otherwise informative survey *Manhood in America*, for example, the concept of "manhood" was born in the laissez-faire social and economic environment of the early nineteenth century and grew up to control men's actions in predominantly negative ways, even after "manhood" changed its name to "masculinity" at the turn of the twentieth century, when one's manhood was no longer a given in the new corporate industrial order but continuously had to be displayed and proven to others.[8] Kimmel's purpose is to hold "American history up to the prism of gender," but by so doing his prism sometimes refracts the light too radically from men's actions and what motivates them, reducing both motives and actions to the assumed internalized concepts of manhood and masculinity.[9] The concepts are the major historical agents, evident in statements like the following one: "American manhood ... suddenly felt desperate, clinging to whatever it could find, just trying to hold on."[10]

Try as these authors do to ground their studies historically, they portray men's actions and motives as resulting primarily from the abstract historical agents of manhood and masculinity rather than from the circumstances of actual men or the characters who represent them. This is especially true of studies that focus on specific historical moments when traditional white-male privileges have declined due to the social, economic and political gains that resulted from the successful struggles of women and minorities. In these studies men respond to such changes but do so in limited and predominantly negative ways, for their responses are restrained significantly by the dominant and controlling historical agents of white masculinity and manhood.[11] Some authors who restrict their analyses to studying these concepts at such moments of change see the concepts as significantly threatened, meaning that the norms associated with the concepts are no longer viable ones for men to live by due to historical changes that reduced but by no means eradicated men's historical position of privilege. These authors describe a white "masculinity" in crisis, a white "manhood" in flux, and a white male "backlash."[12] The purpose of many of these studies is either to document and condemn the racism and sexism associated with "white straight masculinity," as Fred Pfeil does, and, in the process, to participate in its potential "reconfiguration," or to describe a post–1970s white masculinity in crisis due to the successes of the civil rights and women's movements of the 1960s and 1970s, as Sally Robinson does.[13] Those successes, Robinson argues, "marked" white men as "white" in the late twentieth century just as African Americans and women so often have been reduced to being marked by their race or their gender. Robinson claims that the "political," meaning the political successes of the civil rights and women's movements, is "responsible for the marking of white masculinity in the first place."[14]

Soured on the System does not deny that those successes exacerbated men's anxieties, and the book contributes, I believe, to our understanding of them. My focus, however, is on how men are represented in American culture as negotiating, confronting, and sometimes opposing the social and economic realities within which they find themselves, and on how they behave in relation to cultural values they are expected to internalize and act on as natural, values sometimes associated with white masculinity, but also those assumed to be more universal, such as consumerism, and that sometimes transcend race, class, gender, age or other categorizations.[15] I make neither the concept of manhood nor white masculinity central to my analysis in *Soured on the System,* then, because doing so would limit the scope of my analysis and the concept would take on a life of its own, becoming the protagonist in my narrative as it has in the narratives of others. I want to make it clear that I think the two authors, Sally Robinson and Michael S. Kimmel, whose books represent some of the most extensive work on white masculinity and manhood, contribute much to our understanding of white-male culture by discussing the norms associated with masculinity and manhood and by documenting the continued prevalence of some of those norms in American culture. The subject of *Soured on the System,* however, is cultural representations of predominantly white middle-class men, and my purpose is different from Kimmel's and Robinson's. I do not attempt to understand how men's anxieties and frustrations are shaped exclusively by prevalent values associated only with white masculinity or manhood. Rather, I seek to understand the sources of men's discontent and disaffection generally and how men are represented as acting or failing to act when they realize the sources of their discontent. Consequently, when issues such as gender and race are evident in the films I analyze here, and when they are significant to the historical contexts within which particular films were produced, my analysis includes them.

While researching and writing *Soured on the System* it became apparent that men's understanding of the sources of their discontent and their expressions of it are not exclusively shaped by the norms associated with masculinity and manhood. The major sources of men's discontent and disaffection are sometimes the same sources associated with women's discontent and disaffection. For the male office workers in *Office Space* (1999), for example, and for the female temporary office workers in *Clockwatchers* (1997), the source is essentially the same: the men and women exist in corporate cultures that deny them agency; they have little or no control over what they do and how they do it, and that common reality causes them to be both discontented and disaffected. What others might read as a lack of male control in *Office Space,* I see as a lack of control for anyone in such an environment. When the characters' responses to their situations in the two films are sometimes to engage in the Luddite-like destruction of office equipment that contributes to their drudgery, the militancy should be considered neither masculine nor feminine. This is not to deny that the ways characters sometimes express their militancy or other actions are in some ways gendered. They are. But the characters' discontent and subsequent decisions to engage in even minor militant acts result not from masculinity or femininity in the abstract, or from an unrealized ideal associated with masculinity or femininity, but from the structured social environments and the corporate cultures where they spend so many hours of their lives and with so little control of what they do and how they do it.[16]

My analysis, then, is not limited to the facts that the characters in these films are predominantly male and white and middle class. Rather, I emphasize what the characters do when they find themselves accepting, negotiating, confronting and sometimes opposing the social and economic realities they face as they work and live in the increasingly organized system of the twentieth century. Their relationships with women and minorities (much more often the former than the latter) are sometimes represented as significant aspects of men's social realities and their discontent. When they are, I analyze those relationships when they help to further our understanding of men's discontent and disaffection. But I do not restrict my analysis to the prisms of race (white) and gender (male) because doing so would sometimes obfuscate rather than illuminate our understanding of men's discontent and disaffection in twentieth-century American culture.

Cultural Backdrop

That representations of discontented and disaffected men in American culture preceded the development of moving picture technology, the establishment of the motion picture industry, and the corporate reconstruction of American capitalism associated with the last three decades of the nineteenth century is evident in Melville's "Bartleby" tale as early as 1853. Although the pace of social and economic change associated with the commercial and industrial transformation of the country increased significantly after the Civil War, the seeds of that change were becoming apparent before the war and are evident in the Melville story. Cultural representations of men's decreasing autonomy, however, which is directly related to their discontent and disaffection, becomes especially apparent in and widely disseminated through the realist and naturalist literature of the late nineteenth and early twentieth centuries. The publication of this literature coincided with the transformation of everyday life for Americans in these years, and much of the literature emphasizes the experiences of ordinary working-class and middle-class people. I begin with a short discussion of "Bartleby" because I see Melville's tale as the first to represent discontented and disaffected men whose lives are significantly influenced and controlled by others in the changing economy and society of the second half of the nineteenth century. Much of the fiction associated with realism and naturalism in the late nineteenth and early twentieth centuries continues that emphasis, and early filmmakers adapted a variety of these literary texts into film shorts and feature films in the early twentieth century.

Melville, of course, is considered to be an American romantic, along with romantic Transcendentalist authors Ralph Waldo Emerson, Henry David Thoreau and Margaret Fuller, among others. Many of these Transcendentalists were idealistic individualists who believed in people's innate abilities, even deity, and thought individuals needed to get in touch with their inner spiritual selves. But Melville had more in common with Edgar Allen Poe and Nathaniel Hawthorne, romantic writers who, like Melville, rejected the idealism of their Transcendentalist peers and often wrote about the personal demons they saw as motivating men. In their writings the romantics often focus on the individual and emphasize the ability to become self-aware through experiences with nature: Thoreau describing in *Walden* (1854) his self-reliance as he builds and lives in a cabin in the woods at Walden Pond, Emerson advocating in his essay "Nature" (1836) one's ability to become a "transcendent eyeball" in the American wilderness, and Melville emphasizing in *Moby Dick* (1851) the narrator Ishamel's experiences with other men and the sea and its creatures. In contrast to the romantic Transcendentalists, however, Melville sometimes depicts how one's ego can lead to self-destruction and the demise of others. In *Moby Dick* the maniacal Captain Ahab sees nothing beyond the white whale and that he must have it regardless of the potential costs in life and property.

The differences between these romantic authors demonstrate the limits associated with placing authors, or other artists, in a mold and giving it a label: romantic, realist or naturalist, for example. But the romantics wrote in the historical context they shared with their peers; their ideas were in some ways shaped by that context, the context that Michael Kimmel associates with the emergence of the individualistic values he associates with American manhood. And the individualism and autonomy enjoyed by the educated free white men of the northern United States in the first half of the nineteenth century pervades the romantic literature. It should be noted, though, that the Transcendentalist Margaret Fuller — arguably America's first feminist, the editor of the Transcendentalist publication *The Dial*, a journalist, and the author of *Woman in the Nineteenth Century* (1845)—

shared many ideas with her male counterparts, and "manhood" and "masculinity" would no doubt hide more than they reveal about Fuller and her ideas and experiences.

A significant difference between the romantic Transcendentalists represented by Emerson's and Thoreau's writings on individualistic experiences in natural settings and Melville's "Bartleby" lies in the fact that Melville's scrivener exists not isolated and alone in nature but socially in the urban landscape of New York City and Wall Street, where men interact not with the wilderness but with other men in a landscape envisioned, constructed, owned and controlled by other men. Even in *Moby Dick*, a novel set for the most part at sea, Ishmael and the other whalers exist not in nature but in the society represented by the whaling ship *Pequod*, a vessel whose crew is under the complete control of the maniacal Captain Ahab. When men design and build environments where other men work and live, whether those built environments are at sea or in an urban setting, individual agency can be severely restricted, all but completely denied.

In the Melville short story, Bartleby answers an advertisement the lawyer places for scriveners and quickly proves to be an excellent copier: productive, steady, honest, laboring day and night.[17] Bartleby, however, demonstrates after a mere three days on the job a "strange willfulness," for he "prefers not" to check his copy with the lawyer or with the other scriveners in the office.[18] Although Bartleby says little beyond the "I prefer not to" phrase familiar to anyone with a knowledge of American literary history, it is evident from Bartleby's behavior that he comes to reject the mundane nature of his work. He is clearly *walled in* by his job in this tale Melville refers to as "a story of Wall Street."[19] Bartleby's resistance to the authority of his employer expands rapidly as he soon prefers not to copy any more documents and refuses to leave the building when the lawyer no longer employs him. The lawyer must deal with the fact that he cannot get rid of Bartleby unless he has him physically removed from the building. Failing to possess the will to do that, the lawyer goes to the extreme of moving his office, its personnel, furniture and other objects to another building and leaves the melancholy scrivener behind. The new occupant of the office discovers Bartleby there and has him removed and committed to an asylum. Here Bartleby takes control of his life by gradually ending it when he prefers to no longer eat.

Bartleby's existence is not determined, but it is severely controlled by his employer and the nature of the work the lawyer creates for him to do. Bartleby has agency over his life but not over his work other than to refuse to no longer do it, which bewilders the lawyer. The reason for the lawyer's bewilderment is evident in the tale. He sees Bartleby as an object of acquisition. "As days passed on," the lawyer recalls, "I became considerably reconciled to Bartleby. His steadiness, his freedom from all dissipation, his incessant industry ... his great stillness, his unalterableness of demeanor under all circumstances, made him a valuable acquisition."[20] Bartleby is a dependable tool, a reliable machine the lawyer has "acquired." Consequently, when Bartleby ceases to be free "from all dissipation," when he fails to continue to display "incessant industry," the lawyer's universe begins to unravel. Bartleby's existence as an unquestioning scrivener who carries out the lawyer's instructions with "great stillness" and an "unalterableness of demeanor under all circumstances" was understandable. But failing to carry out those instructions under those circumstances, and the scrivener's choice to end his existence rather than submit to those instructions and those conditions any longer, is beyond the lawyer's ability to grasp.

Bartleby's apparent discontent with the mundane nature of his life and with his inability to assert any control over what he does and how he does it foreshadows key aspects of not only the realist and naturalist writers of the late nineteenth and early twentieth centuries, but film shorts like *The Clerk* (1914), silent feature films such as *The Crowd* (1928) and *Modern Times* (1936), and even the films produced in the "organized society" after World War II that are the focus of the following chapters. The realist authors tend to place their more-often-than-not bourgeois protagonists in everyday, even mundane, settings and create situations in which the protagonists must make important decisions, often about moral predicaments. The realists, then, maintain an emphasis on the individual and the possibility of individual agency. The environments within which realist authors situate their characters are important, however, influencing characters' lives, presenting them with significant decisions to make, and constraining their options and, therefore, their agency.

While the naturalist writers share with the realists an interest in portraying characters in actual and sometimes everyday situations, the naturalists tend to be more deterministic, subordinating individual agency almost entirely to seemingly abstract historical forces. Some naturalists, influenced significantly by Marxism and Darwinism, question the possibility of whether or not individual agency even exists. Indeed, an individual's actions are often portrayed as being determined by physiological needs such as sustenance and sex, nature, competition for survival between individuals and species, capitalist economics and business. Although capitalism and business are not "natural" forces but human creations, they are depicted as natural because they are systemic entities within which people must act, although people do not have much, if any, choice regarding how they act, or an awareness of the historical agents driving the forces that seem to determine the conditions of their existence.[21] Naturalist fiction, then, shares something with the romantic literature that many realist authors rejected about the earlier group of writers: an emphasis on the extraordinary rather than the mundane. Just as Melville's Leviathan is an extraordinary force in *Moby Dick*, so are corporations and commercial markets new, extraordinary forces in many naturalist novels.

Much naturalist literature is about people at the bottom of society and their struggles: unskilled and semi-skilled native and immigrant workers competing with each other for dangerous and provisional jobs, middle-class men and women who fall out of the middle class due to some kind of tragedy, farmers fighting corporate interests as they try to remain independent producers in an economy increasingly dominated by monopolistic railroads and landholding companies. The over consumption of alcohol and murder and various other crimes, things largely foreign to the middle-class characters that pervade much realist literature, are associated with characters' struggles in naturalist texts. Naturalist literature tends to be more sensational because the authors often depict seedy characters in situations that would be an affront to middle-class sensibilities. Characters in these texts sometimes take extreme measures to escape their dire situations but struggle against historical forces that overpower them. Consequently, the characters are discontented because they have little control over their lives. Although they may take extreme measures to try to assert control and change their situations, they often become disaffected due to their unsuccessful struggles for survival against forces beyond their control.

While the naturalist writers tend to be more deterministic than the realists and sometimes emphasize extraordinary circumstances, they arguably have more in common than not with the realists. The plots in many realist and naturalist novels revolve around the details of everyday life associated with the social and economic circumstances that emerged with the corporate reconstruction of American capitalism and, most important for my purpose in *Soured on the System*, with the declining agency of individuals in the modern commercial and industrial order. Especially in the realist novels published in the early twentieth century, the choices that the predominantly middle-class characters have are limited, for the characters' options are constrained by the fact that they are not independent but work for others on whom they depend for the middle-class security they believe they have. Moreover, they internalize the values of American business culture and the new consumer society in which they have agency over what they consume rather than what they produce and how they produce it. Whether a character wears a white or blue collar or has a stable or a provisional job, individual options and agency are on the decline in both realist and naturalist texts, a fact that further blurs the lines we sometimes draw to demarcate the genres. That the genre lines are blurred is evinced by the placement of author Frank Norris under the rubric "naturalism" in one anthology of realist and naturalist texts, while an essay on Norris's novel *McTeague* (1899) appears in an anthology titled *American Realism*.[22] The constraints that authors place on working-class and middle-class characters' agency in much of this literature prefigures what we will discover about the agency of middle-class men living and working in the "organized system" represented in films produced from the late 1940s through the end of the twentieth century.

I am not concerned, then, with the genre within which a literary text or film might best be placed. Rather, what is important here is the fact that realist and naturalist writers establish a theme in American culture of discontented and disaffected men who must negotiate life in a modern commercial and industrial society where independent thought and action are constrained, even punished, and dependence and conformity reinforced and rewarded. In much of this literature the expanding national and international market economies and the changing urban and rural landscapes associated with those economies are represented as agents curtailing men's independence in cities and on farms. Some of this literature became the basis for early film shorts and silent feature films in the first decades of the twentieth century. Frank Norris's novel *The Pit* (1903), for example, was the basis for the D.W. Griffith film short *A Corner in Wheat* (1909). In the Norris novel, the second in his *Epic of Wheat* trilogy, and in the Griffith film, a speculator attempts to corner the global wheat market. In the process he is responsible for destroying the lives of many of the world's poor who cannot afford to buy bread to sustain their meager existence. Although we know there is an agent, the speculator, who is behind the crisis, the world's poor only understand their situation to be the result of an extraordinary force, like nature, seemingly beyond anyone's control.

Early filmmakers also adapted some of the realist and naturalist novels to the big screen when they began producing feature films to be shown in the many theater palaces constructed in the late 1910s, 1920s and 1930s. During these years producers sought respectability for their industry by targeting a growing middle-class market in addition to the traditional working-class market of nickelodeon customers in the blue-collar urban ghettos of America's major metropolitan areas.[23] Erich Von Stroheim's silent feature film *Greed* (1924) is an adaptation of Norris's *McTeague* (1899), and Warner Bros. released a silent feature production of author Sinclair Lewis's *Babbitt* in 1924 and followed with a new sound version in 1934.[24]

Many of the realist and naturalist writers believed that democracy was not working, that individual rights were on the decline due to the increasing power and influence of corporate interests and evident in violent confrontations between labor and capital, like the one at Andrew Carnegie's Homestead Steel plant (1892), and in the lack of justice associated with events like the riot at Chicago's Haymarket Square (1886). The writers feared the reality of something industrial titan John D. Rockefeller proclaimed as he worked to solidify his control of the oil refining industry. "The day of combination is here to stay," he announced. "Individualism is gone, never to return."[25] As cultural historian Alan Trachtenberg writes, "the strains and tensions and the violence" of these years influenced *Harper's Monthly* editor and novelist William Dean Howells and writers including the likes of Hamlin Garland, Kate Chopin, Frank Norris, Steven Crane and Theodore Dreiser. These authors often painted "a ragged picture" of the country, Trachtenberg demonstrates, one "of lost hopes, hypocrisy, narrowed and constricted lives, grinding frustrations of poverty and isolation," all things that contributed to rising discontent and disaffection as many working-class people felt increasingly powerless and, as historian Richard Hofstadter once wrote, independent middle-class businessmen felt their status and influence threatened by the growth of corporate power.[26] As late as the 1912 presidential election and President Wilson's inauguration, Theodore Roosevelt, a Republican turned Progressive, and Woodrow Wilson, a Democrat, as well as the Socialist candidate Eugene Victor Debs who won almost one million votes that year, tapped into that middle-class anxiety and working-class concerns when they lamented in their speeches the concentrated power and influence of the new corporations.[27]

Authors William Dean Howells and Edward Bellamy critiqued the increasingly incorporated society with its mundane work, social and political inequalities and declining independence by comparing it to fictional utopian alternatives in Howells' *A Traveler from Altruria* (1894) and Bellamy's *Looking Backward: 2000–1887* (1888). As literacy spread in the late nineteenth century, hundreds of thousands of Americans read these utopian novels.[28] In Howells' story a citizen from the island society of Altruria, Mr. Homos, visits the United States so he can learn about the country that promotes itself as a land of equality and opportunity. But as the Americans that Mr. Homos meets learn more about Altruia, it becomes apparent to them that Altruria, rather than the United States, is the more advanced society, for Altrurian society is based on cooperation and "altruism," America on self-interest and avarice.[29] In *Looking Backward*, Bellamy's protagonist, Julian West, wakes up in a future America where those who do the mundane, repetitive labor necessary in a modern industrial society work a few hours a day and retire at age 45 so they can pursue their creative interests fulltime, where people use credit cards to purchase things and all receive the same amount of credit, and where equality, opportunity and democracy are the realities they are not in Julian West's America of the 1880s.[30] Bellamy's *Looking Backward* was a huge success both in the United States and Europe, out selling other nineteenth-century novels except for Harriet Beecher Stowe's *Uncle Tom's Cabin,* and sparking the development of more than 160 Bellamy Clubs, while Howells' *A Traveler from Altruia* led to a short-lived utopian community, Altruia, in California.[31]

The popularity of Bellamy's utopian novel demonstrates that both middle-class and working-class Americans were concerned about the threat that the emerging corporate order posed to the American individualism that Rockefeller approvingly said was "gone, never to return." The social and political inequalities that disappear in Bellamy's vision of the year 2000 were realities to Americans of the late nineteenth century. To try to maintain some control over their lives in the rapidly changing society, in what Rockefeller referred to as the "day of combination" that was "here to stay," blue-collar workers joined the Knights of Labor, the American Federation of Labor and other unions and battled corporations to try to maintain some control over wages, hours and working conditions.[32] The United States Congress created the Committee on Labor in 1883 to investigate the social conditions that accompanied the corporate reconstruction of American capitalism and the conflicts between labor and capital that erupted.[33] Likewise, many independent farmers, threatened by declining prices and high shipping rates that monopolistic railroad companies established while simultaneously giving discount rates to Rockefeller's Standard Oil and other "combinations," joined the Populist revolt in the 1890s that led to the new People's Party that participated in the 1892 election and then fused with the Democrats under a populist banner and the candidacy of William Jennings Bryan in 1896. These independent farmers called for government ownership of the railroads and telegraphs and for what their opponents labeled as other "radical" changes such as the direct election of United States Senators and citizens' increased participation in the political process at the state level through the adoption of the initiative, the referendum and the recall, all of which became realities during the following 20 years.

But most late nineteenth and early twentieth-century fiction is not about more egalitarian, democratic utopian alternatives to an American society shaped and controlled by "combinations." Novels about working-class struggles such as Upton Sinclair's *The Jungle* (1906), based on Sinclair's muckraking investigation of the meat-packing industry and adapted into a film in 1914, depict the provisional nature of work and the competition between laborers for even a single day's pay in a system that treats them as any other commodity bought and sold in the marketplace. Like Melville's Bartleby, such men are mere "acquisitions" to their employers, short-term acquisitions acquired not by individual business owners like Melville's lawyer-narrator in the 1850s, but by low-level managers who work for the combinations establishing an even greater presence in the first decades of the twentieth century. Sinclair's Lithuanian immigrant protagonist Jurgis Rudkus and his family discover that in America they have no control over what they do and how much they are paid for doing it, and all family members — men, women, and children — must take whatever provisional work they can get in order to keep the family fed.

In contrast to Sinclair's muckraking fiction, literature about the expanding group of white-collar workers and small independent business owners often lumps together a variety of characters that represent what is sometimes referred to as "the new middle classes" and creates what Christopher P. Wilson labels "cultural averaging" or "middle Americanness."[34] Authors do not represent these characters as opposing the system and the values associated with it. Rather, we get a preponderance of characters that accept the nature of everyday life in towns and cities as they negotiate their way through the country's business and social environments and participate as much as possible in the expanding consumer culture. In his novel *Babbitt* (1922), for example, Sinclair Lewis's George Babbitt begins by preaching that the best government is one that serves the interests of business, and Babbitt spends his days selling real estate, trying to impress and influence clients, donating time to his church, and acquiring material things. Although the conservative Babbitt becomes discontented with his mundane life in the town of Zenith, flirts with liberal, even socialist, politics, and has an affair, he chooses conformity in the end and his conformist friends accept him back into the fold. Despite the fact that Babbitt is not an oppositional character, Lewis's purpose is to demonstrate what Americans sacrifice at the altar of middle-class conformity, how they trade independence of mind and life style for middle-class status and the relative security that it provides.[35] Neither *Babbitt* nor similar works by Sherwood Anderson and other authors who were Lewis's contemporaries contain middle-class heroes who become non-conformists and reject permanently the kind of life that George Babbitt leads and the values he represents.[36]

Where the feature films of the teens, twenties and thirties based on such literature were increasingly marketed to middle-class audiences, the earlier film shorts like Griffith's *A Corner in Wheat* targeted predominantly working-class audiences. Consequently, themes of class conflict, the poor's struggles for survival, and the exploitative practices of employers that pervade so many early films resonated with those audiences while facilitating in local, state and federal officials fears of social and political instability. Movie-making in the years before World War I, Steven J. Ross demonstrates, were years when film production was not yet dominated by an established group of filmmakers. As a result, labor unions, businesses and a variety of political organizations with diverse ideologies made movies. When they did, their highly propagandistic films contributed to an open and powerful political dialog embedded in the scenes projected on the rapidly increasing number of movie screens being erected across the country. Ross notes that after a reviewer saw the film adaptation of Upton Sinclair's *The Jungle* in 1914, the critic wrote, "It is possible to read the book and then merely register a vow never to eat tinned goods again." Seeing the movie, however, achieved for the reviewer what Sinclair lamented his novel failed to do: get readers to identify with the plight of workers in Chicago's meatpacking industry. The reviewer continued: "But after seeing the picture we begin to have burned into us that Packingtown made enormous profits not simply out of tainted food, but out of the ruined lives of men and women."[37]

The degree to which realist and naturalist authors influenced early filmmakers cannot be quantified and need not be, for the social, economic and political conditions that provided writers with material for their novels and shaped their ideas had a similar impact on filmmakers. Those conditions that influenced literary content continued to shape film content, evident in additional early production titles such as *Capital Versus Labor* (1910), *The Clerk* (1914), *Making a Living* (1914), and *The Eternal Grind* (1916). This is not to claim that either film or literary content was determined by those conditions; the stories that people and organizations created on both celluloid and paper about those conditions reflect their interpretations and ideologies as well as the conditions themselves. Authors who wrote about individuals' declining independence and agency in the industrializing society prior to the invention and use of motion picture technology increased cultural awareness of the reality. Filmmakers then expanded that awareness while concurrently being influenced by it.

Though the film industry emerged during the years when American capitalism was going through its corporate transformation, filmmaking, for the most part, remained in the hands of diverse independents prior to the country's entry into World War I. Some independents persisted after the war, but production and distribution increasingly became consolidated in the studio system consisting of a group of corporate firms that shifted production from New York to Hollywood in the 1920s. These were years when producers increasingly targeted a middle-class audience, and the incentive to sell films to that audience combined with the centralization of production and distribution reduced the scope of the types of films produced.[38] While producers controlled the resources that went into a film, however, they did not wield complete control over the creativity of the diverse group of directors, writers and actors that they had over the capital they invested in a production. Moreover, the new movie moguls still needed to get the public to buy tickets, so they had to produce films that resonated with people's experiences during the more prosperous 1920s and in the Depression decade of the 1930s.[39] In these years of dramatic historical change, films continued to be released that depict individuals' declining agency in the consolidating corporate order, and in the political system that increasingly represented corporate interests.[40]

Cultural historian Lary May demonstrates that many films produced during the 1920s, best represented in the work of director Cecil B. DeMille, reveal a new theme in American culture. The earlier Progressive-era plots were diverse and included the threat of powerful and menacing corporations, the mundane and provisional nature of work, individuals' declining agency in the consolidating corporate order, and, for May's purposes and best represented in the work of director D. W. Griffith, the reinforcement of middle-class values associated with propriety and restrained passions.

The productions released in the twenties that May describes promoted the "consumer ideal" and exciting sex, albeit within the traditional bonds of marriage. Stories that reinforced values associated with restraining one's physical passions and consumer desires that were at the core of Victorian culture and promoted in Griffith's films were replaced in DeMille productions with plots that depict the pursuit of one's desires and passions as not just acceptable but appropriate and even necessary behavior.

This narrative shift from the diverse social commentary evident in film shorts and some early feature productions is undeniable, despite the fact that labor unrest reached a historical peak in the postwar strike wave of 1919, steel workers and many other employees in the twenties continued to work 12 hours a day and seven days a week, and class divisions and inequality remained significant in what is sometimes referred to as America's "prosperity" decade.[41] Progressive-era legislation reinforced the new corporate order by creating the Federal Reserve Board and other regulatory agencies, and such regulations perhaps made the new order more palatable to more people as Progressive reformers relied on new local, state and federal regulations to begin to create the "organized system" that C. Wright Mills, Paul Goodman and other commentators would criticize in the 1950s, after the New Deal and World War II facilitated further expansion of the system. But even in many of the DeMille films released in the 1920s it's evident that the reason the male characters seek individual happiness through increased, even limitless consumption, as well as through more, and more satisfying, sex is because the nature of their work is not rewarding. Moreover, some films in the twenties continued in the realist and naturalist traditions of portraying protagonists in mundane everyday situations in which the pursuit of personal independence is a difficult, if not a hopeless, endeavor.

In two DeMille films that demonstrate May's thesis about the narrative shift that occurred from Griffith's early films to DeMille's in the twenties, men's search for happiness through satisfying sex within marriage and through material consumption are in large part a consequence of the protagonists' inability to achieve fulfillment in business. In *Forbidden Fruit* (1921), for example, a young man with dreams of economic independence wants to become a self-made man by seeking his fortune in the American West. His desire for independence is thwarted, however, when a conniving monopolistic oil tycoon entices him to work for the tycoon's oil company. To bring the young man into his corporate fold, the tycoon sets him up with a beautiful woman on whom the young man must spend lavish amounts of money in the new consumer culture. The two fall in love and the man forsakes his dream of independence for a position in the tycoon's corporation so he can provide a life of consumption and leisure for his new wife. The sacrifices one must make to become independent would include delaying material and sexual gratification, so the oil tycoon uses the woman as bait to successfully ensnare the young man in his trap. Similarly, in *The Affairs of Anatol* (1921) the character Anatol is a fairly successful "office worker" who, as May describes him, is "bored with life." Unfulfilled by his work and his traditional marriage, Anatol seeks satisfaction in new ways. He takes his wife to cabarets to enjoy modern nightlife, but she demonstrates no interest in the social experiences the cabarets have to offer. Anatol then seeks pleasure with other, more modern women who enjoy the new nightlife, but he eventually returns to his wife, who by the end of the film becomes a more modern woman herself and, therefore, a more satisfying partner for Anatol.[42] Although such films reveal the new pleasure-seeking values associated with personal gratification and the new "consumer ideal," they also demonstrate the barriers to men fulfilling their desires for independence in business and their lack of satisfaction working for others in modern office jobs.

In a feature-length silent film produced at the end of the silent era, director King Vidor associates the birth of a man who has an intense desire for independence with the birth of a nation that fought a war for its independence. The film, Vidor's *The Crowd* (1928), is about the struggles of office worker John Sims (James Murray), who is born on Independence Day in 1900, the dawn of the new century. The people in the anonymous town where John is born celebrate the Fourth of July with parades, picnics and fireworks, and John grows up believing that he, like his country, can achieve independence, separating himself from others and from financial restrictions through determination and hard work. In one scene when John is a child, he and other boys sit on a fence and talk about what they will do when they grow up. John says, "My dad says *I'm* goin' to be somebody big!" To achieve his dreams in what he believes to be the land of opportunity, John moves to New York City, where he secures a job as one of hundreds of bookkeepers for a large corporation. On John's desk rests the nameplate displaying evidence that the company regards him as one of many: the number 137. John and the other male office workers spend their days much like Melville's Bartleby, engaged in mundane, repetitive tasks, only their lives are controlled by managers in a modern corporate bureaucracy rather than by an independent employer like Melville's lawyer. *The*

Crowd depicts these men as indistinguishable members of the modern rat race. In one of many crowd scenes John and hundreds of other men enter numbers in the columns of ledger sheets as they sit at copies of the same desk organized in seemingly endless rows in a massive room with no walls, cubicles or other dividers.[43]

John can do nothing to distinguish himself from the crowd of other bookkeepers, and he remains in the same job after he marries a woman he meets on a blind date with another couple and they have two children. John becomes progressively disenchanted with his job and with his inability to distinguish himself from the other men and fulfill his dream of independence. He then sinks into sever depression when his daughter is struck by a delivery truck and dies. Shortly thereafter, John's manager questions whether or not John is concentrating on his work. Frustrated and depressed, John quits and begins a search that lasts through the remainder of the film for steady, fulltime employment, which he never secures. For the job he has at the end of the film he juggles balls while wearing a clown costume as he walks through the streets of the city carrying a sandwich-board sign that advertises the food at a local diner. In the final scene John, Mary and their son sit in the audience at a variety show, laughing with the crowd in the theater at two clowns performing on stage. The camera

In *The Crowd* (1928), director King Vidor uses multiple scenes like this one of the office where John Sims (James Murray) works to emphasize the decline of independence in modern corporate bureaucracies (Photofest).

pulls back slowly as the Sims becomes indistinguishable from hundreds of other people sitting in the theater, his independence lost in the crowd.

John Sims becomes discontented with his job and his life (he considers suicide at one point), and he is disaffected because he can do nothing to improve his situation. But his love for his wife and his son cause him to renew his hope and his struggle, as futile as Vidor portrays his efforts as being. More desperate situations than John's are represented in many of the films produced during the Great Depression that began one year after the release of *The Crowd*. Interestingly, however, Hollywood's representations of American life became more hopeful as the Depression lingered, not to end until massive government spending for the Second World War created full employment. Robert McElvaine attributes the increased hope represented in Depression-era Hollywood productions in large part to the to the fact that, in contrast to the somber speeches of Herbert Hoover, President Franklin D. Roosevelt instilled hope in the American people.[44] Other factors associated with the cultural phenomenon include two significant developments, one endemic to the industry itself, the adoption of the Motion Picture Production Code by producers and distributors in 1930 and then effectively enforced in 1934, and the other an act of Congress, the creation of the House Committee on Un-American Activities in 1938. Both the adoption of the code and the creation of the committee would influence significantly cultural representations of people and events in American movies for three decades, the code restricting what could appear in Hollywood films, and the possibility of testifying before the committee for engaging in "subversive" activities potentially putting in jeopardy the livelihoods of actors, writers and directors. Although the code was not effectively enforced until it was amended to create the Production Code Administration in 1934, enforcement did not keep films from being released that included scenes and references questioning an economic system that had collapsed and created unemployment as high as 25 percent.

Depression-era films include gangster movies with criminals that audiences could sympathize with because the characters are in part victims of circumstances and otherwise good men. Other, unsympathetic criminals are portrayed as selfish and greedy businessmen who will stop at nothing to get what they want. Americans could also go to a musical for a short time and escape the realities of everyday life, to a drama that followed a family and its struggles during the Depression, or to a screwball comedy that made fun of the rich and their extravagant and wasteful consumption. In the context of the Great Depression, the Cecile B. DeMille theme of middle-class happiness through consumption as a substitute for meaningful work seemed to evaporate with the stock market collapse and high unemployment, but we will see that it reemerges following World War II and that the happiness supposedly associated with consumption is often portrayed as ambiguous.[45] Representing material consumption as a solution to personal problems would be difficult to do in Depression America. Men are more likely to be portrayed as being unemployed than discontented with work in a society where one in four has no job, and employed or not they are not likely to be represented as being disaffected, although many in society became so. Sure, when James Allen (Paul Muni) returns from the Great War in *I Am a Fugitive from a Chain Gang* (1932), he does not want to return to the unfulfilling job he had as a shipping clerk before he became a soldier, noting, "I've learned that life is more important than a stupid, insignificant job."[46] More often than not, however, individuals solve personal and social problems in screwball comedies like *My Man Godfrey* (1936), stand up to business and political corruption in films like *Mr. Smith Goes to Washington* (1939), and have their consciousness raised and fight alongside others against the organized interests and actions of business — California citrus growers — in a movie like the screen adaptation (1940) of John Steinbeck's novel *The Grapes of Wrath* (1939). These films represent conservative, liberal and more radical ideologies, respectively, but all emphasize individual agency, something we will see is represented as being significantly diminished for men with jobs in the organized, corporate bureaucratic system of the postwar years.

High unemployment and the many malnourished adults and children that unemployment created caused working Americans during the Depression to be more discontented with starving than with mundane and unfulfilling labor. Many Depression-era films represent that reality. But Americans who wanted to work for a living and could not became increasingly disaffected from a society and an economic system that produced more food than its citizens could afford to consume and destroyed some of the food that was produced rather than use the food to feed starving citizens.[47] Increasing numbers of Americans saw their lives being controlled by an abstract economic system rather than by themselves or other individuals, a system that Steinbeck referred to in *The Grapes of Wrath* as an invisible "monster" that pushed people off their land and consolidated land ownership in distant eastern banks.[48] The Social Security Act (1935), National Labor Relations Act (1935), Fair Labor Standards Act (1938) and other legislation associated with Roosevelt's New Deal that created the modern welfare state were in part enacted in response to populist Louisiana Senator Huey Long's more radical calls for "share our wealth," Dr. Francis Townsend's plan to provide medical care to America's elderly, and the direct actions of workers who took to the streets across the country to demand the right to bargain collectively with organized employers who worked together to try to ensure they could keep dealing with employees individually.[49]

Some Depression-era films represent the conditions under which people worked and the control employers wielded over them, while at least one suggests an alternative to the system that resembled a plan advocated by Upton Sinclair, the author of *The Jungle* and the Democratic candidate for governor of California in 1934. In *Modern Times* (1936) Charlie Chaplin depicts the mind-numbing, repetitive nature of assembly-line work and attempts by management to control every aspect of employees' lives in order to increase efficiency, even to the extreme of using machines to force-feed their lunches to them and cameras to spy on them to ensure they do not steal precious minutes from repetitive production to have a smoke

Charlie Chaplin's character in *Modern Times* (1936) goes crazy from the monotonous routine of working on an assembly line (Photofest).

when they go to the bathroom. Contrasting this view of discontented workers engaged in repetitive production and whose lives are almost entirely
controlled by management, King Vidor offers in *Our Daily Bread* (1934)
a celluloid vision of a cooperative society of skilled workers engaged in
fulfilling and productive labor, echoing Upton Sinclair's speeches of the
same year when he called for "production for use" and "end poverty in
California."[50] Rather than provide alternatives to that system, however,
more mainstream Depression-era dramas like John Ford's *The Grapes of
Wrath* (1940) and Gregory LaCava's *My Man Godfrey* (1936) instead raise
questions about the values associated with the economic system and about
the social activities and values of the rich. While screwball comedies like
Godfrey propose private, individualistic schemes rather than government
action to resolve the problems of the Depression, they critique the values
of frivolous consumption and unproductive living that so many Depression-era Americans and characters like the Joads could not understand.

From the late nineteenth century to the end of the Great Depression,
then, cultural representations of the declining agency that men in both
blue-collar and white-collar positions had on the job and in society generally emerged in American literature and then became pervasive in both
literature and film. This cultural phenomenon coincided with the increasing centralization of production in large corporate factories and in the
growing corporate bureaucracies where new office jobs were created. In
finance, industry and railroads, a major merger movement occurred at the
turn of the century. Thousands of manufacturing firms were reduced to a
few hundred in a mere six years, 1897–1903, and those are only six years
out of approximately six decades. Corporate empire builders like railroad
magnate James J. Hill and oil tycoon John D. Rockefeller feared competition in a society that, in theory, continued to value it. Hill proclaimed
that consolidation in railroads occurred because he and other railroad
empire builders wanted "to obviate ruinous competition." These captains
of industry sought control not only of production, distribution and market
share, but of decisions regarding wages, hours, working conditions and
work routines, so they created hierarchal corporate bureaucracies with various levels of managers in order to institutionalize that control and maintain
it. The declining control that both blue- and white-collar workers had
over what they did and how they did it is represented in much of late
nineteenth- and early twentieth-century literature and in many of the film
shorts and silent and talkie features produced during the first four decades

of the twentieth century. Moreover, the impact that decisions made by an increasingly smaller percentage of men had on the lives of many farmers and other independent businessmen is also represented in much of the literature and in many of the films, as is the growing influence of a consumer culture in which what one buys and has the ability to buy is valued more than one's independence from working for others or one's agency on the job.[51] Some of these early twentieth-century films contest the nature of the new corporate order. Others reinforce it. The diversity of the films produced in many ways represents the diversity of the political rhetoric and the political actions that emerged in the late nineteenth and early twentieth centuries.

Postwar Culture

We will see that while the scope of that diversity declined significantly after World War II, it did not completely disappear within the postwar liberal consensus that emerged in American political ideology. I discuss that ideology in chapter one as it is represented by two-time Democratic presidential candidate Adlai Stevenson in the 1950s and is represented in a variety of films, but I devote the bulk of my attention there to a detailed analysis of two significant films: Frank Capra's *It's a Wonderful Life* (1946) and Nunnally Johnson's screen adaptation (1956) of author Sloan Wilson's popular novel of the same title, *The Man in the Gray Flannel Suit* (1955). In Capra's production, released in the immediate wake of the war, it is still possible for George Bailey (Jimmy Stewart)—born and raised in the Progressive era and instilled with the independent values of his father—to fight and sacrifice to preserve his own independence and the independence of the working-class and middle-class citizens of Bedford Falls. His foe is the financial and real estate tycoon of the town, Henry F. Potter (Lionel Barrymore), whose sole purpose in life is to consolidate all property in his hands and, consequently, to control both the town of Bedford Falls and its citizens. Immediately after the war it is still possible to openly, directly and successfully confront Potter, a symbol of the consolidating corporate order, as Potter attempts to transform Bedford Falls into Pottersville. Although George is not happy about the sacrifices he must make in his struggle against Potter, and even though Potter unsuccessfully entices George to join that order and become rich himself, with a little help from his friends and a bit of divine intervention George wins his struggle with

Potter. But Potter does not go away, and a somewhat more benevolent version of him is represented as the head of the United Broadcasting Corporation that Tom Rath secures employment with 10 years later in *The Man in the Gray Flannel Suit.* This film represents the emergence of the postwar corporate-liberal consensus.[52] The film demonstrates, however, that the characters are leery of the consensus. Tom Rath must negotiate his way cautiously in what Adlai Stevenson referred to as the new reality of American life. This reality, the politician asserted, was one to which men must adapt, and one for which women must make personal sacrifices by creating middle-class sanctuaries in their homes for their own gray-suited husbands, men whose agency at work and in society is diminished significantly but necessarily in the postwar corporate order.

The films I analyze in chapter two demonstrate that the idea of a coalition of independent business owners and working-class citizens struggling to maintain their independence against corporate consolidation and corporate control remains in American culture well into the 1950s. Such themes are veiled, however, in the western and gangster genres. For the most part, chapter two is devoted to an analysis of two films, *Force of Evil* (1948) and *Johnny Guitar* (1954), movies that reveal stark critiques of the corporate order continued in the postwar years. In the political culture of vehement anti-communism represented by the House Committee on Un-American Activities, the persecution of the Hollywood Ten, and the creation of a producers' blacklist, director Nicholas Ray released the popular western *Johnny Guitar.*[53] The film appeared in theaters one year before Ray's critically acclaimed and hugely popular portrayal of postwar alienated youth starring James Dean: *Rebel Without a Cause* (1955). In *Johnny Guitar* a group of independent business owners and their employees form a coalition against Emma Small (Mercedes McCambridge), the woman who controls much of the western town and opposes the development of independent businesses emerging nearby. Emma's frenzied behavior, her accusations against others, and the pressure she puts on them to admit to crimes also make it clear she represents the anti-communist witch hunter Joseph McCarthy. Like Ray, director Abraham Polonsky used a genre about something other than contemporary mainstream American life in order to critique the loss of independence in the postwar corporate order. The gangster genre went through a transformation as filmmakers departed from the individual ethnic gangster movies of the early thirties to the gangster-syndicate films of the postwar years. A historian of the genre, Jonathan Munby, writes, "Collectively, gangster-syndicate films played on contemporaneous anxieties about the loss of individual (predominantly male) agency in the name of serving the organization."[54] Munby continues, "The gangster-syndicate films of the period played on doubts and fears about the totalizing nature of loyalty to a whole range of 'organizations.'"[55] Such organizations included corporations, labor unions and government agencies. In *Force of Evil* (1948) the word "combination" is used throughout the film to refer to the new business entity organized by the gangster Ben Tucker (Roy Roberts). Tucker consolidates control of the numbers racket under his gangster-syndicate umbrella, destroying the small independent numbers men in the process. The force that is evil in the film is Tucker's new business "combination."

Films like *The Man in the Gray Flannel Suit* reveal that neither filmmakers nor audiences embraced the corporate order unambiguously. Gangster films such as *Force of Evil* and westerns like *Johnny Guitar* indicate that stark critiques and even direct opposition to the new order existed alongside ambiguous acceptance, evidence that the corporate-liberal consensus contained significant fissures.

Chapter three covers the 1960s and 1970s, years marked by many significant events and associated with major historical change. The criticisms of declining independence associated with the postwar corporate order that are represented in the western and gangster genres, combined with the cultural anxieties expressed in films like *It's a Wonderful Life* and *The Man in the Gray Flannel Suit*, reveal that the production of counterculture films in the late 1960s and 1970s was not merely a response to events in those decades: primarily, to the successes of the civil rights and women's movements, Vietnam and Watergate.[56] Rather, the production of a variety of counterculture films in the late sixties and early seventies is rooted in the anxieties, paradoxes and contradictions of postwar American life and culture, and those roots are evident in films produced in the forties and fifties about men negotiating and confronting issues related to work, culture, and society. The events contemporary to the production of the sixties and seventies films opened the cultural doors and enabled the more widespread expression of themes that were extant but repressed in the more immediate postwar years. Moreover, themes related to men's declining agency that are represented in sixties and seventies films are not restricted to productions that can be considered countercultural; they exist as well in what I refer to as urban-avenger films such as *Dirty Harry* (1971) and *Death Wish* (1974), and in films featuring reactionary characters such as *Joe* (1970). This paradox — that films associated with both the left and the right released in the sixties and seventies—is explored in chapter three, where I analyze films associated with the counterculture such as *The Graduate* (1967) and *Easy Rider (1969)*, but also films featuring what are often considered to be right-wing characters, such as *Joe* and *Dirty Harry*.

I discuss these films together because, surprisingly, they share two major features. First, films in each category depict a society of centralized decision-making and little individual control over events and circumstances. Second, the films reveal common criticisms of society but not common solutions. *The Graduate* and *Easy Rider* portray discontented and disaffected protagonists who must escape from society because negotiating a fulfilling life within society is hopeless. In contrast, *Joe* and *Dirty Harry* depict protagonists who are similarly discontented and disaffected but who embrace militant action. The protagonists in the counterculture films see no choices in society worth making other than the choice to flee and explore alternative life styles. Commercialism, corporate influence, political corruption, and a meaningless existence engaged in mundane work routines are too dominant and unappealing to negotiate, so the characters flee to explore alternatives, although Benjamin Braddock in *The Graduate* has no alternatives to pursue and departs on an ambiguous future. Some of those alternatives, however, are quite traditional. For example, in *Easy Rider* Wyatt and Billy explore what it is like to live in a commune, but the alternative lifestyle is not depicted positively. They also visit an independent farmer-rancher, a man who lives a traditional American lifestyle and is in control of his own work, his own destiny, a man Wyatt admires and one Dirty Harry surely would, too. But in postwar America this farmer-rancher exists outside of what has become the mainstream; he is no longer the norm in America that he was still able to be in the early twentieth century. The protagonists in the urban-avenger films are similarly disgusted with the mainstream and with the weak people at its center. The system is corrupt and the people weak but, much like the heroes in *Shane* (1953), *High Noon* (1952) and other traditional westerns, the protagonists confront the outlaws directly and with cunning and overwhelming force, skirting the system to weed out the bad guys and, when necessary, becoming the bad guys themselves so they can get the job done.

Chapter four completes the analysis with a discussion of relevant films produced in the 1980s and 1990s, and with a detailed analysis of three. The films analyzed here continue to represent the discontent and disaffection evident in earlier films. After a discussion of a variety of eighties and nineties productions, my analysis turns to three significant films released at the end of the century: *American Beauty* (1999), *Office Space* (1999) and *Fight Club* (1999). Each film deals with men's lack of independence in relation to work. Two of the three also contain significant critiques of the proposition that men's agency as consumers who attempt to find happiness through the conspicuous consumption of material goods can be a panacea for their lack of agency elsewhere in society. Most films that depict discontented and disaffected men in these years do not have upbeat resolutions. In *American Beauty*, for example, Lester Burnham (Kevin Spacey) quits the job he hates as a middle-class office worker and finds more joy serving burgers and soft drinks at the drive-through window of a local fast-food joint. While his wife — a realtor who strives perpetually to sell more houses and make more money to consume more things — begins an affair with another realtor, Lester pursues his daughter's 16-year-old friend before he is shot and killed by the retired Marine Corps Colonel who lives next door. In the comedy *Office Space,* Peter Gibbons (Rob Livingston) finds his job as a computer programmer so redundant and the oppressive practices of management so bad that he seeks psychological help. The psychiatrist hypnotizes Peter and dies of a heart attack before Peter wakes up, so he goes to work the next day in a half-hypnotized state and tells two outside personnel evaluators exactly what he thinks about the company and management. The evaluators see him as management material himself because of his insight and truthfulness and Peter gets promoted. Now that he demonstrates more control of his life, Peter plans with two other men a scheme to defraud the company of small amounts of money over time so they can eventually become independent of their mind-numbing jobs. Managers detect the scheme, but before they discover who planned it another disgruntled worker burns the corporate headquarters to the ground, along with any evidence that could connect Peter and his friends to the scheme. Although Peter no longer works for the corporation, he accepts a position as a general laborer. The chapter ends with an analysis of the *Fight Club* film described at the beginning of this introduction, a movie with a radical critique of American consumer culture and of men's almost complete lack of agency at work and in society generally.

I do not claim that the themes I explore here represent themes that all or even most men identify with at any time in American history. There is no way to quantify how people felt or what they thought when they viewed a particular film. Rather, my analysis of cultural representations of men's discontent and disaffection reveals some significant sources of that discontent and disaffection, sources that emerged with the corporate reconstruction of American capitalism in the late nineteenth century and persisted throughout the twentieth century. New historical developments — the civil rights and women's movements, for example — and new social and economic circumstances — declining blue-collar jobs, mindless and repetitive white-collar positions, and the dominance of corporations rather than independent businesses in the increasingly global economy — sometimes fuel men's anxieties and the discontent associated with those anxieties. This is particularly evident in the movie *Joe*. Cultural representations of race and gender relations, for example, change significantly during the 150 years of cultural history studied here. References to those changes as they are depicted in particular cultural texts appear in the following pages. But short-term studies that focus on those moments of change tend to miss the continuity evident here. Issues related to controlling one's labor and one's destiny, to being involved (or not involved) in rewarding and creative labor, and to having agency at work and in society generally emerge in the late nineteenth-century texts and remain in many of those created throughout the twentieth. Men's declining independence and increasing need to conform to corporate life and to a culture of consumption as just compensation for repetitive and mundane labor are direct and significant causes of their discontent and disaffection.

1
Negotiating Corporate Life
Adapting to the Organized System
in the 1940s and 1950s

Some historians have referred to the years directly following World War II as "the proud decades," the years of the "vital center" in American politics, and the time of a postwar "consensus" culture. Others have more accurately described these years as ones filled with class conflict, racial strife, and intense anxieties about a rapidly changing American society and culture and an increasingly dangerous world. These latter historians have documented the many cracks that existed in the cold war consensus, the vitality of political ideas and cultural expressions at the margins rather than the defined center of American life, and the numerous events and policies for which no one should be proud.[1] Even many of the cultural artifacts of the postwar years, however, those one might assume helped to reinforce the consensus culture that has received so much scholarly attention, reveal some of the intense anxieties that permeated American society. Most of the space in this chapter is devoted to two widely popular films that reveal some of those anxieties.

The Second World War accelerated trends in the economy and society that had been shaping social and economic life since the mid nineteenth century. Corporate consolidation and influence reached new heights, and women entered the labor force at unprecedented numbers and in traditionally male occupations, demonstrating clearly their abilities to compete with men on traditionally male terrain and fueling anxieties among men and women regarding gender relations and gender roles. Moreover, "organization" took on new meaning for the increased number of men who worked for corporations, for blue-collar workers who joined unions, and for all Americans who interacted with the new government bureaucracies created as a result of the war and the New Deal. For these reasons men became increasingly anxious about the declining control they had on the job, the increased questioning of their authority in the home despite intense propaganda crafted to reinforce their authority in that sphere, and diminished independence in general. Although politicians and the government waged ideological campaigns to portray the home as woman's proper place and working for corporations as a natural aspect of American life, tensions about that reality and about gender relations in the postwar years pervade American films of the 1940s and 1950s.[2]

The two major films I discuss here are *It's a Wonderful Life* (1946) and *The Man in the Gray Flannel Suit* (1956). Control issues permeate each of these films. The first demonstrates an old pre-war, Progressive-era theme evident in the 1912 presidential campaign speeches of Democrat Woodrow Wilson and former Republican turned Progressive Party candidate Theodore Roosevelt.[3] Director Frank Capra's movie classic posits a coalition of working-class citizens and small independent business owners against a villain who clearly represents the concentrated economic power of a corporation out to centralize the control of all property under one big umbrella. Corporate power and the control over people's lives that power represents exist in society but can still be confronted and kept at bay, enabling small businessmen and homeowners to wield some control over their lives and over the future of the country. Ten years later, *The Man in the Gray Flannel Suit* depicts a much different reality. Corporations dominate society, and the men who spend their daily lives working for them have little control over what they do and how they do it, depending on their salaries and, therefore, the corporations for their security. The opposition to concentrated economic power and the social control associated with it that is displayed by a coalition of working-class and middle-class citizens in *It's a Wonderful Life* is replaced by a narrative of individual gray-suited salaried employees negotiating corporate life. This latter theme of individuals negotiating positions within the corporate order becomes the dominant one in postwar films, although we will see in the next chapter that significant criticisms of that order are evident in some westerns and gangster-syndicate films of the 1940s and 1950s, veiled in these genre films but evident just the same.

The Man in the Gray Flannel Suit reveals this narrative shift and demands much of the attention here. This Darryl F. Zanuck production, based on Sloan Wilson's novel (1955) of the same title, was released at a key moment in the history of American work routines, economic development, and gender relations, a time that Illinois Governor and two-time Democratic presidential candidate Adlai Stevenson defined as a moment of "crisis" in his 1955 commencement address to graduates at Smith College, the prestigious women's college.[4] The social changes that made the 1950s a moment of crisis for Stevenson are represented in *The Man in the Gray Flannel Suit*, but the protagonist, Tom Rath (Gregory Peck), is a more complicated corporate employee than Stevenson implied to Smith graduates their future husbands would be. And Tom's wife Betsy (Jennifer Jones) does not represent the happy and contented housewife Stevenson encouraged the Smith women to become, for she does not create a domestic refuge for Tom, a place free of conflict and stress where he can escape the unfulfilling labor and the culture of conformity at his new employer, the United Broadcasting Corporation (UBC). Rather, although positioned in the domestic sphere as Stevenson advocated, Betsy is an assertive, creative, and entrepreneurial woman, arguably the conductor of the Rath family train. The fact that she, unlike Tom, is untainted by the corporate culture at UBC enables her to criticize Tom when he starts to become just one more corporate yes-man, another gray-suit willing to compromise his values and not speak his mind in order to keep management happy and his job secure. That Betsy exists outside of the corporate culture that threatens to corrupt Tom enables her to encourage him to maintain his honesty and integrity in a corporate environment inhospitable to those values. Although Betsy's position in the domestic sphere causes her to depend on Tom for her economic security, her freedom in that position to critique the corporate culture at UBC causes Tom to depend on Betsy for his moral security and, in the language of some contemporary social and cultural critics, for the preservation of his manhood.[5] Moreover, Betsy's independence from the negative influences of postwar corporate life described by Stevenson also enables her to imagine economic opportunities for the Raths that could eventually lead to their financial independence.

The domestic sphere as it is depicted in *The Man in the Gray Flannel Suit* is therefore much more complicated than Stevenson portrayed it, and Betsy's position in it more dynamic than cultural historians sometimes describe the domestic sphere of the postwar years.[6] Betsy does not work outside of the home, but she is not a model homemaker, nor are her thoughts and activities confined to domestic responsibilities such as creating a haven for her husband and physically and emotionally nurturing the Rath children. Her agency in the domestic sphere reveals it to be a place where critiques of corporate culture are nurtured, and where ideas for an entrepreneurial venture are germinated and hatched. Although the film ends before all of Betsy's financial plans are realized, her idea to develop land that Tom inherits represents the potential for the Raths to achieve economic independence and, consequently, freedom from the corporate culture that threatens to strip Tom of his independent thoughts and actions as he considers trading his honesty, integrity and individualism for economic security in a corporate bureaucracy where authority is centralized in a managerial elite.[7]

When Stevenson spoke at Smith College that June of 1955, he was accelerating his second of two presidential campaigns against President Dwight D. Eisenhower and, consequently, thinking about a wider audience while focusing his comments on the Smith women. Smith was and is a women's college, the one Betty Friedan, the author of *The Feminine Mystique* (1963), graduated from in 1942. Smith graduates also contributed to the book. Friedan sent questionnaires to 200 of her classmates. That data provided her with much of the material she relied on to write the book.[8] Although the impact of Stevenson's speech, if all women at Smith and elsewhere in 1955 had followed his advice, would be to keep women out of the labor market and from competing with men, Stevenson is also a significant public figure who commented on the social realities of work in the corporate bureaucracies of the second half of the twentieth century, realities represented in *The Man in the Gray Flannel Suit* and numerous films throughout the remainder of the century.

In Stevenson's commencement address he told some of the most highly educated young women in the country that the western world was in "crisis," and that crisis was one of "collectivism colliding with individualism." He did not refer to a crisis associated with the conflict between communism and capitalism in the cold war but to the collectivism and increasing centralization of the specialized industrial capitalist society of postwar America. Stevenson lectured the Smith women that, due to the centralization of authority and the specialized tasks assigned to men in corporate bureaucracies, men were no longer the individuals they used to be; their values as well as their activities were being shaped by the centralization of authority and the homogeneity of behavior and values in the corporate bureaucracies where men lived from nine to five.[9] Stevenson accepted these realities of modern life, but he warned that the spread of specialization within centralized bureaucracies caused men to lack meaning and purpose in their lives. Purpose would now need to be created and nurtured not at work but at home for both men and women, albeit in different ways. What the sphere of work now lacked for men, women could compensate for by creating a domestic haven into which men could retreat at the end of each day. Stevenson instructed the Smith women, "I think there is much you can do about our crisis in the humble role of housewife." In that role American women were "to restore valid, meaningful purpose to life in your home; ... to watch for and arrest the constant gravitational pulls to which we are all exposed — your workaday husband especially — in our specialized, fragmented society." "But I am told," Stevenson continued,

> that nowadays the young wife or mother is short of time for such subtle arts, that things are not what they used to be; that once immersed in the very pressing and particular problems of domesticity, many women feel frustrated and far apart from the great issues and stirring debates for which their education has given them understanding and relish. Once they read Baudelaire. Now it is the Consumer's Guide. Once they wrote poetry. Now it's the laundry list. Once they discussed art and philosophy until late in the night. Now they are so tired they fall asleep as soon as the dishes are finished. There is, often, a sense of contraction, of closing horizons and lost opportunities. They had hoped to play their part in the crisis of the age.

"And they do," he concluded, "although it might not be what they had envisioned." Stevenson instructed the graduates, "women 'never had it so good' as you do. And despite the difficulties of domesticity, you have a way to participate actively in the crisis." That "way," for Stevenson, was to create a domestic refuge where men could escape what Stevenson described as the new realities of modern life.[10]

Stevenson was not alone in describing a "crisis" of modern life in postwar America. A mainstream politician and presidential aspirant, Stevenson defined but did not critique the crisis or its causes. Others did. While Americans flocked to theaters to see *The Man in the Gray Flannel Suit* in 1956, many also read cultural critic Paul Goodman's new book *Growing Up Absurd*. Here Goodman laments "the disgrace of the Organized System of semimonopolies, government, advertisers, etc., and the disaffection of the growing generation."[11] He justifies focusing on disaffected young men because they are the ones who struggle to discover "how to be useful and make something of oneself." "A girl," Goodman asserts, "does not *have* to, she is not expected to, 'make something' of herself. Her career does not have to be self-justifying, for she will have children, which is absolutely self-justifying, like any other natural or creative act."[12] While writing a critical analysis of the disaffection of male youth, Goodman reveals he had internalized the same cultural assumptions about females that Stevenson made evident in his Smith College address. Goodman writes that his "purpose is a simple one: to show how it is desperately hard these days for an average child to grow up to be a man, for our present organized system of society does not want men. They are not safe. They do not suit."[13] Stated simply, what Goodman means by "real" manhood is evidence of individual agency, the willingness and the ability to say what one believes needs to be said and to do what one thinks needs to be done, regardless of the consequences. But life in the highly organized postwar society demanded conformity to the system rather than this central trait of what Goodman associates with American manhood.

It is important to recall that cultural anxieties about men's declining independence and authority existed long before the 1950s. In her book *Manliness and Civilization*, Gail Bederman demonstrates that politicians, psychologists and other commentators, Theodore Roosevelt being the most notable example, feared the demise of "manliness" as early as the late nineteenth century, although they did not speak and write about the problem in the same way. Roosevelt and his contemporaries saw the problem as being the increasing softness of American life due to the close of the frontier and the rise of large urban centers where it was no longer necessary for men to live Roosevelt's much lauded "strenuous life."[14] By the 1950s, commentators like Goodman and politicians like Stevenson recognized that the corporate reconstruction of American capitalism evident in Roosevelt's years but accelerated by the Great Depression, World War II, and postwar reconstruction robbed men of the autonomy their ancestors had enjoyed to a greater degree. Stevenson's description of the "crisis" was not as direct as Goodman's critique, but the private bureaucracies to which Stevenson referred were clearly corporate, the fragmentation and specialization he lamented but accepted clearly the same. The anxieties necessarily on the lips of some of the country's most prominent politicians in the 1950s and in the prose of its harshest cultural critics were not only evident but also central to many of its most popular films.

We have seen that anxieties about corporate life and about declining independence were voiced by prominent politicians and evident in popular culture prior to the 1950s: in the speeches of Progressive-era politicians like Theodore Roosevelt and Woodrow Wilson, and in the many social problem short films of those years; in feature films of the 1920s like King Vidor's *The Crowd* (1928); in Depression-era political rhetoric like Franklin Roosevelt's critique of "economic royalists"; in the campaigns of more populist politicians of the 1930s (such as Huey Long and Upton Sinclair); and in the screwball comedies and proletarian dramas of the 1930s. The first year after the war ended found Americans anxious about the possible return of the Depression due to the end of the war economy, and about the concentrated economic power and growing influence of corporations that resulted from the government contracts awarded to big business during the war, a phenomenon that continued throughout the cold war.[15]

The major theme of the popular film *It's a Wonderful Life* is significant in relation to the quickly changing cultural climate of the postwar years. By the 1950s, the pervasive influence of corporations in the American economy is represented in *The Man In The Gray Flannel Suit* as a reality of American life to which men like Tom Rath must adjust, just as Adlai Stevenson lectured Smith College women to do. A mere 10 years earlier, however, director Frank Capra's protagonist in *It's a Wonderful Life*, George Bailey (Jimmy Stewart), directly confronts Henry F. Potter (Lionel Barrymore), "the richest and meanest man in the county," and the symbol of concentrated economic power in the film. Potter's purpose is to dominate totally both the society represented by the town of Bedford Falls and the citizens who live there, and only an independent-minded and self-sacrificing character willing to act, George Bailey, can stop him.

It's a Wonderful Life was (and is) popular with audiences, and many critics liked it as well. Capra claimed to have received "thousands of letters" from Americans who told him the film "touched their hearts."[16] It touched many critics' hearts, too. A reviewer for *Variety* applauded the film's "April-air wholesomeness and humanism,"[17] and the reviewer for *Time* declared, "*It's a Wonderful Life* ... is a pretty wonderful movie." The *Time* reviewer went on to assert that even though the film was a fantasy it was "twice as lifelike as most Hollywood whimsies which are offered with straight faces as slices of reality."[18] The film did well at the box office, although Capra pointed out that it struggled to make a profit due to high production costs.[19] It was also nominated for Best Picture, Best Actor and Best Director, but that year the highly acclaimed film about American servicemen readjusting to civilian life, *The Best Years of Our Lives,* won all three categories.[20]

This most popular of Frank Capra's films spans the years 1900–1945. Potter is a financial titan, clearly representative of the Gilded Age captains of finance and industry, evident by the ornate wheelchair he gets around in and the elaborate horse-drawn carriage he travels in during one of the flashback scenes that enable us to learn about George Bailey's childhood experiences. Potter is a financial Captain Ahab who *must* have his whale.

His leviathan is a small building and loan institution, the Bailey Bros. Building and Loan, run by a mild mannered, middle-class man, Peter Bailey. This independent financial institution is the only thing keeping Potter from achieving the total economic dominance of society that he desires. Peter Bailey runs the building and loan with no interest in or thought of profit. He dedicates his life to using the institution to enable the working-class citizens and small business owners of Bedford Falls to own their own homes so they do not have to live in Potter's slums and pay their hard-earned money to him in the form of rent. The independent middle-class hero who follows in his father's footsteps and stands between Potter and the average citizens of Bedford Falls is the self-assured, ambitious and intelligent George Bailey. George dreams of fleeing this two-bit town by saving enough money to go to college and then exploring the world and making a million dollars by designing modern bridges and buildings. One cannot fulfill George's dreams if he remains rooted in a community, so George talks about marriage as if it is the 1919 flu virus that kills the drugstore owner's son. Alas, however, Bedford Falls and its citizens have George in a moral vice from which he cannot escape. His father dies when George is finally prepared to leave for college after saving for years to be able to go. George buries his father and then attends what he thinks will be his final board meeting at the building and loan, where he has worked with his father since leaving his childhood job at Mr. Gower's (Henry Byron Warner) drugstore.[21]

At this meeting George learns that Potter plans to gain control of the building and loan and then dissolve it so he can keep the people of Bedford Falls from owning their own homes. Potter attacks Peter Bailey's character. He tells the men at the meeting, "Peter Bailey was not a businessman. That's what killed him. He was a man of high ideals, so called." The issue of Ernie Bishop's (Frank Faylan) loan comes up. Potter points out that Ernie has no credit and that the bank turned down his application. George says he approved the loan because he knows Ernie personally. (Ernie is the taxi driver waiting outside the office to drive George to the train that will finally take him out of Bedford Falls). George tells the men he can vouch for Ernie's character. Potter responds, "If you shoot pool with some employee here you can come and borrow money. What does that get us? A discontented, lazy rabble instead of a thrifty working class." He then adds that Peter Bailey was a dreamer who filled people's heads with impossible ideas. George comes to his father's defense, arguing that Peter Bailey kept people like Ernie out of Potter's slums:

Just remember this, Mr. Potter, that this rabble you're talking about, they do most of the working and paying and living and dying in this community. Well, is it too much to have them work and pay and live and die in a couple of rooms and a bath? Anyway, my father didn't think so. People were human beings to him. But to you, a warped, frustrated old man, they're cattle! Well, in my book, he died a richer man than you'll ever be!

Potter's response is "sentimental hogwash." George leaves the room and paces nervously in the lobby of the building and loan while the board members deliberate with Potter. The men vote against Potter and decide not to dissolve the building and loan on the condition George remain as Executive Secretary in his father's place. One man leaves the meeting to tell George the board will not grant control to Potter if George agrees to stay and manage the building and loan. George is torn between following his own interests or forsaking them for the interests of the society in which he lives.

After his father dies, in *It's a Wonderful Life* (1946) George Bailey (Jimmy Stewart) defends citizens' right to own their own homes as he confronts Henry F. Potter (Lionel Barrymore), the "richest and meanest man in the county" and the symbol of concentrated economic power in the film (Photofest).

This scene is significant because of the explicit tension between Potter's unmitigated greed and the community interests for which George sacrifices his own interests. It is also significant because of the social positions of George and Potter. Potter is an economic elite, a person of extensive wealth and influence who wants to own everything and control everyone. He has invested a significant amount of capital in many businesses in the town, even in the building and loan, although he does not have a controlling interest. Potter wants to dissolve the building and loan so he can control the housing market in Bedford Falls. George, on the other hand, has always worked for a living. Although he does not drive a cab like Ernie, walk a beat like Bert the policeman, or own a small business like the Italian immigrant Martini's tavern or Mr. Gower's drugstore, he has worked since his childhood days at the drugstore. He understands the value of work and of small business ownership. George is clearly middle class, which is apparent by his position between Potter and working-class citizens like Bert and Ernie.

The physical position of George's eventual home with his wife, Mary (Donna Reed), further demonstrates his social position. Potter is at one extreme: we never see him outside of and are led to believe he lives at the center of town. The workers and small business owners like Martini, however, live in Bailey Park, a development of modest homes erected in a field outside of town. George and Mary's house is in a position between these two extremes. It is not outside of town nor is it downtown; it is in an intermediate position. Just as George mediates the tensions between Potter and the working class and small businessmen with a working-class clientele, he lives in a physical position between them. Moreover, as George is in a social position between Potter and the workers and independent business owners, he has the values of both, and the tensions between Potter's interests and those of the other residents of Bedford Falls are the tensions within George.

Although these tensions exist within George himself, it is a mistake to conclude, as Raymond Carney does, that the film is basically "a kind of psychodrama in which each of the major characters around George externalizes an imaginative contradiction or division of allegiance that already exists within him."[22] Such a conclusion abstracts the individual, in this case George, from the social context within which he lives and develops his values. It implies that the very real conflicts and contradictions in society are merely personal psychological conflicts. It reduces *all* conflict to psychological conflict, and it leads Carney to assert that in contrast to

Capra's earlier films — *Mr. Deeds Goes to Town* (1936), *Mr. Smith Goes to Washington* (1939), *Meet John Doe* (1941) — "the drama has moved away from confrontation, coercion and the attempted manipulation of a central character to become a psychodrama of contradictory imaginative tendencies within one figure."[23] Carney has uncovered one subtext to the film, the psychological tensions of postwar culture, but he has done so at too great a cost: by emphasizing characters' personal anxieties over the social relations that produce those anxieties, social relations with which audiences could identify. George's anxieties are related to the two different social and economic possibilities depicted in the film: Bedford Falls with George in it, a society where George checks Potter's power and influence and average citizens can own their own homes and independent businesses, and Pottersville, the society George learns Bedford Falls would have become had he not been there to check the centralization of economic power in Potter's hands and Potter's subsequent control over how and in what people live. Anxieties about these two possibilities exist within George because they exist outside of him, in the society where George and the other citizens live and work everyday. These anxieties and social tensions surely resonated with audiences in the immediate postwar years.

Following the board meeting, George remains in Bedford Falls and his life there is one of perpetual sacrifice and frustration. He gives his younger brother Harry his college funds, and Harry agrees to return to manage the building and loan after he graduates so George can then go to college. But Harry gets married in college and has the opportunity to work for his wife's father after he graduates, so George doesn't have the heart to make him keep his commitment. George then marries a local woman, Mary, who has recently graduated from college herself, has had a crush on George since she was a small girl and George made her sundaes at Mr. Gower's drugstore, and has returned to Bedford Falls for the sole purpose, apparently, of fulfilling her destiny by marrying George Bailey. George then lives the life of his father, sacrificing his ambition and the opportunity to acquire personal wealth in order to keep Potter at bay. Only when George contemplates suicide is he saved by divine intervention: his guardian angel, Clarence (Henry Travers), who earns his wings by showing George he has actually lived a wonderful life because he is the richest man in the county based on how much he is loved and appreciated by the people in the community.

It's a Wonderful Life portrays George and Peter Bailey as independent, paternalistic middle-class heroes who sacrifice their self-interests to check the unmitigated greed and concentrated economic power of Potter. As long as the building and loan remains under the control of virtuous middle-class citizens like Peter and George, small businesses can exist, even thrive, working-class citizens can achieve the American dream (if that dream is defined predominantly as home and small business ownership), and the concentrated economic power and influence represented by Potter can be contained if not eradicated or completely controlled. At one point when Potter is frustrated in his attempts to gain control of the building and loan, he tries to entice George to compromise his values and join him rather than oppose him. He offers George a position with a large annual salary and, appealing to George's life-long interest in seeing the world, regular business trips to Europe. For a brief moment, George considers taking the bait but then turns on Potter. He tells Potter he recognizes his plot to gain control of the building and loan and refuses the offer. He chooses a life of independence from Potter's control, albeit one of fewer opportunities and significantly less material well-being, so he can remain true to his values and protect the average citizens of Bedford Falls from the influence Potter would wield over their lives if he gained control of the building and loan.

The society represented in *The Man in the Gray Flannel Suit* is significantly different from that depicted a mere decade earlier in *It's a Wonderful Life*, for people must now work within the corporate order and adapt to the new realities of American life that Adlai Stevenson accepted but referred to as creating a postwar crisis. The corporate order and the empire builders and their managers who run it are to be negotiated, not opposed as George Bailey opposes Henry F. Potter. Even in 1946, however, Capra had to look to the past, to the early twentieth-century world of Peter Bailey and the values he instilled in George, to create a character who considers opposing the concentrated economic power and social control represented by Potter. By 1956, Tom Rath and the other men in gray suits carry out the specialized tasks defined by others that Adlai Stevenson alluded to in his address to Smith College women; they report to a cadre of corporate managers in the centralized bureaucracies that Stevenson accepted as the new reality of American life. Although that new reality is not symbolically confronted and opposed in *The Man in the Gray Flannel Suit* as it is when George confronts Potter and dedicates his life to opposing Potter's interests, the values of conformity and dishonesty for the sake of economic security associated with it are. That opposition, however, and the values of honesty, integrity, and independence exist not in the corporate order itself but in the home, with Betsy, who pushes Tom to resist the pressure to become another gray-suited corporate yes-man and to support her plans for them to become independent entrepreneurs while Tom continues working at UBC.[24]

When *The Man in the Gray Flannel Suit* begins, Tom Rath works for "the foundation," a position with no opportunity for advancement but one that, as Tom puts it, is "safe." Tom, due to the recommendation of a man he commutes with on the train into New York every day, and, most important, to the constant pressure of his wife to take the necessary risk to improve their lot in life, secures a job in public relations at the United Broadcasting Corporation. It is in this corporate environment that the themes of the Stevenson speech are so apparent. Tom's supervisors tell the founder and head of the company, Mr. Hopkins (Frederic March), exactly what they think he wants to hear. They are "yes-men" and expect Tom and all UBC employees to be the same. Tom's social reality is conformity, keeping the bosses happy, behaving as his superiors do. It is due to Betsy, clearly the more independent thinker, that Tom maintains his integrity and honesty in his relationship with Hopkins.[25] (The fact that these values reside in Betsy and that she is the staunchest advocate of them reveals that the values are not associated exclusively with concepts of manhood and masculinity.) Hopkins literally sacrificed his relationships with his family so he could dedicate his life to creating a corporate empire at UBC. By the end of the film, Tom's honesty and integrity, his willingness to tell Hopkins the truth against the pressures of his immediate superiors, combined with his insightful ideas (and Betsy's) about a speech Hopkins is scheduled to present, win Hopkins over. Hopkins wants to groom Tom to be his right-hand man and perhaps his successor at UBC. In one scene the two men discuss family and what Hopkins has sacrificed, and Hopkins says that if he had it to do over again he would choose to spend more time with his wife, son and daughter. His daughter elopes at age 18 with a man old enough to be her father, his estranged wife tells him she never wants to see him again, and we learn his son died in World War II. He gives Tom a chance to take the place of one of his superiors at UBC, but Tom tells him he cannot take a business trip with him due to family matters. Hopkins says he understands and we are left thinking that Tom will continue in a nine-to-five position working for Hopkins.

The home in the film is a space that simultaneously nurtures both resistance and accommodation to the postwar realities of American life. Betsy's impatience with Tom for even considering to behave like the other men wearing gray suits is possible because the social space of her home, created by the independent physical space of the house that she detests, frees her from the daily pressures on Tom to conform to the corporate order and become a calm and obedient cog in a corporate bureaucracy. Although Betsy is confined to the home, it would be a mistake to interpret her character as operating as the kind of self-sacrificing "true woman" that Adlai Stevenson attempted to revive in his Smith College address: the dedicated wife and mother and moral guardian of the family, a woman shielded in the home from the corrupt, self-seeking realities endemic to business and politics.[26] Betsy does not resist the materialism of postwar society, nor, directly, does she challenge her place in it as a homemaker or Tom's as a loyal corporate bureaucrat. But her freedom from the corporate-bureaucratic life that Tom must lead enables her to think and act much more like George Bailey than as a submissive wife or like Tom and the other gray-suits at UBC. Betsy's honesty and integrity save Tom from losing his, and her ideas and plans provide them with the possibility of future economic independence, further evidence that such independent traits are not exclusively masculine.

Although she does not spend her days trying to save working-class Americans, small businessmen, and an entire town from the economic control of a character like Henry F. Potter, Betsy shares George Bailey's values in two significant ways. First, she is not only willing but compelled to speak truth to power, which for her is to speak truth to Tom (and Tom, as a result, to his superiors at UBC, including Hopkins), much to his chagrin. But her absolute disgust with Tom's apparent willingness to be just like the other gray-suits and not rock the corporate boat directly influences Tom's future actions. Second, Betsy is every bit as entrepreneurial as George Bailey dreams of becoming before he faces the reality that he is stuck in Bedford Falls for life. George wants to build bridges and new buildings and make a million dollars before he turns thirty. Betsy likewise wants to move up the socio-economic ladder and demonstrates she has the character that undoubtedly would enable her to thrive as an independent businesswoman. When Tom and Betsy inherit Tom's grandmother's house and land, she tells Tom of her plans to move into the grandmother's house and, once there, pressure the zoning board to change the zoning laws so she and Tom can divide the 23 acres of land into one-acre parcels, take out construction loans, and build houses on the lots and sell them. Betsy shows every sign of becoming the prosperous, independent developer that George Bailey only dreams of being. (This fact is even more evident in the novel.) George does become a developer, but a self-sacrificing one, continuing in the footsteps of his father, forsaking profits and personal wealth so people can achieve the dream of home-ownership in Bailey Park and, consequently, independence from Potter. Betsy's values are clearly more self serving, but they represent the entrepreneurial ethic of an independent business person who would not be happy in the culture of conformity endemic to the corporate bureaucracy that Tom Rath finds himself negotiating every day.

The tensions between Tom and Betsy become evident in the first scenes in the Rath home, where repeated references to death, concerns about financial and job security, conflicts

Tom Rath (Gregory Peck) in one of many scenes in *The Man in the Gray Flannel Suit* (1956) where his wife Betsy (Jennifer Jones) encourages him and sometimes lectures him to take risks and to speak his mind rather than conform to the corporate culture and become another gray-suited yes-man (Photofest).

between Tom and Betsy and between parents and children establish a dark and anxious mood. Americans sitting in theaters across the country in 1956 could relate to that mood. Adults had lived through the Great Depression and World War II. Many had experienced financial insecurity and continued to fear it. They also lost family members during the war and became part of the first generation in human history to face the potential of nuclear annihilation as the cold war heated up between the United States and the Soviet Union. Some now had to guard what they said to ensure they were not branded as communist subversives in the extreme culture of political conformity known as McCarthyism. Risk aversion, as it is depicted in Tom's character in these scenes, is something many Americans understood first hand.

In the first scene at the house, one of the girls says repeatedly that she thinks her sister will die from the chicken pox and Tom scolds her for saying so. In another scene the boy gets mad at his father because Tom won't let him sleep with the family dog and shouts at him to "shut up" after the boy says he doesn't care if his parents die "a hundred million times." The tensions between the children and their parents cause similar tensions to develop between Tom and Betsy throughout the evening. These tensions eventually erupt into a full-scale war of words, one in which she attacks his character for being too cautious and indecisive, and his willingness to sacrifice his courage and independence for security in the post-war organized system.

What finally ignites the conflict is a phone call Tom receives about his grandmother's estate. He learns that his grandmother apparently lost the money his grandfather had left her. (We discover later that the butler who had been taking care of her embezzled the money.) The small amount of money they would get if they sell the grandmother's house Tom would like to put in the bank. Betsy wants to sell their house and the grandmother's place and buy a "nice" house. He's cautious, unwilling to take risks to create a better future. She's a risk-taking optimist, someone who wants to shape their lives rather than merely take things as they come and respond passively to circumstances as they develop.

The argument about the house evolves into one about his job at the foundation. Tom tells Betsy many people are worse off than they are and that he's lucky to be making the $7,000 salary he earns. Betsy replies, "But you can't look at things like that, Tommy. You've got to believe that things are going to get better. Promotions. Opportunities. Some good breaks. That's what life is, hope and the breaks. You can't just accept the way things are now." Tom asks her if she's ever considered what would happen to her and the children if he "dropped dead," and he defends his job at the foundation as an "absolutely safe spot" when she asks if he plans to stay there forever. He tells her they should put what money they get for the grandmother's house in the bank and buy some insurance, and she replies with emphasis and emotion: "I'm sorry, Tommy. You know how I hate this house, but you don't know how much I hate it. It's *ugliness*! It's *depression*! But most all, it … it's *defeat*! Don't you feel that at all?" He admits, "Well, it's not exactly a palace." She then proceeds to drive a stake through his heart as their conflict mounts: "It's a graveyard, Tommy, a graveyard with everything we used to talk about: happiness … fun … *ambition*. And I want to get out of it." "But if we put it all in the *bank*," he replies as she cuts him off and says, "And go on living here the rest of our lives?" When she complains that their house is "not a happy house," Tom doesn't agree and Betsy blames his unwillingness to take risks on the war. "Ever since the war," she gibes. Tom tells her the war's been over for 10 years and he just doesn't think "this is any time to be taking chances." "Then if it wasn't the war," she asks, "what has happened to you?" Tom replies, "What do you mean, what's happened to me?" "I don't know," she says, "except that you've lost your guts and all of a sudden I'm ashamed of you." The stake reaches its target as that line concludes their argument and Tom takes his drink with him while he goes upstairs to say goodnight to the kids.

Tom's experiences during the war, depicted in a series of flashback scenes, are a significant part of the film and demand comment here, for although Betsy is correct that those experiences made Tom more cautious, his risk aversion is a personal issue related in part to his wartime experiences that he brings to a new postwar structural reality. Once he is hired at UBC, Tom becomes one of many employees at the company, and he must negotiate his way through corporate life just as the other gray-suits must do. Betsy pushes Tom to be independent-minded and take risks, but it's not as if every other man at UBC takes risks and Tom does not. When Tom does take risks, he is the extreme exception rather than the rule, for the corporate culture at UBC denies such agency to most men who work there. That lack of agency is central to the crisis that Stevenson, Goodman and other commentators in the fifties described as a reality of postwar life. In the end, Tom stands out from *all* of the other gray-suits for his honesty and his integrity, for his willingness to risk even his job and the security it provides for himself and his family by telling his boss something Tom knows he may not want to hear. And it is clear that Betsy, rather than Tom himself, is the key reason he finds his independent voice.

Taking risks, especially the risk of death in time of war, which Tom did on multiple occasions in both the European and Pacific theaters, is a traditional characteristic of an idealized American manhood associated with historical figures like Theodore Roosevelt and his conception of manhood.[27] We learn that Tom killed multiple men during the war, including a good friend who happened to be in the wrong place when Tom threw a grenade. Tom lives with his memory of that tragic event, and with his memories of the many enemy soldiers he killed. Those memories cause Tom to see his own life as insignificant in the larger scheme of things and to value security in an insecure world.

It is not men's wartime experiences, however, that cause Tom and other UBC employees to avoid taking risks in the postwar corporate order. Rather, the central issue related to men adjusting to the corporate life depicted in *The Man in the Gray Flannel Suit* is one that Paul Goodman recognized in 1956 when he wrote that the "organized system of society" no longer wanted "real men" because "They are not safe. They do not suit."[28] It is not memories of wartime experiences, then, that cause corporate employees to become gray-suited yes-men in the postwar years. Rather, it is their declining independence and lack of agency in the postwar corporate order. Tom's wartime experiences changed his life, but those experiences do not explain the realities of daily life at UBC that Tom and the other gray-suits must constantly negotiate. All the gray-suits do not have flashbacks of wartime experiences. All do work at UBC. Corporate life, not memories of war, causes them to lack independence of thought and action.

The argument that takes place between Tom and Betsy establishes the differences between them and also provides us with hints of how each will respond to the corporate culture at UBC once Tom secures a job there. Betsy is assertive and a risk taker. She has principles and is someone who questions things and authority. She looks to the future and is willing to take risks to shape that future to make life better for herself and her family. She does not merely complain about how things are; she envisions how things might be and what she and Tom can do to make them that way. In contrast to Betsy, Tom appears to believe no risk is acceptable to take as long as the Raths have security, a roof over their heads, and food on the table. Her personality is dynamic, his as bland and conservative as the gray suit he wears. She seems to be the more sympathetic character, someone audiences could admire for her courage, strength of character, and determination to seize the day, much like George Bailey a decade earlier. But Tom's aversion to risk, his emphasis on security and safety, are traits that resonated with postwar audiences as well.

When Tom secures a job at UBC, some of his anxieties are reinforced in the corporate environment where what he does and how he does it are determined and scrutinized by a cadre of mid-level corporate bureaucrats. The values of George Bailey and of Betsy — honesty, integrity, speaking truth to power regardless of the personal consequences — are values that UBC employees must compromise unless they have direct access to the man at the top, which is extremely rare due to the centralization of authority described by Adlai Stevenson and 1950s social critics, but is the case for Tom due to the nature of his position at UBC. And when Tom does speak truth to power at the company, he does so because of Betsy's influence, because of the values she is able to hold and nurture in an independent space, a place where she is free from the corporate culture at UBC: the American home.

We begin to learn about the corporate culture at UBC when Tom has a series of interviews with the bureaucrats who decide which candidates will eventually be interviewed by Hopkins himself, although the candidates do not know that the person who gets the position will be a special aid to Hopkins. In his first interview with Gordon Walker (Gene Lockhart), Walker instructs Tom to go into another room and type a statement about why UBC should hire him, a statement that emphasizes the most significant thing about him. He composes a brief statement in which he simply says, "I believe I could do a good job." He continues without mentioning anything about his significance and ends by stating he "will be glad to answer any other questions relevant to this application for employment." He also says he fails to see "that any further speculation on my importance could be of any legitimate interest or value to the United Broadcasting Corporation." There is nothing in the statement that would make him stand out other than the fact that he must see himself as the most insignificant person on the planet. When Walker reads the statement, he appears dumbfounded by Tom's failure to discuss his significance.

That insignificance, however, suits perfectly the corporate culture at UBC, a culture shaped and protected by Walker and other bureaucrats who prize conformity of ideas and behavior over innovative thinking and independent action. Tom suits these middle managers because of his apparent insignificance, not despite it. But he believes he will hear nothing more from the company and tells Betsy he will not get the position. He is surprised, then, when he secures another interview with Walker, Bill Ogden (Henry Daniell) and Hopkins himself. Ogden is Hopkins' personal assistant, and he tells Tom, "Mr. Hopkins was quite impressed with the *tone* of your application." Tom asks, "Ralph Hopkins?" Ogden's reference to the tone of Tom's application reveals that the company doesn't prize men who think they are important. Tom's question about Hopkins demonstrates that Tom did not realize he might be working for the man who devoted his life to building the corporate empire that is the United Broadcasting Corporation. When Hopkins joins the others, he tells Tom about the national mental health campaign he wants to begin and asks Tom if he has any ideas about how to get it off the ground and garner public support, especially the support of people in the medical profession. Tom notes that he would need to give it some thought but makes some immediate suggestions. Hopkins says he likes Tom's ideas. (We learn later that he also likes Tom because Tom reminds him of his deceased son, who died in the war.) One of the other men agrees immediately, the first sign that confirming what Hopkins thinks rather than telling him the truth is an important component of everyday life at UBC.

When Tom arrives at home that evening, he finds Betsy in bed; she has contracted their daughter's chicken pox. The scene is important because it establishes Betsy's role as an innovative and entrepreneurial risk taker whose criticisms of her husband's cautious behavior stem from her own independent personality. Her illness does not keep her from telling Tom about her plans for his grandmother's property and the Rath family's future, including Tom's employment possibilities. Tom reluctantly agrees to listen as Betsy tells him they can live in his grandmother's house for a while and divide the 23 acres into one-acre lots, build houses on them, and sell the houses. She says one-acre lots in the area sell for $1,000. She wants to become developers, says they can borrow the money from the bank to build, and the least they will make is $100,000. (In the novel, soon after the Raths move to the property a contractor gets them to consider smaller, one-quarter-acre lots and figures total sales will be $800,000.00.[29] By the end of the novel it's clear the Raths will get their development.) Tom remarks, sarcastically, "And just to think, only a week ago we were facing the poor house." Betsy replies, sternly, "I'm not kidding, Tommy." Tom asks how she thinks they can afford to keep up the new house and pay the bills while they carry out Betsy's plan. She says they will be able to do it on the new $10,000 salary he will earn working at UBC. He reminds her he has not been offered a job at UBC and insists he will not be offered a job at the company. She tells him the people at UBC would not have discussed salary with him if Mr. Hopkins didn't want him, and that Tom can get the full $10,000 if he has the "nerve to hold out for it." She hesitates when she says this, seeming to recall their last argument when she said he lacked "guts" and she was "ashamed" of him. This scene does not depict Betsy as an emotional, irrational woman, the way Tom seems to want to view her in order to justify his own cautious behavior and pessimistic attitude. Rather, it depicts Betsy as a calculating, determined, rational entrepreneur and acceptable risk taker, a person, unlike Tom, with dreams but also plans to turn those dreams into realities.

Betsy's optimism is justified in the next scene as Tom walks to his new office escorted by Walker and Ogden. They tell him his new title will be "Special Assistant to the President." His first responsibility is to work on a speech Hopkins is scheduled to deliver at a convention of physicians where Hopkins will discuss the national mental health campaign he wants to launch. Tom asks Ogden, "You mean you want me to write this speech for him?" Ogden informs Tom, "Nobody writes Mr. Hopkins' speeches but Mr. Hopkins. We simply do the research, kick around ideas with him, and kick out a rough, preliminary form." He then leans over Tom's desk and looks him straight in the eyes: "And if the speech is right, it will not even mention a national mental health campaign. But at the end of it, the entire audience will rise as one man and demand, not only that such a campaign be launched at once, but that Mr. Hopkins should head it." Tom says, "Is that *all?*" Ogden replies, while exiting, "And I wouldn't be facetious about it if I were you."

Tom's experiences on the job that first day teach him about the stifling nature of corporate life, about a business culture that represses independent thought and rewards conformity and banality. He tries that evening to explain to Betsy what he's learning about the corporate culture at UBC. While she drives him home from the train station he tells her about the corporate game he is learning to play. He says he is writing a speech for Hopkins but stops himself and says, "No, no, no. That's not it. Might as well get used to this double talk from the beginning. I'm *not* writing a speech for Mr. Hopkins. I'm providing the rough material, so that he can write his own speech." She tells him he's being "bright and cynical" about his new job and says she is "tired of being bright and brittle and broke. There's no way to tackle a new job or anything else but honestly." Tom replies, "Well, I'm going to tackle it honestly, but I have an idea that things are going to be a little more complicated on Madison Avenue." He then notices she's not taking the usual way home and asks where they are going. He learns Betsy has been implementing her plan for the grandmother's estate. She tells him they are going to the grandmother's house to talk to Edward, the man who took care of Tom's grandmother and her house for decades, because Betsy sold their house that day to a man who said he would give them $14,000 cash if he could move in immediately. Betsy has them scheduled to move into the grandmother's house on Thursday. While Tom's new position in corporate America stifles his independent thoughts and actions, Betsy's position in the home provides her with the freedom to think in innovative ways and to take quick and independent action when necessary.

Because Tom is hired to be Hopkins' special assistant, he learns about the personal sacrifices Hopkins has made to build his corporate empire, and he is soon faced with the possibility of making choices that involve the same sacrifices. The men's first private meeting together is cut short when Hopkins' 18-year-old daughter, Susan (Gigi Perreau), arrives. Hopkins' estranged wife, Helen (Ann Harding), called him earlier to tell him their daughter refuses to go to college and is involved with older men. Helen lives in a house they built in the same Connecticut neighborhood where Tom now lives in his grandmother's house. Hopkins lives at the top of a New York apartment building overlooking Central Park. Their different residences reveal that, while still married, they lead separate lives. In their conversation Helen lets Hopkins know that if he can't reach Susan she will hold him responsible for the damage he's done to Susan by making UBC a bigger priority than his family. The impact of Hopkins' choices on his family is evident in Susan's rebellion against everything he values and the way he lives his life.

Susan rejects her father's attempts to advise her about her own life because the choices he has made have been self-serving and reveal that he loves nothing and no one more than the wealth, power and influence that his position at the pinnacle of corporate America provide him. She refuses to work for him or go to college, and she lashes out at him when he tries to educate her about the money she will one day inherit and the power she will have as a consequence of her wealth. She tells him if he is trying to get her to understand that money is power, she's not interested. "I'm not going to let money ruin my life the way it's ruined yours and mother's," she says. "It's really stupid the way you live, working all the time, ever since I can remember. You must have a guilt complex. Or you're a masochist!" The more he tries to talk to her, the more critical and enraged she becomes before she storms out of the room: "Why this all of a sudden? You've never paid any attention to me before." When he says she's still his "little girl" and he loves her, she calls him a hypocrite and says, "You've hardly bothered to see me since I was born." Just before she storms out of the room she says he doesn't love her or her mother or have the capacity to love anyone and shouts, "And I don't want to be like that!" He catches up with her at the elevator and tells her to be reasonable, but she takes the opportunity to criticize him one last time: "I don't want to be reasonable. I don't want to have anything to do with you! That's the way you and mother have been all your lives, reasonable, and I don't want anything like that. I'm going to try something else." Like we will see about the character

Benjamin Braddock (Dustin Hoffman) in *The Graduate* (1967) a decade later, Susan rejects the values of her affluent parents and criticizes the idea that she should have a myopic focus on planning for the future. Although she is clearly immature, she elopes with a bohemian artist (a playwright) and foreshadows both the alienation that Ben Braddock represents and the more countercultural characters in movies like *Easy Rider* (1969), *Joe* (1970) and other counterculture films of the late sixties and early seventies, characters that reject conformity and value independence and freedom.

While Tom's first days at UBC teach him that a member of the rank-and-file gray-suits is expected to conform to how corporate bureaucrats like Ogden and Walker want him to think and act, his increasing knowledge of Hopkins' private life reveals the personal sacrifices he would have to make to move out of the rank-and-file and into the class of elite corporate managers.

Tom's immediate discontent with his job, however, is due to the fact that he is supposed to write a speech for which someone else will get credit and, more significantly, for which he will actually have little, if any, input. Tom meets with Ogden in Ogden's office after his new boss finishes reading the last in a series of drafts Tom writes of the speech Hopkins is scheduled to deliver on mental health. Ogden tells Tom the speech is awful, worse than the previous drafts, that it lacks "oomph." Tom, frustrated by remaining engaged in the redundant, unproductive labor of composing multiple drafts of the speech without any clear suggestions from Ogden about the direction Ogden thinks the speech should go, stands up to Ogden. He tells Ogden he is not giving him any intelligible input other than the speech lacks "oomph," and he says he thinks Mr. Hopkins should have the opportunity to read it for himself and decide if it has "oomph or not." Tom snipes that he could get better comments from his six-year-old son. Ogden reminds Tom of the power he wields over him when he tells Tom he could find himself out on Madison Avenue if he isn't careful. When Tom says that's all right with him, Ogden says he'll take care of the speech himself. Ogden then turns away from Tom, ignoring Tom as he begins a phone conversation and acts as if Tom isn't even in the room. Tom rises and exits, not sure if he still works at UBC, and clearly aware of the consequences of speaking honestly and independently in a corporate bureaucracy that demands conformity and submission. The only thing that saves Tom from being crushed by one of the biggest cogs in the wheel that is the corporate structure at UBC is his direct access to the man at the top, Ralph Hopkins.

Tom meets with Hopkins shortly after his contentious meeting with Ogden, and Hopkins asks him how the speech is coming along. Tom tells Hopkins he's no longer working on the speech and says he'll have to ask Bill Ogden if he wants to know why. Confused, Hopkins says he doesn't understand; he then gives Tom a copy of the speech that he says he and "the boys" have composed. Hopkins asks Tom to read it and tell him what he thinks. When he asks Tom if something is wrong, Tom says he just didn't understand that was how the speech was to be written. He tells Hopkins he will be glad to read it that night. Once Tom leaves, Hopkins immediately calls Bill Ogden and asks him if Tom prepared anything on the speech. Ogden tells Hopkins that Tom did some work on the speech but what he wrote was worthless and he didn't want to bother Hopkins with it.

Tom's contentious discussion of the speech with Betsy that evening reveals the fragile nature of Tom's position at UBC and the reasons for his discontent with his new job. Tom reads the speech and takes it home to have Betsy read it, too. She does, and they discuss it while they sit in the kitchen at Tom's grandmother's house, where they now live. The scene demonstrates Tom's growing awareness that corporate life is a strategic game of self-preservation in which the most successful players are those who best wield the tools of ingratiation, ambiguity and deceit.

He refuses to tell Betsy if he wrote the speech until she lets him know what she thinks about it; he wants her honest opinion regardless of who wrote it. She confesses that she thinks it is "boring" and some parts are "silly." He tells her he didn't write it and thinks it's "dribble." She agrees, and he tells her he's supposed to tell Hopkins what he thinks. When she learns he's reluctant to do so, she can't understand why. Tom's justification for considering being dishonest about what he thinks demonstrates how corporate life at UBC creates out of new employees like Tom the gray-suited yes-men that Betsy learns to despise. "Well, one thing I've learned already," Tom says,

> is you've got to protect yourself in the clinches. The thing to do is to sort of feel your way along. I mean, when they call you in to give a report like this, you begin with a lot of highly qualified, contradictory statements and watch your man's face to see which one pleases him. For instance, you can begin, "I think there are a lot of wonderful things in this speech." Then you pause for a second or two. If that seems to make him happy, then you can go on, "and I have only a few minor alterations to suggest." But if he looks a little startled on the word "wonderful," then you switch, and say "but on the whole, I don't think it quite comes off." If you've been smart

enough about it, you can wind up by telling him *exactly* what he wants to hear.

Betsy responds to Tom's description of what she considers to be the appalling reality of the corporate culture at UBC by asking, "But that's not what you're going to do, is it?" Tom confesses, "I don't know!" Betsy, incredulous, shoots back, "You don't know!" "Well," Tom says, "I've got to protect myself, haven't I?" She looks away from him, down at the table, and says, with disgust, "Well, I'll tell you what I think about it. I think the whole idea is sickening." When they continue their argument in another room she says, "This is a speech that can make or break a very important health campaign for this country, isn't it?" He says it could and she continues to voice her disgust as he justifies forsaking his independence and his values to adapt to the corporate culture at UBC. Betsy asks, "And are you going to tell him the truth about it or not?" Tom says, "But how do you know that that's the truth? How do you know that this isn't precisely the way to appeal to those people?" "Oh, Tommy," Besty criticizes, "you don't even believe that yourself." Tom says, "Well, it's exactly the sort of appeal that sells a billion dollars worth of cars in this country every year." She counters, "That's entirely different. That's some kind of math nonsense. These are very intelligent men you'll be talking to. They'll throw up at that muck!" Tom, even though he asked for her opinion and agreed with it, now belittles her judgment. "Oh, you don't know anything about it one way or the other," he says. She wants to know if he's going to give Hopkins his honest opinion, and he says he is, that he will tell Hopkins "I honestly don't know. But that this sort of approach has been successful in other sales campaigns and now I see no reason it can't work in this one." "Are you trying to kid me?" she asks, and he responds by telling her that is the "exact truth, as a matter of fact."

The arguments Tom makes to Betsy are those of a man frightened by the prospect of losing his job and being unable to provide for his family, fears that men like Bill Ogden are well aware of and use to foster the dependence and conformity they demand. But Betsy is a bigger risk taker than Tom and lets him know she wants him "to go out and fight for something again, like the fellow I married. Not to turn into a *cheap, slippery, yes-man.*" Tom defends himself as he describes the necessity of conforming in order to ensure security for his family. "When a man's got plenty of security, money in the bank, other jobs waiting for him," he lectures her, "it's a cinch to be fearless and full of integrity. But when he's got a wife and three children to support, and his job's all he's got, what do you think he ought to do about it then?" Betsy is emphatic: "I know what I'd do." Tom reminds her she should also think about the fact that they might not even own the house they live in because his grandmother's butler is contesting the will. (We later learn that the butler had the grandmother sign a document leaving the house to him when she believed she was signing one of a number of checks to pay some bills.) Betsy concedes and tells Tom to go ahead and do what he thinks he needs to do: "Alright. You can try it. But I don't think it will work." Tom tells her to leave it to him and concludes his justification by describing himself as a rational player in the game of corporate life. "I never wanted to get into this rat race," he asserts, "but now that I'm in it, I think I'd be an idiot not to play it the way everybody else plays it." Betsy tells him she believes he's a decent man and supports what he will do "because for a decent man there's never any peace of mind without honesty." But just before she exits the room she lets him know she's beginning to question his honesty when she says, "Right now it just makes me wonder how long it'll be before you decide that it will be *simpler* and *safer* not to tell me the truth." Her last line foreshadows what is to come when Tom learns from his old army comrade that he has an illegitimate Italian child, a boy he fathered with a woman he had an affair with during the war.[30] Betsy fears that the lack of honesty and integrity in corporate life, where deception and conformity are the norm, threatens to infiltrate the American home.

Tom meets Hopkins at his apartment the following day to discuss the speech, and he learns that Hopkins' daughter has eloped and his marriage is over because Hopkins' wife blames him for Susan's irresponsible actions and her attitudes toward her parents. Hopkins' failures as a father and husband are clearly on his mind as he discusses the speech with Tom. Where other scenes reveal that average middle-class citizens like the Raths question and criticize the social relationships of the postwar corporate order and the values associated with it, this scene with Tom and Hopkins divulges that even the people at the top, the corporate empire builders, question what they create and control, the social costs associated with the system.

Hopkins asks Tom a leading question about the current form of the speech. "So," he says, "you like that approach, huh?" Tom does what Betsy told him he should do: he tells Hopkins the truth. "No," he says, "I didn't. I don't think that's the right approach at all." Hopkins says he's asked six men (clearly the corporate yes-men the system produces so copiously) about the speech and Tom is the first one "that wasn't actually enthusiastic about it." Tom replies, "Well, I could be 100 percent wrong, of course, but you asked me what I thought about it, and that's it." Hopkins asks him what he doesn't like and Tom defines two problems with the speech that are inappropriate for an audience of intelligent physicians: It describes in depth the mental health problem they already know exists, and it's filled with false humility the physicians will see through immediately. Tom tells him the speech states numerous times "That you're a very simple, unin-formed man who, in effect, doesn't really know what he's talking about." He says if the doctors really believed that they would never want him to lead the campaign for mental health. Hopkins asks Tom how he would write it, and Tom says he would tell them he is willing to use the resources of UBC to publicize the campaign for mental health. Hopkins tells Tom it's a very interesting idea and then puts his head in his hand, seeming to contemplate the news about his daughter and his relationships with his daughter and his wife. When Tom gets his briefcase, Hopkins asks him to stay and have a drink. He shifts the conversation to his son Bobby, a young man who, like Tom, insisted on doing the "right" thing and playing it "straight."

After Hopkins instructs Tom to spend a lot of time with his kids, he slips into a self-justifying rant that reveals his attitude about the vast major-ity of the men he employees and the ego that caused him to sacrifice family for wealth, status and power in corporate America. With a rising voice he tells Tom, "You know where I made my mistake. Yep. Somebody's got to do it." He stomps his foot on floor and continues:

> Somebody's got to dedicate himself to it. Big, successful businesses just
> aren't built by men like you — nine to five and home and family. You live
> on 'em, but you never built one. Big, successful businesses are built by
> men like me, who give everything they've got to it. Live it, body and soul.
> Lift it up regardless of anybody or anything else. And without men like
> me there wouldn't be any big, successful businesses. My mistake was in
> being one of those men.

Hopkins catches himself, looks over at Tom, and raises his hand to his forehead as he apologies for his rant. "I'm terribly sorry," he says. "Why don't we take this up some other time." Tom replies, "Not at all. Aren't you feeling well?" Hopkins tells Tom he just needs to lie down and get a little rest and thanks him for coming. Hopkins' "mistake" was not in cre-ating a corporate empire but in forsaking his family to do it. But one cannot have both, and some men just "got to do it." If they don't, lesser men will not have jobs; the social order itself depends on men like Hopkins making the kinds of sacrifices he makes.

Here the corporate order, with its bureaucratic culture of conformity and platoons of gray-suited yes-men who forsake their independence and integrity for security, is not challenged as it is in the earlier social problem short films of the Progressive Era produced for and marketed to niche audiences. Nor is it directly criticized and confronted by virtuous working-class and middle-class heroes as it is in some of the Depression-era feature films or even as late as the immediate postwar war period in a film like *It's a Wonderful Life*. Rather, employees accept the corporate order but they do so leerily, and even corporate empire builders like Ralph Hopkins have doubts.

Tom negotiates the needs of his family with the demands of his job, and he will not move up as far as he could within the corporate bureaucracy because he privileges family over career. He knows and works with the man at the top and is liked and respected by him, so his job is secure; Bill Ogden cannot fire Tom because Hopkins will protect him. Tom will continue as Hopkins' special assistant but will not have Ogden's success because he is "nine to five and home and family." Without direct access to Hopkins, however, Tom would need to do what all the other gray-suits do: comply with Ogden's demands and conform to the corporate culture that Betsy and Tom detest. But Tom works directly with Hopkins. He discovers that because of his relationship with Hopkins he can speak his mind and influence the final product of his labor — the speech. In the end, Tom does not compromise his values and does not need to escape into a domestic refuge created by his wife (Betsy never actually creates such a refuge), as Adlai Stevenson emphasized in his speech to Smith College graduates. He learns he can be honest with Hopkins, and Hopkins provides him with some autonomy over his labor, so he is no longer as discontented with his job or completely disaffected from corporate life at UBC. He occupies a rare and privileged space within the corporate bureaucracy.

The corporate culture at UBC will continue to reward what Betsy refers to as a "cheap, slippery, yes-man," one like any of the six men Hopkins says read the speech before Tom did, a man like either Gordon Walker or Bill Ogden. These middle- and upper-level managers forsake honesty and integrity as they try to figure out what Hopkins and their immediate superiors want and give it to them without question. Their security, as demonstrated in the scene between Ogden and Tom when Ogden removes Tom from the task of writing the speech and threatens him with unemployment, depends on reinforcing their superiors' opinions, even ingratiating them. Tom is prepared to fit into that culture, as much as it disgusts him, to play the game like everyone else plays it, because he knows his family's security depends on it. The opposition to that culture exists outside of the bureaucratic structure at UBC, in the independent space of the home, where Betsy is free to criticize both Tom and the corporate reality he must negotiate every day as she pressures him to maintain his honesty and integrity in the new corporate order where, as Stevenson noted, authority had become centralized and independence reduced, in the organized system that Paul Goodman lamented for no longer valuing "real men." Betsy's values are paramount in the film, however, and reveal that the system would not value "real women" in Tom's position either, if it did not confine them to the role of secretary and let them in at the level of the gray-suits.

The Man in the Gray Flannel Suit received positive reviews, and the themes of the film resonated with postwar audiences filled with veterans and other Americans adjusting to the increasingly organized nature of postwar life, at least the white, middle-class members of those audiences; the only minority in the film is the black domestic servant who serves Ralph Hopkins his breakfast, just as the only African American who seems to reside in Bedford Falls is the domestic who works in Peter Bailey's home. The critics loved the movie. *The New York Times* reviewer referred to it as "a mature, fascinating and often tender and touching film." He focused, however, on what he portrayed as the "personal" issues that various characters deal with rather than on the structural realities of corporate life that disgust Betsy and create so much tension in the Rath family home. He noted that while Hopkins talks to Tom "the whole rotten fabric of the boss' personal life is ripped," and he emphasized that Tom has to deal with the "crooked caretaker" of his grandmother's estate and the pain associated with telling Betsy about his wartime affair. He merely mentioned in passing that the film contains "some intimations of the harried life of other people," but he did feel compelled to point out that characters' "feelings and mental processes are truly conditioned by the patterns of their lives." He made no reference, however, to what those patterns are.[31] The woman who reviewed the movie for *The Chicago Daily Tribune* similarly called the film "delightful," but she said a little more than her male counterpart at *The Times* about Tom's struggles with corporate life, noting that Tom "encounters the infighting among the yes-men, and soon begins to wonder if integrity pays."[32]

Although these contemporary reviewers focused on personal issues, in his study of American dystopian literature in the postwar years David

Seed points out that *The Man in the Gray Flannel Suit* shares some of the themes central to that literature. "Despite being an apparently successful executive," Seed writes, "Thomas Rath registers a tension between satisfaction and its opposite which recurs throughout fifties dystopias." Moreover, Seed informs us, "the protagonists of dystopias are usually defined in relation to organizational structures." Seed notes that in Aldous Huxley's novel *Brave New World* the author incorporates into the narrative "an abiding fear which runs through American dystopian fiction of the 1950s that individuals will lose their identity and become the two-dimensional stereotypes indicated in two catch-phrases of the period: the 'organization man' and the 'man in the gray flannel suit.'"[33] Although movie critics focused primarily on what they referred to as personal issues in *The Man in the Gray Flannel Suit*, references to the declining independence associated with the increasingly corporate nature of American life soon pervaded American culture in the postwar years. Gregory Peck's gray suit came to represent much more than a pair of slacks and a jacket, and "yes-man" became a hyphenated noun, symbols of declining independence and increasingly obligatory conformity, realities of postwar life that dystopian writers associated with anything but progress, and that politicians like Adlai Stevenson insisted were new realities to which American women and their husbands must adapt.

In *It's a Wonderful Life* (1946), opposition to Potter and what he represents — centralized economic power and the ability to control the lives of average citizens — exists in the independent building and loan managed by the virtuous middle-class Bailey men. By the time *The Man in the Gray Flannel Suit* (1956) is released just one decade later, the corporate reality represented by the United Broadcasting Corporation and its founder is not opposed by virtuous men in an independent business institution or by the employees who depend on the company for their security. Like Adlai Stevenson, the characters accept that reality and negotiate life in the system rather than oppose it. The honesty, integrity and agency associated with George and Peter Bailey are now associated most prominently with Betsy, who exists not in an independent business institution but in the American home. The home is not a refuge for Tom Rath as Stevenson lectured Smith College women they should make it, but it is an independent social space where the conformist corporate culture is critiqued and what is left of individual integrity nurtured. It is also the space where ideas for small, independent business ventures are created and plans for their realization executed. Such small business ventures would now exist within, and without being opposed to, the postwar corporate order.

All is not bliss in the Raths' domestic sphere, however, illustrating that cultural representations of postwar gender relations often depict more accurately the reality of those relations than did prescriptive lectures by public officials like Adlai Stevenson, a prominent political figure who admonished even the most highly educated women in the country to forsake careers to create a domestic refuge for their husbands as men negotiated the problems associated with corporate life. Betsy's sharp criticisms of Tom for considering to compromise his values, and her biting insults of his character, combined with her entrepreneurial spirit and her influence over the family's future subvert the closure on the narrative in the final scene, where she forgives all sins and is elevated to the position of someone who should be "worshipped." She forgives Tom for the affair he had during the war and agrees they should help support Tom's Italian son. For her forgiveness and her sacrifice, the final line in the film is Tom's: "Do you mind if I tell you, I worship you?"

Although *The Man in the Gray Flannel Suit* is a film about a man dealing with the anxieties and negotiating the realities associated with postwar corporate life that Adlai Stevenson described and Paul Goodman and other commentators criticized, it ends by elevating that man's wife to the position of someone deserving secular, domestic sainthood. This closure on the narrative therefore demands commentary. The fact that Tom implies that he "worships" Betsy in the end, combined with the fact that she is positioned in the domestic sphere and is seemingly the human repository of virtuous values, can cause us, incorrectly, to read her character as a traditional "true woman" so much lauded by late nineteenth- and early twentieth-century upper-class and middle-class Americans.

These defenders of "true womanhood" both defined specifically and defended excruciatingly the concept in a society changing rapidly from the consequences of the corporate reconstruction of American capitalism as increasing numbers of elite and middle-class women attended college and as more women worked as shop girls in factories, as sales representatives in major department stores, as telephone operators, as secretaries and in various other jobs in the expanding national economy — places other than the domestic sphere. Clear definitions of what a "true woman" was supposed to be emerged in the early nineteenth century, but ideological defenses of the concept intensified in the late nineteenth century and well into the twentieth as many social and cultural elites did not like what increasing numbers of women were doing: participating in the new economic (various jobs), social (women's clubs), cultural (movie theaters and other new "cheap amusements"), and political (campaigns for suffrage and various reform movements) spheres outside of the home and beyond the influence of husbands, fathers and mothers who controlled behavior in the home.[34]

Ironically, many elite and middle-class men sent their daughters to colleges like Smith, where they became more independent thinkers.[35] Such men believed that true women were supposed to forsake their self-interests in order to create harmony in the home, were to avoid the self-seeking spheres of business and politics and nurture in their children the same virtuous values they supposedly embodied themselves.[36] The men defended the concept of true womanhood well into the twentieth century because anyone who visited a major city realized how many "new women" were walking the streets, that, increasingly, women were not confined to the home but were out in the world and acting in it. The anxieties that such advocates of "true womanhood" revealed in their speeches, sermons and essays reflect the fact that American society and women's place in it were not everything those advocates wanted them to be.

Similar anxieties about woman's place were also intense in the 1950s, and many moviegoers sitting in theaters across the country and watching Gregory Peck and Jennifer Jones as Tom and Betsy Rath battle it out in their home on the big screen harbored those anxieties.[37] Politicians like Stevenson in their speeches and government agencies through the propaganda films they produced asked women to sacrifice their career aspirations and all other aspirations beyond that of becoming domestic saints who would enable their husbands to deal with the "crisis" that Stevenson defined. But that, of course, does not mean that women did or that the ones who did were happy doing it. If that were true, then Smith College graduate Betty Friedan would have never defined another "crisis" of the postwar years, the one with no name that she labeled in the title of her book, *The Feminine Mystique,* which sold millions of copies to Americans with anxieties about work, home and gender relations. Government propaganda produced for the war effort in the early 1940s told women "You can do it!" and asked them to work riveting, welding and otherwise constructing ships, planes and other weapons of war to defeat the Germans and the Japanese. In glaring contrast just a decade later, government propaganda films that educators showed to high school students in the 1950s depicted young women attending home economics classes and helping mom in the home while brothers studied math and science before dinner. "Rosie the Riveter" was no longer needed; women could be mothers, nurses, teachers, and flight attendants, taking care of others' needs. But women who became WACCs and WAVES in the army and the navy during the war, women who welded and riveted and sweat as they did, and women who attended Smith and other colleges where they learned to think critically, logically organize their thoughts, and defend their ideas with evidence did not all retreat into the home, forget their studies of Baudelaire, embrace the *Consumer's Guide,* and attempt to create domestic bliss, although evidence reveals that some clearly did.[38]

It is implied at the end of *The Man in the Gray Flannel Suit* that "all's right with the world," as Judge Bernstein (Lee J. Cobb), who arranges for Tom to make regular support payments for his Italian son, says Tom and Betsy's values and actions make him feel. But we should not believe it, nor should we think that former WACCs, WAVEs, Rosie-the-Riviters and other women did. Neither, should we assume, did many American men in 1956 who identified with Tom Rath's character, but who, unlike Tom, did not have a direct line to the man at the top and who daily found themselves in situations where they had to compromise their values in ways that Tom, in the end, did not have to do. The evidence in the film itself reveals that all is not right with the world, for although things change for the Raths, the Gordon Walkers and Bill Ogdens still walk the halls at the United Broadcasting Corporation, supervising all of the other gray-suits, insisting they conform and defining and controlling the tasks they do.

We now turn to chapter two and other films produced in the postwar years that do not resolve the crisis that Adlai Stevenson described in such an upbeat way at Smith College in 1955. Some films in the gangster and western genres depict a corporate order with little or no room for negotiation, of unbridled corporate greed and power and little room for individual agency. Others portray stark confrontations between characters that represent concentrated corporate power and control over people's lives and other characters that represent struggling independent businessmen (and, albeit rarely, businesswomen). Filmmakers who were Adlai Stevenson's contemporaries sometimes turn the presidential hopeful's vision of the postwar corporate order and postwar gender relations on its head. In some cases their films and critics' responses to them reveal that men's' anxieties in postwar society and about postwar gender relations were more intense than what is evident in either Stevenson's speech or in a film like *The Man in the Gray Flannel Suit.* The tensions associated with work, individual agency and gender relations represented in *The Man in the Gray Flannel Suit* are starker in other films produced in these years, and they remain in popular culture and in American society during the turbulent 1960s and beyond. New tensions also emerge. Sometimes the resolutions to the tensions addressed in later films are just as contradictory, sometimes far more menacing.

2
Gunslingers and Gangsters in the Age of Corporate Combinations
The Veiled Struggle Against the Force That Is Evil in Joe McCarthy's America

We saw in chapter four that cultural representations of discontented and disaffected men took some new and interesting twists following the Great Depression and the Second World War. By the 1950s, characters like Tom Rath in *The Man in the Gray Flannel Suit* negotiate their lives in the modern corporate bureaucracies that politicians like Adlai Stevenson accepted as the new reality of American life, while Paul Goodman and other cultural critics lamented the problems associated with America's "organized system." In the year directly following the war, however, Frank Capra portrayed in *It's a Wonderful Life* the continued possibility of an old Progressive ideal: a coalition of virtuous middle-class and working-class citizens united in a common effort to check the concentrated economic power of Henry F. Potter, a man who seeks to consolidate all property ownership in his hands and by so doing significantly control the lives and the livelihoods of working-class and middle-class citizens. Potter and the threat he represents to individuals' ability to own property and to maintain a degree of control over their lives exist in society, but that threat is checked by virtuous citizens, especially George Bailey, who forsake their self-interests for the greater good of society represented by Bedford Falls. Capra's 1946 classic, then, represents opposition to Potter and what he represents while simultaneously legitimating Potter's social and economic position. Potter is not depicted as someone who should be eradicated from society. Rather, he represents someone with legitimate interests but whose desire to consolidate property and power over citizens' lives must be constantly checked in order to protect the limited but vital interests of working-class and middle-class citizens.

One decade later, society as it is represented in *The Man in the Gray Flannel Suit* is not filled with small businessmen like Martini, independent financial institutions like the building and loan, and working-class guys like Bert and Ernie. Instead, corporations dominate the urban landscape and men like Tom Rath work within the corporate entities that together comprise the organized system. The man at the top of the United Broadcasting Corporation is not depicted as the evil, self-interested man that Potter represents. In contrast, Ralph Hopkins is a somewhat benevolent, albeit power-hungry, man who has sacrificed family to create a business empire, a corporation that most other men depend on for their livelihoods but in so doing sacrifice their individuality, honesty and integrity as they negotiate life in a corporate bureaucracy managed by men like Bill Ogden. The individual agency evident in George Bailey, an agency nurtured by the values of his father and in the small and independent institution of the building and loan, is not evident in UBC employees. That agency exists in Betsy, however, someone untainted by the corporate culture at UBC that Tom must negotiate everyday. Due to Betsy's influence that agency becomes evident in Tom. In this domestic melodrama about everyday life in postwar America, corporations and the powerful men who found them and hire managers to run them are not confronted and opposed, their interests and power not checked by working-class citizens and small, independent businessmen. Instead, the powerful men and their business empires represent a reality that must be accepted and negotiated on an individual basis, happiness and fulfillment coming not from working in the organized system but from domestic relationships and domestic life. Negotiating life in the system is a major theme of many such melodramas of the postwar years.[1]

All films produced in the postwar years, however, do not merely depict men like Tom Rath negotiating their way through corporate and family life while, in the spirit of Adlai Stevenson, leerily accepting the corporate order and their lack of independence and control in it. Some filmmakers in the late forties and fifties made films in which characters that represent individuals who display the desire to control their own destinies must do so by confronting and resisting others' attempts to control them and to control society itself. If they do not, they risk becoming corrupted by society, for organized society is devoid of honesty, integrity, and the self-sacrificing actions of a character like George Bailey.[2] Increasingly in the postwar years, characters that exhibit such values have little or no power in society. Those who do hold power are self-interested, greedy, and usually corrupt. Society as it is often depicted in these films has become so controlled by powerful interests that society itself must be opposed, often by a lone hero working on his own or sometimes by a coalition of independent business owners and working-class citizens, people who represent an alternative to the dominant order. These themes, evident in the films *Force of Evil* and *Johnny Guitar* and analyzed in this chapter, establish significant aspects of the narratives apparent in the counterculture films of the late sixties and early seventies, the urban-avenger films of the seventies, and in variants of both the counter-culture films and the urban-avenger films produced in the last decades of the twentieth and into the twenty-first century.

The critical themes evident in *Force of Evil* and *Johnny Guitar* made it into the films despite increased enforcement of the Motion Picture Production Code, the intensifying hearings of the House Committee on Un-American Activities (HUAC), the initial round of Hollywood blacklisting, and the efforts of extreme anti-communist ideologues determined to repress films that in anyway critiqued social and economic practices endemic to postwar corporate capitalism. Indeed, by the late forties and fifties the cultural and political climate had become so extreme that even producing a film like *It's a Wonderful Life* probably would have been suspect. Just one year after the release of the Capra classic, cultural historian Stephen Whitfield writes, "The movie industry was conscripted into the Cold War in 1947 when HUAC was invited to Los Angeles."[3] Ayn Rand, the ardent anti-communist who opposed collectivism in any form and, ironically, wrote popular novels with individualistic heroes whose individuality and creativity are threatened and stifled by the institutionalized conformity associated with corporate bureaucracies, was a friendly HUAC witness who testified that even the much loved and seven–Academy-Award–winning (including Best Picture, Actor, Director and Screen Play) film *The Best Years of Our Lives* (1946) disseminated the Communist Party line. Rand claimed the film about World War II veterans adjusting to postwar life was unacceptable because of a scene in which a banker is leery about granting a G.I. loan to one of the veterans. She said the scene makes it seem as if business is against the veterans. Rand also testified that the Russian people were not able to "smile," at least in the "social" sense, because of their "system." A former screenwriter herself, Rand composed *Screen Guide for Americans* (1950), a pamphlet instructing Hollywood writers to never refer to "the common man" or "the little people." Despite the realities of the country's diverse social and economic life, Rand believed it to be immoral to portray Americans as being common or to depict industrialists in a negative way. The conservative Motion Picture Alliance for the Preservation of American Ideals ensured the pamphlet was widely disseminated in Hollywood and reprinted in major newspapers.[4] The activities of virulent anti-communists like Rand, the government repression of free artistic and political expression through HUAC, and the motion picture industry's blacklisting of actors, directors and writers caused many filmmakers to hide their direct critiques of the American system and individuals' declining control of their lives in that system behind the veils of the western and gangster genres.

In the late forties and fifties, discontented independent business owners and their employees and other average citizens are often represented as struggling to protect or regain control over their lives in an increasingly corporate and bureaucratic society. It is important to point out, however, that such struggles against the centralization of authority and power in corporate entities is also evident in characters that symbolize an earlier, more individualistic rather than corporate form of wealth and power. These characters represent the last vestige of the nineteenth-century captains of industry so much lauded by ardent individualists like Ayn Rand. As they are represented in films like *Citizen Kane* (1941), such men rant about the influence and power of corporations and the politicians that the "trusts" control and pay to do their bidding, making the world a worse place for the wealthy independents as well as the "common man." Even the ardent individualistic, capitalistic publisher Charles Foster Kane (H. G. Welles) is accused of being a communist by characters representing corrupt politicians who do the bidding of the trusts. Kane may be a capitalist, but he hates corporations, so he must be a communist disguised as a capitalist. The politicians' anti-communist attacks on Kane in the film are designed to get people to believe that Kane is a communist, for, according to the politicians' distorted logic, being a communist could be the only reason for Kane's attacks on capitalist corporations.[5] Likewise, in *Fountainhead* (1949), a film based on Rand's popular novel of the same title, the ardent individualistic and creative architect Howard Roark (Gary Cooper) is a non-conformist who rails against the mediocrity and lack of creativity endemic to the corporate bureaucracies that represent a non-communist form of collectivism. Although Roark does not possess Kane's wealth and power, it is only because his ingenious, creative work is not recognized and rewarded by a society that privileges conformity and mediocrity.[6] Such films share with the urban-avenger films of the late twentieth century the glorification of an ardent individualistic hero of indefatigable resolve who cannot be corrupted by a bureaucratic society that values conformity and, increasingly, consumerism over individualism and creativity. For the most part, however, the heroes in the late-twentieth century films represent more average Americans like those in *Force of Evil* and *Johnny Guitar*.

In addition to the prominent theme of the individual's declining agency in an increasingly organized and bureaucratic society apparent in the postwar films discussed here and in chapter one, the gender issues evident in the earlier analysis of *The Man in the Gray Flannel Suit* become even more complicated in *Johnny Guitar*. In 1946, George Bailey's wife, Mary, although college educated, is depicted in a traditional domestic relationship and stands by her man in a time of crisis. Betsy Rath's character 10 years later is a more complicated one. Although she, too, is in a traditional relationship, Betsy is not an ideal mother or wife, nor is she merely someone who provides moral support for her husband. She is Tom's harshest critic, the source of his moral integrity, and the author of an entrepreneurial scheme that has the potential to provide the Raths with the resources to become independent of UBC. In *Force of Evil* (1948) the major female character, Doris Lowry (Beatrice Pearson), is a young working-class woman who falls in love with the protagonist and, somewhat like Betsy Rath, becomes his moral compass. In contrast to the characters in these other three films, however, the two most independent-minded and economically and politically powerful characters in *Johnny Guitar* are women, a fact that caused some reviewers in 1954 to express bewilderment about the film. While the male characters in *Johnny Guitar* accept women in such positions, some male reviewers did not, evidence of men's anxieties about women's changing social, economic and political roles in postwar American society at the same time that public officials and government agencies waged an intense ideological campaign to contain women in the domestic sphere.[7]

Force of Evil (1948) is set in contemporary New York City and more than anything else is about a business entity the characters refer to as "the combination," "the corporation," or "the organization." The characters' use of these terms throughout the film recalls John Steinbeck's use of "monster" in *The Grapes of Wrath* to refer to the seemingly invisible force that drives farmers off their land and consolidates landholding in ever-larger combinations, eroding farmers' independence in the process.[8]

Force of Evil makes it clear, however, that real men with real interests control such "combinations," and we learn who and what they are.

Joe Morse (John Garfield) is a corporate lawyer from a working-class family whose parents died in his youth and whose older brother Leo (Thomas Gomez) sacrificed so Joe could go to college. Joe wants to be rich and recognizes that to achieve his goal in postwar America one must join "the combination" rather than resist it. One of his clients, a gangster named Ben Tucker (Roy Roberts), made a fortune bootlegging beer during Prohibition and used his old partner Ficco's "Chicago shooters" to consolidate the beer trade in his hands, literally killing the competition. Tucker now wants to control the numbers racket in New York. Joe will help him make the numbers racket legitimate and consolidate control of the business in a legal corporation.[9]

Force of Evil was directed by a strong, eventually blacklisted auteur, Abraham Polonsky, who had joined the American Communist Party in the late 1930s. He joined the party in part because of his strong anti-fascism during the thirties. More important, however, were the social and economic conditions that Polonsky witnessed in the United States during the Depression. "I came of age in a country that had come to a standstill," he recalled, "with fifty million people unemployed and the banks closed. I voted for FDR, and the New Deal was 'left' enough for many of us." Polonsky noted, "I was always a materialist and a leftist."[10] This fact clearly influenced Polonsky's filmmaking.[11] The themes in *Force of Evil* are popular ones, however, themes evident in other postwar films and rooted in American literature and film since the late nineteenth century. *Force of Evil* shares with many earlier and later cultural texts an emphasis on the declining agency of workers and independent business owners in an increasingly organized society dominated by large corporations.

The film's popularity is evident in the fact that local theaters played it on their screens throughout the winter and into the spring. The dates when local theaters placed ads for the film and the dates when reviews appeared in newspapers and magazines reveal that *Force of Evil* enjoyed a long run at the box office, despite the fact that Enterprise Productions and Metro-Goldwyn-Mayer failed to spend much on publicity.[12] The movie was released in late December, 1948, and ads and reviews appeared through April, 1949.[13]

The four months that *Force of Evil* played in local movie houses also demonstrates that audiences appear to have responded more favorably to the film than some reviewers did. The reviews were mixed, the negative ones commenting little or not at all on the plot and the fact that the "corporation" Tucker and Joe Morse create and the power it wields over independent businessmen and their employees represents more than crime drama. Reviewers failed to even mention the film's emphasis on corporations and combinations in relation to criminal activities let alone larger social and economic trends. Although the Library of Congress recognized *Force of Evil* as being historically and culturally significant when it added the film to the National Film Registry in 1994, the reviewer for the *Chicago Daily Tribune* walked out of the theater confused and suggested others would do likewise: "Throughout the film every one gabs on and on in a senseless sort of double talk, and unless you wish to be driven to same, take my advice and steer clear of this one."[14] The reviewer for *Newsweek* also missed the central theme of the film and focused instead on the language, unable to understand why an educated corporate lawyer with working-class roots has not adopted the language of his Harvard educated and more socially privileged law partner.[15] The *Variety* reviewer remarked, "A poetic, almost allegorical, interpretation keeps intruding on the tougher elements of the plot." This reviewer never mentioned what that allegorical interpretation is, however, nor did he define the "tougher elements of the plot."[16] The reviewer for *Good Housekeeping* got the basic story right but failed to make any connection between the capitalism practiced in the numbers racket and that practiced by the "legitimate" corporations on Wall Street, which is what Joe Morse and Ben Tucker want to make the numbers racket.[17] In contrast to these reviews, the one that appeared in *The New Republic* applauded the directing, the acting, and the photography, calling the movie "the best crook drama of the year." This reviewer alluded to, but did not mention directly, some of the working-class themes in the film by referencing Clifford Odets, the author of the Depression-era agitprop play *Waiting for Lefty* (1935). Although these contemporary reviewers either missed or ignored the fact that the numbers racket in *Force of Evil* is meant to symbolize problems with the legitimate capitalist enterprises represented on Wall Street, Joseph Breen surely did not. The Breen Office enforced the Motion Picture Production Code and did not approve the script until Polonsky revised it to conform to Breen's interpretation of the Code.[18]

The numbers racket as it is represented in *Force of Evil* is composed of a series of independent and illegal financial entities that people involved in the racket call "banks." These independent banks take bets people place on what an unpredictable daily number will be. Basically, the numbers game is an illegal lottery. The bankers pay the few winners each day and keep the money from the bets that all the "suckers" place. Joe advises Tucker that things have changed and they do not need to use the old violent gangster tactics to control business in the numbers racket. Instead, they can rig the system to bankrupt all of the independent banks, refinance a select few to continue business as part of a new combination, and ensure that the bulk of the profits from these refinanced institutions flows into a new "corporation." Joe advises Tucker they can create a legal corporation and make the numbers racket legal by paying corrupt politicians to pass legislation to make lotteries legal just as they are legal in Ireland and Cuba and as betting on horse races is legal in the United States.

The plan is to fix it so the three-digit lottery number that hits on the Fourth of July is the one that most of the "suckers" pick to hit every Independence Day: 776. The lottery number will be the number that reflects the odds after the last bet is placed on the third horse race at a particular track on July 3. If all the patriotic "suckers" who bet their nickels and dimes on 776 every year actually win the Independence Day lottery, then all the independent banks will have to cover those bets and will go bankrupt. When they do, Joe Morse and Ben Tucker will be ready to infuse a select number of banks with enough capital to keep them operating. As a result, those banks will become part of a new combination of banks controlled by Tucker and Joe, the bankers will be paid a percentage of future profits to keep managing the banks, and the majority of the profits will flow into the new corporation. To carry out the plan to crush the independent banks, Joe secures the services of a man who has a gift for figuring odds. Joe calls this man "Two-and-Two" and gives him $25,000 to place a bet. One of Tucker's men arranges for Two-and-Two to be able to place the final bet in the third race on July 3. He will know the odds before he bets and will compute what bet he will need to place for the odds to result in the number 776.

As Joe Morse puts into place the various steps of his plan to consolidate into one big corporation the numerous independent numbers banks that operate in the city, we learn that he has a conflict of interest. His big brother Leo (Thomas Gomez) operates a small bank in the working-class neighborhood where Joe and Leo grew up. Although Leo and Joe are somewhat estranged, Joe cares for his brother and wants Leo to benefit from his scheme. Implementing Joe's plans, however, will crush Leo's small bank along with the other independents. At first Joe wants to tell Leo about 776 so Leo can make enough money from the knowledge to retire. Leo has a heart condition and needs to get rid of the stress in his life, and Joe sees the Independence Day plan as a way for that to happen. But Tucker insists that no one be told of the plan to fix it for 776 to hit on July Fourth. Instead, then, Joe agrees with Tucker that Leo's bank will become one of those they include in the new combination, a bank Leo will run for the new corporation but will no longer control as control is centralized in the new corporate entity. As Tucker explains to Joe: "We only want to finance 12 of the banks, Joe. The big ones. And your brother's little bank, of course. That makes 13. The rest can go to the wall and the combination will take over their trade."

The problem is that Leo values his independence and his employees and does not want his business or the people who work for him to be incorporated into the new combination. Leo represents an earlier America where independent individuals own and control most businesses, care for the people who work for them, and treat with respect the people they serve in those businesses, much like George Bailey and the independent building and loan in *It's a Wonderful Life*. Joe Morse and Ben Tucker represent the new order of centralized authority and control as the former independents are either crushed or combined into one big corporation. If Leo knows what is good for him, according to Joe, he will become a manager in that corporation, for Joe and Ben will succeed where Henry F. Potter failed. Consolidating formerly independent businesses into new centralized corporate entities is the new way of life, the new social and economic reality, a "force" that cannot be resisted and whose ability to become the dominant social and economic reality can no longer be checked. Henry F. Potter represents that threat in *It's a Wonderful Life*, but Frank Capra created flashback scenes of an earlier America to make it appear as if that old order can exist alongside the new centralized corporate order represented by Potter. *Force of Evil* portrays the new order as evil and critiques it directly, but the critique is veiled in a gangster-syndicate film about an illegal business, albeit one that millions of Americans participate in everyday. Although Leo Morse is himself involved in the numbers racket, he, like George Bailey, holds traditional values about independence and responsibility to others that are foreign to the new order represented by his brother Joe, Ben Tucker, and the new corporation they create.

After a meeting between Joe and Ben in which Tucker gives Joe a not-too-subtle warning about what will happen to Joe if he tells Leo about 776, Joe goes to see Leo for the first time in years. This meeting between the two brothers is important because it establishes the differences between Joe and Leo and the values they represent, between Joe's unmitigated self interest as he strives to amass wealth and influence in the corporate order, and Leo's roots in a traditional America of independent businessmen who sacrifice financial reward for the ability to remain independent and for the employees for whom they feel responsible. The life Leo lives is the life Joe has worked to escape. The place Leo lives is one Joe would like to erase from his memory.

Joe narrates as he walks through the neighborhood and into Leo's building. Referring to Leo he says, "And here he was, back in the slums, where we were born." As Joe walks through the building to his brother's office, he tells the audience about how small banks like Leo's operate and why they are called banks. He compares Leo's bank to any small, independent business: "He ran a small numbers bank the way another man runs a restaurant, a bar. These collection offices were called 'banks,' and they were like banks because money was deposited there. They were unlike banks because the chances of getting money out were a thousand to one. These were the odds against winning." When Joe enters the dilapidated apartment that serves as Leo's business offices, the main room is filled with modestly dressed people from the neighborhood who work counting coins with hand-operated coin-counting machines, filling bags with coins, and keeping the books in notepads. Leo's employees look much like they walked in off of one of the streets in George Bailey's hometown of Bedford Falls. The sound of the coins churning in the machines fills the room. As he narrates Joe informs us, "The banks were located behind pool rooms, in lofts, cellars, or hidden in slum apartments like Leo's."

Joe moves through the apartment to Leo's office, a shabby room where Leo sits at a small wooden desk. Depicting some of the classic features of film noir, light fixtures hang low from the ceiling, objects create shadows throughout the room, and dilapidated shades drape the windows — evidence of Leo's struggle to make ends meet and symbols of what is left of the America of small independent businessmen he represents. Joe does not tell Leo about number 776, but he warns his brother of the possibility of a combination taking all the business from Leo and the other independent bankers. As he paces next to Leo's desk, Joe warns him, "Now, you listen to me. Something very serious is about to happen to your business." As Leo listens, Joe describes the realities of Leo's situation and what would happen to him if the banks involved in the numbers racket faced competition from a new combination. "You're one of twenty or thirty numbers banks in the city," he tells Leo, "one of the smaller ones. Suppose a combine moves in." Joe takes a moment to ensure Leo is listening and then lectures him on economies of scale: "Suppose it reduces the overhead, legal fees, bail bonds; suppose it reduces the costs and guarantees the profits — a man like you would be out of business, wouldn't you? You couldn't compete, could you?" Joe leans against Leo's desk and bends forward, looking into his brother's eyes as Leo stares blankly into space: "But suppose you had a brother, and this brother made your bank the number one bank in the combination, in the merger, in the corporation." Leo asks, sarcastically, "What corporation? Tucker?"

Before Joe can answer they are interrupted by a knock on the door. Leo tells the person to come in. After Leo's secretary, Doris Lowry (Beatrice Pearson), enters the room, Leo asks Joe, "And what does this corporation expect from me, brother Joe?" Joe hesitates to answer in front of Doris, but Leo says he has no secrets from her. Joe continues, "In return for the organization's service, in return for taking you into the combination, the corporation gets two thirds of the profit and you get one third." Leo becomes increasingly upset as he responds to Joe's proposal, sometimes feeling his chest and sipping a glass of milk. He barks, "Two thirds for Tucker, brother Joe, and one third for me, my own business! Do you know what that is, Joe? Black mail! That's what it is, blackmail! My own brother, blackmailing me!" Joe tells him he is crazy and Leo shouts, "I don't want it!" Joe insults Leo, "You're a small man. Because if it's a small thing you're a tiger, you're a tiger! But if it's a big thing, you shout and yell and call me names. 'Oh, no, a million dollars for Leo. Oh, no. It must be the wrong address. It must be somebody next door.'" Leo says "no" repeatedly and emphatically as he rises out of his chair and goes to the door to let Joe out: "The answer is no." Joe replies, "You understand your 'no' won't stop the merging of these banks, yours included." Joe rushes to the door and grasps Leo by the arm and puts his other hand on his brother's shoulder as he begs Leo in a hushed voice to accept the deal: "Leo, Leo, this is your chance, the one I've got for you!" Leo opens the door for Joe to leave as he says, "You take your chance, Joe, and get out of here." Joe pulls the door closed and tells Leo, "Are you telling me, a corporation lawyer, that you're running a legitimate business here?" He reminds Leo he is making payoffs for illegal lotteries and gambling, and he cites the sections of the penal code that Leo is violating. Leo counters, "I do my business honest and respectable." Joe replies, "Honest? Respectable? Don't you take the nickels and dimes and pennies from people who bet just like every other crook, big or little, in this racket? They call this racket 'policy' because people bet their nickels on numbers instead of paying their weekly insurance premiums. That's why, 'policy.' That's what it is and that's what it's called. And Tucker wants to make millions, you want to make thousands, and you," turning to Doris, "you do it for 35 dollars a week. But it's all the same, all 'policy.'" Leo tells Joe that Doris is like a daughter to him, demonstrating his disgust with Joe for implying that she is a criminal. He then tells Joe he wanted to be the lawyer and could have been if he had thrown Joe out of the house when their parents died, but he stayed there with Joe and worked so Joe could live in the house and go to school. He calls Joe "a crook, a cheat, and a gangster!" Joe tells Leo he needs to be calm and sensible, that "Tucker will make you honest. Tucker will make you respectable. He's giving me a quarter of a million dollars to raise public sentiment, to make 'policy' legal like Bingo, Bango, and the Irish Sweep-

In *Force of Evil* (1948), corporate lawyer Joe Morse (John Garfield), left, tries to persuade his brother Leo (Thomas Gomez), right, to give up his independence and join the new corporate combination that Joe creates, but Leo vehemently resists what Joe tells him is inevitable. Leo's secretary, Doris Lowry (Beatrice Pearson), looks on as her boss wages a final and futile effort to remain independent (Photofest).

stakes. I'm paying you back, Leo. I'll make you rich. With an office on Wall Street, up in the clouds!" Leo then tells Joe his answer is positively "No! No! No!"

To justify his actions in his quest for wealth and power in the postwar corporate order, Joe convinces himself and tries to convince Leo that there is no difference between what Leo does with people's pennies, nickels and dimes when they place small lottery bets with his independent little bank and what Tucker does with millions of dollars to create combinations, control markets, influence politicians, and crush independent businesses and people's lives, both financially and literally if they stand in his way. In Joe's mind it is merely a difference of scale. Independence, he believes, comes with increasing one's net worth, and the way to do that is to be connected to the new corporate order represented by Tucker and the combination Joe helps him establish and make legitimate by purchasing political influence and, if necessary, resorting to strong-arm tactics. It's the law of the jungle and all are animals in it whether they acknowledge it or not. Joe would concur with Gordon Gekko's (Michael Douglas) famous statement in *Wall Street* (1989) four decades later when he tells investors "Greed is good."[19]

Joe believes that Tucker's business is no different than any other big business represented on Wall Street, Tucker's tactics no different than the founders of other corporate firms. Greed is not only good but also natural, and those, like Leo, who act on any motive other than self-interest are somehow behaving unnaturally, irrationally. In contrast, Leo still values his independence, something Joe is giving up without realizing it when he ties his future to that of the new corporation he helps Tucker create. Leo understands that once his bank becomes part of the corporation he will merely manage the bank's affairs while others make critical decisions about profit margins, about who will work and who will not, and about what kind of business tactics will be implemented. Leo realizes that linking his future and the futures of his employees to the new corporate combination means losing control and, therefore, independence in exchange for money. Leo's discontent, then, is related to the power that Tucker and others who control such combinations have to force independents like Leo out of business. As such combinations come to dominate society, Leo and others who share his values are increasingly disaffected from that society of diminished individual agency, more personal and independent business relationships, and the primacy of greed over all other motives for behavior.

Joe believes that Leo doesn't know what's good for him, so he decides to force Leo to join the combination. When he leaves Leo's office, Joe makes a call from a phone booth. He arranges to have someone inform the police that a small numbers bank is operating at his brother's address and to have the police raid the bank the first thing the next morning. Joe tells the person on the phone, "I want my brother to know that Tucker's running 'policy.' I want to force him in." Joe eventually succeeds: Leo realizes the corporation has beaten him and he reluctantly joins the combination, albeit for a very short time. This does not happen, however, until after 776 hits on the Fourth of July and Leo goes bankrupt along with the rest of the numbers banks. The police raid does cause Leo to realize he wants to get out of the numbers racket but does not push him into business with Joe and Tucker in the new combination they form.

When Joe pays Leo's fine (along with those of all Leo's employees) and gets him out of jail, it is July 3. At the police station Leo tells Joe he will settle his accounts and quit business the next day: "I'm taking my capital; I'm getting out. I'm through; I'm finished." Joe knows Leo will go bankrupt if he waits until then to get out, so he pleads with Leo not to wait, to get out immediately. But Leo, thinking of his responsibility to his clients, says people have bets in his bank so he will wait until tomorrow and pay off whatever he owes and then close forever. He tells Joe there is one thing Joe can do for him: get Doris a job. He blames Joe for Doris's new circumstances, for the fact that she got arrested in the raid and now has a misdemeanor and bad references. "You got fancy friends down on Wall Street," he says. "She's a good secretary. Get her a job. I'll thank you for that, for her, not for me." Joe agrees to do it and, thinking about what will happen when 776 hits the next day, he warns Leo that something might happen that could cause Leo to need his help. Leo replies sarcastically, "What could happen that I would need *your* help?"

Leo escorts one of his employees home and Joe offers Doris a ride. When she refuses he tells her he promised Leo he would take her home. She says he is lying and he acknowledges that he is, but she accepts his offer when he points out it is raining and says, "You tell me the story of your life and maybe I can suggest a happy ending." Their conversation in the cab serves to distinguish further that although Joe's belief in the primacy of crass self-interest entrenched in the corporate order associated with Tucker and the combination is dominant in society, opposition to Joe's values and to what Tucker and the combination represent continue to exist in people like Doris and Leo, even though Joe considers them "perverse" for their willingness to deny themselves for the sake of others.

In order to live with himself and the choices he makes, Joe must view others as evil in order to believe that his work with Tucker to form the combination that will destroy people's lives, including his brother's if Joe does not give him special treatment, is no different than what everyone does. Doris tells Joe she knows how much Leo did for him, that Leo sacrificed for Joe. But Joe thinks that sacrifice itself is evil, that people who sacrifice for others do so to try to make others feel guilty. Joe's entire philosophy of life is based on the belief that people are takers, and that even when they give they do so because they want something in return. He believes that people who don't accept his philosophy live their lives feeling guilty all the time and trying to make others feel guilty along with them just because they don't abide by Doris's principle of self-sacrifice. He makes his ideas about self-sacrificing clear to Doris: "It's perverse. Can't you see what it is? It's not natural. To go to great expense for something you want, that's natural. To reach out to take it, that's human, that's natural."

Other, seemingly more virtuous characters than Joe also refuse to accept the guilt that others try to place on them. People make decisions based on the limited options available within the system, a system that forces them to choose between unappealing alternatives. While Leo condemns Joe for forcing him to accept membership in the new combination, Leo defends himself when his bookkeeper, Freddie Bauer (Howland Chamberlain), condemns Leo for forcing him to accept employment in the corporation once Leo's bank becomes part of the new combination. The system, rather than the individuals acting in relation to it, is indicted as a force that both limits people's choices and encourages them to make immoral choices. Moreover, in contrast to the corporate capitalism represented by Tucker and the combination, the seemingly more moral and self-sacrificing small, independent capitalism that Leo represents, with its concern for employees' welfare and for businessmen's independence from the central authority but greater financial rewards associated with Tucker's organization, is not portrayed romantically and idealistically, as an unblemished model of an untainted social and economic system that should be resurrected. Rather, embedded in the nature of that earlier form of capitalism are the seeds of the corruption associated with the postwar combinations presented as the new reality of American life. That earlier system, too, forced people to do things they would rather not have done. This becomes evident in a scene at Leo's apartment.

When 776 hits on Independence Day and the numbers bankers become insolvent, Joe goes to Leo's apartment to make him a proposition that will not only enable him to survive the situation but to prosper from it. Joe can ensure that Leo's bank becomes the number one bank in the new combination after the corporation pays Leo's debts to all the "suckers" for betting on 776. Leo's wife, Sylvia (Georgia Backus), implores Leo not to listen to Joe. She says, "Don't have anything to do with him, Leo. You're a businessman." Leo remarks, "Yes, I've been a businessman all of my life, and honest, I don't know what a business is." Sylvia counters, "Well, you had a garage; you had a real estate business." Leo replies, "A lot you know. Real estate business. Living from mortgage to mortgage. Stealing credit like a thief. And the garage. That was a business. Three cents overcharge on every gallon of gas. Two cents for the chauffeur and a penny for me. A penny for one thief, two cents for the other." At one level it appears that Joe is correct, that what Leo has done all his life is no different from what Joe is offering him now and what Joe is doing himself. It is only a matter of degree, of the amount people allow themselves to make. Leo does not have to be a petty thief, a cheap crook any longer. Leo continues, "Well, Joe's here now. I won't have to steal pennies anymore. I'll have big crooks to steal dollars for me." He agrees to Joe's proposition and arranges to meet him at the numbers bank in the morning, noting he has to go to the office anyway to get his books in order even though he is now what he refers to as "a bank-rupt." Joe says, "I'll be there, Leo, with a new set of books for you."

Historian Robert Sklar notes that Polonsky added much of this dialog to appease the Breen office. Breen worried that "audiences might sympathize with the small, independent, picked-upon Leo."[20] Sklar appropriately asks us to consider that while *Force of Evil* was in production the Supreme Court prepared to rule against monopolistic practices in the motion picture industry. As a result of the *Paramount* case, the production companies could no longer own both the production companies and the theaters where the films would be shown. Sklar recognizes that the major production companies had an interest in depicting small independent businesses, represented by Leo, as "petty grafters" just as willing as corporations to take the public for what they could get. This added dialog, however, could also be read as revealing an inherent problem with capitalism in all its stages, not just the corporate phase accelerated by the Depression and World War II and emerging from the economic and military crises seemingly unchallenged in the postwar years. Polonosky may very well have used Breen's desire to portray independents like Leo as petty grafters as an opportunity to critique the profit motive inherent to capitalism in all stages of its evolution.[21]

The new corporation wins. It rigs the system, forces Leo and the other independents out, and takes control of Leo's bank and a few others that the formerly independent bankers now manage for the corporation controlled by Tucker and his crafty lawyer, Joe. It's clear, however, that although the corporation is merely part of a larger system of combination and consolidation, real men direct the actions of the corporation, for Joe and Tucker create the situation that causes Leo and some of the other bankers to become managers in a new corporate order in the numbers racket. Despite the fact that when Joe called someone to arrange the raid on Leo's bank he said he wanted to "force him in," the raid failed to cause Leo to join the combination. But bankruptcy achieves what jail could not, and men operating within and controlling the system arrange Leo's bankruptcy.

A scene at Leo's office demonstrates that Joe and Tucker create a system that leaves men with little control over their lives in the new corporation that now controls them. The scene also demonstrates that once Leo joins the combination people under him in the corporate structure see him as forcing them to do things they do not want to do. Leo's bookkeeper, Freddie Bauer, nervously enters the office. The rooms are filled with Leo's other employees and with men who work for the new combination. Joe sees Bauer, slaps him on the back and says, "You're a bookkeeper now for a big organization, Mr. Bauer." Bauer enters a room where Leo sits reading to his employees the conditions for the corporation to take over the bank and inject it with the capital required to cover the debts the bank owes people who bet on number 776. Bauer tells Leo he has to talk with him immediately. Leo takes him into another room and Bauer tells him that he can't work at the bank anymore, that Leo must get someone to replace him before the next day. "This place makes me sick," he says. Leo retorts, "You've got eyes, Freddie. You can see for yourself. I'm not alone in business anymore." Bauer blames Leo for his new situation. "Mr. Morse," he says, "what did you put me into?" Leo counters, "I didn't put you into anything. They put me!" Bauer asks, "Did you put me into this without my knowing or saying? Did you do a thing like this to me?" Leo reminds Bauer of how Bauer came to work for him in the first place: "You came to work in a racket because you wanted the extra money. Now you'll get a raise. You're working for a big corporation instead of a little man. You're a bookkeeper for 13 banks instead of one." Leo ads, sarcastically, "You're getting ahead in the world!" Noting the apparent loss of any control he has over his life as a consequence of Leo joining the corporation, Bauer says, "I don't want it. I'm not your slave." When Bauer rushes out the door and into the lobby, some of Tucker's men stop him, and Joe makes it clear to him that the new combination demands loyalty. Bauer asks Joe, "How are you gonna stop me?" One of Tucker's thugs sitting in a chair lets him know: "The combination will stop you, Bauer. Stop you dead, in your tracks." Joe says, "You see Mr. Bauer, I'm just trying to help. What do you say?" The thug rises out of the chair, takes Bauer by the arm, and escorts him to the door while he says, "Now, if you have any more trouble, just let me know and I'll try to straighten it out for you. That's my job."

Although Bauer wants out from under the corporate control the new combination imposes on him, the threats of corporate thugs reveal the risks he'll take if he tries to quit his job. He decides, then, to give information about the combination to the state prosecuting attorney's office and help the prosecutor destroy the corporation before it crushes him. Alone in the office later, Bauer uses the pay phone to call the prosecutor's office and tell him to raid the bank first thing in the morning. He says if the bank relocates after the raid he'll call and give them the new address and the addresses of the other banks as well. When Bauer leaves the building, he is stopped by a thug who works for Tucker's old partner, Bill Ficco (Paul Fix). Tucker and Ficco made a fortune selling beer during prohibition. The man tells Bauer that Ficco wants to set up a meeting with Leo to get information about the combination banks; he wants in on the action. Bauer tells him, "I don't want to have anything to do with gangsters." The man replies, "What do you mean, gangsters? It's business."

When Joe learns that Ficco wants part of the action, that Tucker refuses to let Ficco into the combination and will fight him with guns, if necessary, to keep him out, Joe fears that his brother will get killed and tells Tucker he will take over Leo's bank and run it himself.

Joe's desire to protect Leo, his developing love interest in Doris, and problems associated with making the numbers racket a legitimate, legal business if old-time gangsters like Ficco get involved cause Joe to decide to get out of the corporation himself. He takes potentially fatal risks to get Leo out of the corporation, especially with Ficco's new interest in the combination, and the risks lead to the deaths of Leo, Tucker, and Ficco, and to Joe, reunited with Doris, cooperating with the prosecutor. Viewers are left thinking that the transformed hero can work with the government to end corruption, that the government itself, except for a few self-serving politicians on Tucker's payroll, is undefiled by the corruption that permeates society. This ending, Polonsky later acknowledged, reflects the director's need to comply with the Breen Office's efforts to enforce the Motion Picture Production code, achieved by making Joe a hero, destroying the combination and the criminals associated with it, and portraying the government — represented by the prosecutor's office — in a positive light.[22]

Although the protagonist in *Force of Evil* is Joe Morse, similar to *It's a Wonderful Life*, the film depicts an independent, middle-class individual, Joe's brother Leo, struggling against the historical force of corporate consolidation and the declining autonomy associated with the rise of what Paul Goodman and other postwar social critics referred to as "the organized system."[23] A character representing a more modern version of the much-lauded nineteenth-century cultural icon of the independent individual is "forced" to become the mid–twentieth century "organization man." The circumstances pushing Leo to become an organization man — the development of a powerful business combination and the power and influence of the men who found and run it — are similar to the circumstances working on George Bailey to join Potter rather than resist him. Potter, however, never gains control of the building and loan while Tucker's new corporation becomes the entire banking system in the numbers racket.

In 1946 *It's a Wonderful Life* presents a coalition of working-class and middle-class citizens led by a virtuous middle-class hero, George Bailey, who sacrifice and work together to check the centralization of authority and the consolidation of property in the person of Henry F. Potter as he attempts to control all banking and finance in society as it is represented by the town of Bedford Falls. Potter is not depicted as the head of a postwar corporate empire but as an old Progressive-era robber baron. The concentration of authority and property in such figures causes men to become discontented with their loss of control and disaffected from the society in which their agency is increasingly and significantly diminished, which is apparent when Bedford Falls becomes Pottersville. But Pottersville is a threat rather than a reality. The coalition of average citizens with George Bailey at its center keeps Potter at bay.

Like in *It's a Wonderful Life*, in *Force of Evil* working-class and middle-class citizens, represented by Leo and his employees, engage in a similar struggle against consolidated property ownership and the concentrated social and economic power associated with it. Veiled in the transformed gangster genre, however, there exists in *Force of Evil* a stark critique of the social and economic realities associated with a society dominated by "combinations," "corporations," and "organizations." These entities must be crushed, for they represent the force that is evil in society, a force restricting people's options, concentrating wealth and power in fewer hands, threatening independent businesses, and reducing if not obliterating individualism in general. When *The Man in the Gray Flannel Suit* is released approximately a decade later, the film depicts life in a society completely transformed, one where individuals depend on employment in corporate bureaucracies and lead lives in which they are not supposed to question management let alone the "organized system." The order is not opposed, the power of the "combinations" neither checked nor overtly critiqued, and a coalition of independent business and working-class interests not an alternative.

Despite the emergence of postwar melodramas like *The Man in the Gray Flannel Suit* that depict the postwar organized society as an unopposed reality, the independent American struggling against historical forces and powerful interests out to rob him of his independence and incorporate him into the organized system does not disappear from American popular culture. In the postwar years, such independent characters increasingly exist in opposition to society rather than within it; they tend to be cultural outsiders as the compliant organization man takes center stage. This does not mean that characters representing the organization man, such as Tom Rath in *The Man in the Gray Flannel Suit*, accept uncritically the life of diminished agency and reduced control associated with being organization men. Rather, the organized system becomes dominant, and the organization man negotiates his way through the system to the best of his abilities given his diminished control over his life in the system. And he may very well critique the system as he negotiates his way within it. But direct opposition to that system does not exist in domestic melodramas as it does in a reformulated postwar gangster film like *Force of Evil,* where a new combination or corporation is represented as an organization of gangsters, corrupt lawyers and politicians.

This type of critique is not limited to the gangster-syndicate films, however. It also emerges in the American western, a genre that enables filmmakers to critique contemporary issues by setting them in a romanticized time and a romanticized geographic space, when and where many Americans assume independence was paramount: independent life the norm, independent business activity pervasive, individual agency both practiced and cherished, and bureaucratic organizations that stifle individualism foreign to the American experience. For these reasons *Johnny Guitar* (1954) is a significant countercultural western released during the height of McCarthyism and long before the emergence of counterculture of the late 1960s. The film also is important for the gender issues it raises and addresses in a much more oppositional, even radical, way than gender issues are represented in postwar films like *It's a Wonderful Life, Force of Evil*, and *The Man in the Gray Flannel Suit*. Discontented and disaffected men are represented in the film, but the characters with the most wealth and power are women. And the men are not discontented because women have power; they are discontented with the way one woman wields the power she has, and this character represents the same concentrated social and economic power associated with Henry F. Potter and with Ben Tucker's new corporation.

Johnny Guitar is a Nicholas Ray western. Compared to a film like *It's a Wonderful Life*, which is shown on television every year during the holiday season, the number of people who have seen *Johnny Guitar* is relatively small. For this reason some readers may question my use of the film as a significant cultural artifact that has something important to tell us about postwar American culture. *Johnny Guitar* was popular with American movie-goers in 1954, however, even though it was released when the motion picture industry experienced a general slump in ticket sales due in part to rising competition with television and to a long winter, and even though male critics disliked the film.[24]

The film was released in early May and was usually in the top five movies playing in cities across the country through June. In late May, *Variety* reported, "*Johnny Guitar* is best bet of the new films around here this season in a week marked by continued doldrums at most mainstream houses."[25] Even during Memorial Day week, with competition from the newly released box office hit *Dial M For Murder, Variety* noted, "*Johnny* was still in fifth position overall."[26] Professional male reviewers did not agree with moviegoers that the film should be a top selection at the box office. For example, the reviewer for *Time* wrote that the film "is one of those curious composite animals, like the tiglon, the hipplope and the peccadillo, that most people would rather talk about than see."[27] Other reviewers disliked the film for various reasons: because women were cast in traditional male roles, because reviewers found it difficult to sympathize with the characters, and because the film was full of love, hate and violence. (There were surely other things causing this last reviewer to dislike the western since it held no monopoly on love, hate and violence in the genre or in American films in general.[28]) That the film was not popular with professional male critics does not overshadow the fact that Americans across the country had it near the top of their to-see lists. On the contrary, it demonstrates that the film spoke to popular audiences in ways the professional critics did not understand. This makes *Johnny Guitar* even that much more of a significant cultural artifact deserving analysis.

Johnny Guitar is about a woman saloon owner, Vienna (Joan Crawford), and her relationship to a town and to the men in her life, particularly Johnny Guitar (Sterling Hayden). Vienna's relationship with Johnny develops within a social context that represents much about American society in the 1950s. Vienna owns a saloon on the outskirts of a western town, which represents society in the film. She is new to the area and the location of her business outside of the town symbolizes her distanced relationship to society. She has connections to society — she has a bank account in town and she knows all of the people there — but she is not actually a part of it. This society is corrupt and controlled by a selfish and neurotic woman, Emma Small (Mercedes McCambridge), who, much like Henry F. Potter, cannot deal with the fact that Vienna owns her own business. Emma is also jealous of the attention men, particularly the Dancin' Kid (Scott Brady), show Vienna. Vienna is a shrewd, independent businesswoman who struggles with Emma and with her own desires for power and wealth. She is introduced as a cold, self-interested individual, much like Emma, who purchased her land after learning from a surveyor that the railroad would come through the area and would foster economic growth. Throughout the film, however, Vienna's greed is tempered as she discovers that wealth is empty unless it is shared.[29] Like George Bailey in *It's a Wonderful Life* and Leo in *Force of Evil*, Vienna develops relationships with working-class characters and independent businessmen, sacrifices for the good of those characters, and forms a coalition with them as they collectively oppose the concentrated wealth and power represented by Emma, who attempts to control society and the people in it. That control is so complete it must be confronted and opposed. Trying to keep it in check, as George Bailey does in *It's a Wonderful Life*, is out of the question.

Although most of the characters in the film are discontented and disaffected men, the fact that two women play traditionally male roles is a major reason professional male critics disliked the film in 1954. Their responses are best understood in relation to the social and historical context of the 1950s. As World War II production demanded increased women's labor power, more women entered the work force in large numbers, and their experiences caused them to challenge more broadly the traditional assumption that women's place was in the home. After the war ended, however, and returning soldiers were reintegrated into the work force, many women lost their jobs to men or had to give up their skilled jobs for unskilled jobs or clerical office positions. Of course, some women chose to return to the home, which films like *It's a Wonderful Life* depicted as women's proper place.[30] But women's wartime experiences increased the number of both single and married women in the workforce, and this increase continued after the war, even though women lost jobs to returning soldiers. Women's wartime experiences and increased employment opportunities caused many to learn that the value of their labor need not be determined solely by their productivity in the home. Moreover, they represented an increasing competitive threat to men in the work force, and postwar employers did not value or reward their labor equally with that of men.[31]

In her studies of American families in the cold war era, Elaine Tyler May argues that professionals dealt with this threat by prescribing traditional women's roles in order to contain women within the traditional family structure. The influx of women into the workforce during and following the war caused physicians, psychiatrists, clergymen, sociologists, writers for women's magazines such as *The Ladies Home Journal* and other professionals, both male and female, to voice concerns that the moral fabric of society was ripping.[32] May writes that such professionals assumed that

> Stable families conforming to respectable behavior held the key to the future. In keeping with the American tradition of republican motherhood, it was up to women to achieve successful families: if they fulfilled their domestic roles as adapted to the atomic age, they would be able to rear children who would avoid juvenile delinquency, stay in school, and become future scientists and experts to defeat the Russians in the cold war.[33]

Many professional critics who reviewed *Johnny Guitar* in 1954 fit within May's field of experts who feared the female threat and prescribed traditional roles for women in films. In his review in *The New Yorker,* John McCarten called the film "the maddest Western you are likely to encounter this year. It has not only male but female gunfighters."[34] Women are not professional gunfighters in the film, however. Emma and Vienna do shoot it out at the end, but the gunfight is a short scene in the film. That women in the film own property and are in positions of power over men were the real reasons this reviewer disliked the film, which is apparent in the way he concluded his review: "Back to *Kinder, Kuche. Kirche*" (children, kitchen, church). The reviewer for *Time*, demonstrating his angst over sexual issues, wrote, "The menace is not a man but a woman.... What's more, she is not just the usual jealous woman but a real sexological square knot who fondles pistols suggestively and gets unladylike satisfaction from watching a house burn down."[35] *The Newsweek* reviewer, noting that Crawford "is still one of the slinkiest of the six-gun operatives," never actually reviewed the film and could not get his mind off the actress. He ended with this observation: "Summing up: Joan Crawford shapes up well in her levis."[36]

The plot of the film develops around a stagecoach holdup. Emma's brother is killed in the holdup and she falsely accuses the Dancin' Kid and his men of committing the crime. The Kid and his men work and own a silver mine that cannot be reached without taking a secret trail through a stream and behind a waterfall. Emma uses the crime as an excuse to vent her wrath on the Kid and on Vienna. She associates the Kid and his men with the holdup and Vienna with the Kid, therefore condemning them all without any evidence. The Kid did not hold up the stage, but he and his men decide later to rob the bank. They figure they might as well since leaders in society already blame them for a crime they did not commit; they are consequently corrupted *by* society and further alienated from it.

As in *It's a Wonderful Life*, there are tensions between the social groups in this film as well as tensions within groups and within particular group members. No room exists in Emma's corrupt society for those who hold to traditional values of independent property, community and public virtue. These values are only evident in some members of the two groups — the Dancin' Kid's gang and Vienna's employees — that exist outside of the society Emma controls.[37] In addition to the tensions between social groups, we learn that tensions also exist within Vienna and between Johnny and Vienna. Vienna has sent for Johnny, an old acquaintance and a gunfighter, to protect her and her property from Emma and the townspeople. At one time in her life she wanted to settle down with Johnny, but he did not want to be tied down to a wife and a home. Standing in front of a model of the city she wants to develop, Vienna tells Johnny that five years earlier she wanted to build a future together but he needed his independence. The future society that Vienna wants to build could have had a place in it for Johnny, but he was unwilling to sacrifice his self-interest to be a part of it, something he now regrets. He asks her, "What do ya suppose'd happen if this man were to come back?" She replies, "When a fire burns itself out, all you have left is ashes." The tension is between his self-interest then and her self-interest now, between her past desire to have a relationship and his searching to see if that relationship is still a possibility. Thus the tension between groups, and between Emma and Vienna, also exists within groups, apparent in this scene with Johnny and Vienna. The only way for self-interest to be controlled is to share and moderate one's interests with the interests of others, something both Johnny and Vienna learn during the course of the film, and something impossible in the society represented by Emma Small and her cohorts.

This tension between group members is evident throughout the film. For example, in one scene the Dancin' Kid and his men are at their silver mine debating where to go and what to do. The mine has been exhausted and they think Emma and the townspeople will be looking for them to blame them for the stagecoach holdup. The Kid wants to stay because he has feelings for Vienna. Bart (Ernest Borgnine) tells him he is a fool, that

A marketing poster for *Johnny Guitar* displays the conflict between the independent characters represented by Vienna (Joan Crawford) and Johnny Guitar (Sterling Hayden) and the mob controlled by Emma Small (Mercedes McCambridge), and the lengths to which Emma will go (burning Vienna's business to the ground) to maintain control of the society she and the townspeople represent (Photofest).

he should not waste his time on Vienna. The Kid asks if there is anything in life Bart likes and Bart says, "Me, I like me!" This same intra-group tension is also evident later in the film when the Kid wants to turn back and look for Turkey, who is hurt by an explosion and falls behind the rest of the group when they are trying to escape. Bart tells the Kid they should not risk their own necks looking for Turkey. The Kid thinks of the welfare of the group but Bart thinks only of his own skin.

Unlike Bart's character, which remains the same throughout the film, Vienna's cold and bitter nature changes as she, similar to Joe Morse in *Force of Evil*, sheds the self-interest that makes her want to build a city and realizes that the men who work for her depend on her and she on them. One scene illustrates that Vienna has come to think of her group as a community, much like the bank-run scene with George Bailey at the building and loan in *It's a Wonderful Life*. The posse is searching for Vienna because she was in the bank withdrawing her money when the Kid and his men robbed it. Because the Kid's men did not take Vienna's money, Emma assumes that Vienna also is guilty. Vienna goes to her saloon and gives her three casino employees six months' pay and tells them to come back when the time has passed. She promises them a share of her business when they return, and she gives one of them extra money to take care of the cook, Tom (John Carradine). Unlike Emma, Vienna now understands that they depend on one another, and she is willing to let her employees have a share of her business. The future community she comes to envision will not be the extant society based on unmitigated self-interest and concentrated property ownership that Emma controls. The intra-group tensions are thus developed within a social context, and on one level the film can be read as a social and economic struggle as some characters attempt to build a social group opposed to the concentrated power and wealth that Emma represents, and to the corrupt townspeople who do her bidding.

The contrast between Emma's values and those that Vienna comes to embrace is further apparent in a scene at Vienna's when Emma and the posse arrive looking for Turkey. They find Vienna sitting alone at the piano wearing a white gown, a stark contrast to their own black funeral clothes. The white gown symbolizes her newfound virtue, compassion and morality. Emma accuses Vienna of taking part in the bank robbery when Turkey rolls out from beneath a table. (Tom found him wounded and brought him there to hide.) Emma's people pull Turkey up to a kneeling position and hold his arms outstretched as if they are crucifying him; blood covers his neck, chest and shirt. Emma tries to get him to say that Vienna was in on the bank robbery: "Just tell us she was one of you, Turkey, and you'll go free!" Turkey pleads to Vienna, "I don't want to die! What'll I do?" Vienna says, "Save yourself." He then asks what they will do to Vienna and Emma replies, "The law will take its course." One of Emma's men, McIvers (Ward Bond), tells Turkey he does not have to say anything, just nod. "Was Vienna one of ya?" he asks him; then Emma screams, "Well, was she?!" Turkey gasps as if taking his last breath and nods his head forward to infer that she was.

In this scene, Turkey, to ensure he will be dealt with less severely, is forced by Emma and her cohorts to say an innocent person took part in a crime. As in Arthur Miller's play *The Crucible* (1953), the scene is a parable about the HUAC hearings during the 1940s and 1950s, when in order to protect themselves people named others as being involved in subversive activities.[38] Emma, with her short, dark hair and her neurotic personality, is a parody of Senator Joseph McCarthy. What is important about the scene, however, is the contrast between Vienna's values and those of the posse, of Emma, and even of Turkey. Emma and the posse want to hang an innocent person in the name of justice for their own warped satisfaction. Turkey saves himself (he thinks) by incriminating Vienna. In contrast to her character early in the film, Vienna does not think only of herself.

At the end of the film, Johnny, Vienna and the Kid defeat Emma and her cohorts in a shootout at the Kid's hideout. In the final scene, Johnny and Vienna (the Kid is killed) emerge from behind the waterfall that hides the entrance to the Kid's place. They stand in the stream embracing, soaking wet from the water, as if cleansed through baptism of their past sins and now ready to begin a new life together free from the concentrated power and corruption displayed by Emma and the townspeople and endemic to the society Emma controls.

Johnny Guitar is a low-budget film that received negative reviews, but its success at the box office suggests that audiences related to the tensions in the film that the critics either missed completely or did not understand. Critics do not usually have a historical perspective and often separate the films they review from the historical climates within which the films are produced. The changing assumptions surrounding women's work and women's social roles and, more importantly for my purposes here, the increased threat to small business owners by the centralization of big business during the Depression and the war were surely reasons for the production and popular reception *of Johnny Guitar* in the 1950s. These were social realities people lived with in the 1950s, realities evident in the film.

Much of the secondary literature on *Johnny Guitar,* however, like Raymond Carney's work on *It's a Wonderful Life,* focuses on the psychological tensions in the film.[39] Peter Biskind and Michael Wilmington argue that *Johnny Guitar* is about personal, usually psycho-sexual, problems. In his auteur study of Nicholas Ray, Biskind downplays the socio-economic conflict between Vienna's coalition with independent men and Emma and her cohorts. To Biskind, Vienna "is punished for her independence from men by losing her casino (set afire by the posse), and must vanquish Emma, her evil, desexed other half so that she can accept the loving embrace of Johnny Guitar...."[40] Biskind sees the essential conflict of the film as a psycho-sexual conflict within Vienna, one played out externally with Emma, whom he apparently sees as the other half of a schizophrenic personality. There is no evidence in the film, however, as we will see in chapter seven there is in *Fight Club,* that the protagonist is indeed schizophrenic. Wilmington reads Emma's character in a similar way. "Celibacy," he informs us, "has apparently driven her mad; she seizes on the murder as an excuse to banish and possibly lynch Vienna, whom she envies, and the Kid, for whom she has a wild, repressed love."[41]

My point is not that these psycho-sexual conflicts are absent in *Johnny Guitar,* or in other postwar films for that matter. Biskind and Wilmington, as well as Carney, reveal the psychological tensions in the films they study. My concern is that in such studies the social terrain becomes submerged beneath the psychological terrain and that the social conflicts that often foster psychological conflicts are not adequately addressed. I would agree with Biskind, for example, when he asserts that "Ray's films share with other films of the fifties a fondness for psychological and occasionally mythic categories...." He goes too far, however, when he concludes that these categories "replaced the social and political ones of the thirties and forties."[42] In the politically repressive environment of McCarthyism, filmmakers such as Ray did make less overtly political and subversive films than, say, King Vidor's *Our Daily Bread* (1934). But because they created films in a more censored and oppressive environment, they had to be more ingenious in devising ways to critique America's dominant institutions and values, business and political practices. Carney, Biskind and Wilmington suggest that the hegemony of America's socio-economic structure and dominant institutions is so complete that opposition is impossible, that all tensions must be psychological rather than sociological and historical; conflicts and problems become individual rather than social, and social conflicts are merely internal conflicts externalized. Such a focus causes Biskind to acknowledge that Nicholas Ray was "a serious director concerned with social problems," but leads him to conclude, "to see [him] as fundamentally subversive to [America's] central institutions is the reverse of the truth."[43]

The evidence in *Johnny Guitar* related to social conflicts, to people and groups of people with competing values, and to issues related to concentrated economic and political power is too strong to dismiss as mere external manifestations of characters' individual psychological problems. Ray's film does not call for the demise of corporate capitalism and the dictatorship of the proletariat, which would be an extreme example of subversion and, perhaps, is the kind of example some need to enable them to see the film as in some way subversive or, in other words, what later in the 1960s would be considered countercultural. But even Ray's casting of female characters in traditionally male roles is subversive, evident in the fact that the casting clearly challenged the perspective of many male critics. Wilmington points out that the title suggests the film is about Johnny Guitar when it is actually about Vienna.[44] The movie has a traditional western façade that veils some significantly nontraditional, even subversive, content. It challenges not only assumptions about traditional gender roles but also increasingly dominant assumptions about the social and economic relations of the postwar corporate order, even though these challenges are veiled behind the setting of the late nineteenth-century West.

In *Johnny Guitar*, as in *It's a Wonderful Life* and *Force of Evil*, there are social groups and tensions between them. Emma owns the town and threatens the existence of Vienna's independent business, which Emma eventually destroys by fire. She, like Henry F. Potter, owns most of the town and wants everything for herself. That which she cannot have she must destroy, just as Potter wants to gain control of and then dissolve the building and loan and pursues that objective as maniacally as Melville's Captain Ahab chases his leviathan in *Moby Dick,* and just as Tucker seeks to crush the independent banks in the numbers racket. Emma, like Potter, wants to consolidate all property in her hands and destroys Vienna's saloon and casino. The Dancin' Kid and his men are too independent to be incorporated into Emma's society, as are Leo Morse and his employees too independent to be incorporated successfully into Tucker's combination. The Kid and his men are independent business owners but also independent workers, men who both work their claim and own it as they labor in their small silver mine, much like the Bedford Falls tavern owner Martini and the small numbers banker Leo. Moreover, the Dancin' Kid and his men live on the land farthest from town, farthest from Emma's domain, like

Martini and those who share his social position live farthest from Potter in Bailey Park. It is also important to remember that it is only after Emma's corrupt society wrongly accuses the Kid and his men of a crime that they become totally disaffected from society and actually rob the bank. And they do not take the small independent saloon owner's (Vienna's) money, only that of their accusers. Just as the workers and small business owners in *It's A Wonderful Life* only turn into Potter's "discontented rabble" when society becomes totally controlled by Potter and bears his name, Pottersville, the Kid and his men only resort to crime when the society controlled by Emma unjustly makes them criminals.

That the Kid and his men do not take Vienna's money when they rob the bank demonstrates that she holds a social position between the Kid and Emma. Her saloon is on the outskirts of town, between Emma's town and the Kid's gang's silver mine, just as George Bailey's house is between Potter and Bailey Park. Further, like George, Vienna helps the working class in their struggles with Emma and her cohorts and they help her. For example, she hides Turkey from Emma and the posse, and she tells Turkey to save himself at the potential loss of her own life. She also flees to the Kid's domain for protection when she's in trouble, just as Potter's "rabble" protect George from Potter's attempt to have George imprisoned for embezzlement when George's uncle inadvertently leaves a building-and-loan deposit with Potter without knowing it. Moreover, Vienna has the same tensions within her that George Bailey has within him. In the beginning of the film she thinks about building a city and she avoids the romantic attentions of Johnny, just as George Bailey wants to build cities and bridges and avoids the romantic attentions of Mary. When Vienna does get involved with Johnny again, her clothes change from the black pants and shirts that the townspeople wear, to a red nightgown, to a white dress, and finally to the more colorful clothes of the Kid's gang. In the end she actually wears the Kid's clothes, symbolizing her eventual solidarity with the gang, a solidarity created by their mutual opposition to Emma and the corrupt society she controls. What all three films depict, then, are coalitions of small independent business owners with the working class as they confront the organized interests of centralized economic power.

The male characters in *Johnny Guitar* who are not part of Emma's cohort are not opposed to Vienna being a non-traditional woman, a successful and ambitious independent businesswoman who wants to control her own destiny and has men on her payroll. They are, however, opposed to Emma's influence and power, not because she is a woman but because she wields her power in order to control Vienna as well as the Kid's men. Together they confront the concentrated economic power and political influence represented by Emma and the townspeople. The threat to Vienna's independent business by Emma's exploits, then, represents the same kind of corporate threat to small, private business that Tucker's new corporation in the numbers racket represents to Leo Morse's independent numbers bank in *Force of Evil*. In *It's a Wonderful Life, Force of Evil* and *Johnny Guitar,* the concentrated economic power and the authority of what *Force of Evil* refers to as "corporations," "combinations" and "organizations" threaten characters' independence. Potter wants to gain control of the building and loan in order to consolidate all financial business within a combination of banking institutions under his control. Tucker and his corporation lawyer, Joe Morse, successfully consolidate all banking in the numbers racket under the umbrella of the new corporation. And Emma literally destroys Vienna's independent business by burning it to the ground. The continued independence of the building and loan in *It's a Wonderful Life* is associated with average citizens living better lives and having more control over the lives that they lead; the men become "discontented rabble" when that control is lost. In *Force of Evil* Leo Morse wages a futile struggle to remain an independent businessman and to keep his employees as well as his bank from being incorporated into Tucker's new combination, where the employees are threatened by corporate-gangster thugs and do not even have the ability to quit their jobs, to stop working for the corporation. In *Johnny Guitar* the disaffected men in the Kid's gang fight against the power and influence concentrated in Emma and in the corrupt society she controls and represents.

In the two films of the late forties, *It's a Wonderful Life* and *Force of Evil,* the possibility for evil to be checked in society is still possible. In the former, George Bailey wins his struggle with Potter. In the latter, Joe Morse has a conversion experience following his brother's death, kills Tucker and Ficco, and commits to helping Prosecutor Hall battle the "force of evil" in the future. Protagonists in these films can still exist in society and work against the evils associated with combinations, corporations, and organizations, although director Polonsky only made that possible in *Force of Evil* due to the political power of the Breen Office to make him do so. In 1946, George Bailey merely needs to keep Potter's power in check. In 1948, Joe Morse realizes he must work to help Prosecutor Hall eradicate that kind of concentrated economic power from society. The resolution to *Force of Evil* is therefore a more radical solution to the problem of concentrated economic power that is central to the plots of both films.

By the mid-fifties, the centralization of power and influence in corporations and the negative consequences associated with that centralization are represented as being victorious. In 1956, gray-suited men like Tom Rath in *The Man in the Gray Flannel Suit* are not independent but must negotiate their way through the organized system, playing the games others who manage their lives in the system design for them to play. In 1954, *Johnny Guitar* likewise portrays the centralization of authority and power represented by Emma as victorious; she controls society as the town represents it. Opposition exists at the periphery of society, however, evident in the Kid's gang's independent mine, in Vienna's independent saloon and casino on the outskirts of the town, and in the coalition the characters associated with Vienna and the Kid develop to confront and battle Emma. Emma and her black-clad henchmen must destroy these characters that represent alternatives to the social and economic order that Emma controls, and Vienna, Johnny and the other men in the Kid's gang must directly and violently confront them to maintain their independence.

3

Similar Criticisms, Dissimilar Solutions

The 1960s and 1970s

We have seen that critiques of individuals' declining agency in the increasingly organized and bureaucratized society of the 1940s and 1950s appear in mainstream films like *The Man in the Gray Flannel Suit*, but that characters in such films are represented as negotiating corporate life in the organized system rather than confronting and opposing the symbols of corporate consolidation and influence evident in gunslinger and gangster films such as *Force of Evil* (1948) and *Johnny Guitar* (1954). Although such opposition remains evident immediately after the war in *It's a Wonderful Life* (1946) as George Bailey stands up for the rights and values of vulnerable individuals against Potter's attempts to obliterate those rights and values and gain control of all property in Bedford Falls, that kind of direct opposition becomes veiled in the gunslinger and gangster films of the forties and fifties. Such opposition remains evident in gangster and western films released since then, but the veil drops in the 1960s and 1970s as critiques of dominant social and economic practices and the values associated with those practices become more apparent in mainstream dramas and comedies as well. Similar to *The Man in the Gray Flannel Suit* (1956), many films released in the sixties and later take the postwar corporate order for granted, depicting men, much like Tom Rath, as negotiating their way through the daily grind of corporate life so they can make their bread and play their roles as consumers in America's postwar economy. But late sixties and seventies films often are more overtly critical of the system and the values associated with it, portraying men as either dropping out or engaging in acts of violence as the only viable actions they can take to display even a modicum of agency. The replacement of the Motion Picture Production Code with a rating system and the declining control that the studios wielded over production, combined with the demise of McCarthyism, the continuing struggle for civil rights, the mounting evidence of President Johnson's failed policy in Vietnam, and the increasingly pervasive values and behaviors associated with American consumer culture created a historical context in which filmmakers had the liberty and the reasons to make more overtly critical films.

The adoption of the 1968 rating system and the growth of independent filmmakers are industry-specific developments that facilitated creativity and impacted significantly and positively film content in the 1960s and 1970s. The studios adopted The Motion Picture Production Code (1930) in response to cultural conservatives' attempts since the early years of the motion picture industry to control film content. The producers sought to regulate their movies before those who wanted to control what Americans could see and hear on the big screen demanded government regulation. The code is a long list of "don'ts," things filmmakers could not include in their movies, such as portraying ministers negatively, criminals positively, and sex in any way at all. Filmmakers skirted the code in various ways from the start, and they increasingly did so in the fifties and sixties as their European counterparts made movies with more mature content and Americans struggled to do likewise. A code adopted during the waning years of prohibition could not last in a society swimming in corporate martini lunches, more explicit discussions of sex, magazines like Hugh Hefner's *Playboy*, and a youth culture associated with sex, drugs and rock 'n' roll. In 1966, the Motion Picture Association of America (MPAA) hired President Johnson's special assistant and advertising man Jack Valenti to be its president, and the organization replaced the code with the rating system. Control of what people could see and hear now rested with individual moviegoers; the new code just required they have an idea of what they would be getting.[1]

The significant control that the major studios exerted over filmmakers also waned in the postwar years, creating opportunities for more independent productions, facilitating creativity, and enabling filmmakers to engage in more overt social, cultural and political critiques. The five major studios — Warner Bros., Paramount, RKO, MGM-Loew's, and Twentieth Century–Fox — owned a mere 17 percent of theaters in the country after the war. In 1947, however, the Supreme Court ruled in the *United States v. Paramount, Inc. et al* that Paramount and the other studios wielded too much control over the initial exhibition of new films in America's highly populated urban centers. In 32 of the 94 largest cities, the Court stated that no independent theaters existed. Moreover, the Court concluded that "70 percent of first-run theaters are affiliated with one or more of the five majors" in cities with populations that exceeded 100,000. A lower court had ruled that the vertical integration of major studios did not need to be dismantled but competitive bidding among exhibitors should be protected. When that case reached the Supreme Court, the high court disagreed with the lower-court ruling because the studios fixed prices, demanded block booking (if an exhibitor wanted a blockbuster film the studios forced the exhibitor to purchase less-appealing movies as well), and engaged in "other unlawful restraints of trade" in their business with theaters. The justices sent the case back to the lower court, and that court decided to break up the vertically integrated studios, which was completed by the end of 1954. The growth of independents did not occur overnight. By the early sixties, however, independents accounted for approximately two thirds of films produced in the United States. Two decades earlier, the production of two thirds of American movies rested with only seven companies. *Easy Rider* director Dennis Hopper put it this way: "The studio is a thing of the past, and they are very smart if they just concentrate on becoming distributing companies for independent producers." *Star Wars* creator George Lucas described the consequences of the studios' decline a little differently: "The studio system is dead.... The power is with the people now. The workers have the means of production!"[2]

If in 1947 a filmmaker had uttered Lucas's words, he surely would have found himself sitting before the House Committee on Un-American Activities (HUAC) with the Hollywood Ten and blacklisted along with the hundreds of other actors, writers and directors whose careers were either put on hold or destroyed by the political oppression known as McCarthyism. Although the committee did not disband until 1975, the political culture had changed significantly by the late sixties with the successful struggle for civil rights, the unsuccessful war in southeast Asia, and the media images of the brutality and violence associated with each as local officials beat, cattle-prodded, and police-dogged innocent men, women and children at home, and federal officials ordered Asian civilians to be carpet-bombed, fire-bombed and Napalmed abroad. Such violence caused Dr. Martin Luther, Jr., to condemn his government's militant actions to achieve its political objectives abroad after black youth justified to him their use of such actions on American streets to achieve their goals at home. "They asked," King announced exactly one year to the day before he was murdered by an assassin's bullet, "if our own nation wasn't using massive doses of violence to solve its problems, to bring about the changes it wanted. Their questions hit home, and I knew that I could never again raise my voice against the violence of the oppressed in the ghettos without having first spoken clearly to the greatest purveyor of violence in the world today — my own government."[3] Just as Dr. King became more openly critical of his government in the late sixties, the turbulent history of these years and the changes in the motion picture industry provided filmmakers with the ability and the reasons to make more overtly critical films.

Characters in such films who drop out reject society altogether. They realize that to exist in society they must conform to unappealing and meaningless work, to a life of incessant striving in order to accumulate more material things, and to a regimen of hours and days designed and controlled by others. Rather than accept such a reality as their destiny, they turn their backs on the nature of everyday life in the postwar organized system. But these non-conformist dropouts often cannot imagine an alternative and are left alienated and confused. Or, they do what becomes a staple of such films and engage in illegal activities that, if successful, provide them with the financial means to be independent. For freedom in postwar America requires either capital or vagrancy to enable men to become independent from the organized system to which most are tethered. But that independence does not necessarily provide them with cultural freedom; men who drop out are represented as rejecting the regimented time and materialistic values of corporate society but often have no alternative values to embrace.

In contrast to the dropouts, those who confront the system from within often continue to be gunslingers and gangsters of sorts. Organized gangsters, like the Corleone family in *The God Father* trilogy, represent the organized system; they repeatedly say "it's business" as they carve up market share with other "families" and use their illegitimate gains in industries like bootlegging and prostitution to become legitimate corporations that run casinos and other legal businesses. They also simultaneously crush some "families" as they consolidate their holdings through militant horizontal integration, all the while paying politicians and cops to do their bidding.[4] The small, independent criminals, on the other hand — like Wyatt (Peter Fonda) and Billy (Dennis Hopper) in *Easy Rider* (1969) — commit crimes so they can acquire enough capital to take control of their lives and achieve independence from life in the system. The gunslingers, however, are either cops, like Harry Callahan (Clint Eastwood) in *Dirty*

Harry (1971), who work in law enforcement agencies where they are hampered by bureaucracies that restrict their ability to do their jobs and must therefore fight the system as well as the criminals. Or they are vigilante outsiders, like Paul Kersey (Charles Bronson) in *Death Wish* (1974), who take the law into their own hands as they become judge and executioner in a bureaucratic society where corrupt lawyers, judges and politicians negotiate justice rather than seek it.

In the introduction to this book, I argue that authors who claim that men's discontent and disaffection in the late twentieth century were responses to the successes of the civil rights and women's movements and from the country's defeat in Vietnam contribute to our understanding of men's anxieties as they were manifested in society and represented in American culture. My central claim, however, is that men's discontent and disaffection are evident well before the successes of those movements and the failed policy in Vietnam, and that the discontent and disaffection continue well beyond those successes and that failure. Clearly, race and gender issues were significant in these years, as was for some filmmakers the catastrophe of American policy in Southeast Asia. Those realities, however, only demonstrate my point that the new developments exacerbated men's anxieties and discontent but did not create them. Moreover, another development, the emergence of the counterculture, also fueled conservative male discontent with alternative values and behaviors while other men participated in countercultural activities due to their discontent with established society and culture, with "the establishment." We have to remember, too, that many filmmakers who created the celluloid representations of reactionary men identified with aspects of the counterculture. Consequently, some of the extremely racist, bigoted, misogynistic and violent super-patriot characters that appear in American films are sometimes more caricature than character. The same can be said of how characters associated with the counterculture or opposed to American foreign policy are depicted in films created by more conservative filmmakers.[5]

It is important to point out that "counterculture" is a problematic term, one that authors use frequently and loosely to refer to the values and activities of anyone or any group in the sixties that questioned the values and practices of "the establishment." Interestingly, some authors use "counterculture" in conjunction with the term "movement" even though a wide variety of countercultural "movements" existed and had very different goals and distinct strategies, if any, for attempting to achieve their goals. It should be clear that "doing one's own thing" is too radically individualistic to be the guiding principle of a "movement." As one author who studies the sixties notes, "the counterculture included everyone, excluded no one."[6] That said, "counterculture" is most often associated with "hippies" and diverse groups of activists, but those groups were not united by a common purpose or a shared set of values; they separately and distinctly revealed their opposition to some aspect or aspects of the established order. A more disparate "counter" rather than a unified oppositional "culture" existed.[7]

We have seen in previous chapters that anxieties about and criticisms of postwar society and culture are evident in films produced in the forties and fifties, especially in regard to individuals' declining agency and influence in what Adlai Stevenson and various social critics referred to as the realities of America's organized system and men's lack of independence in that system. Anxieties about men's inability to "do their own thing," then, emerged long before the sixties began and continued after the decade ended. Such anxieties pervade many forties and fifties films and, we will see in chapter four, remain central in a variety of films released in the final decades of the twentieth century. But the criticisms become more overt in sixties and seventies films, especially in movies set in contemporary mainstream American society rather than in the western and gangster genres. Moreover, my analysis here of the countercultural film *Easy Rider* (1969), of the avenger-cop film *Dirty Harry* (1971), of the comedy-drama *The Graduate* (1967), and of the tragic drama *Joe* (1970) reveals that the theme of men's declining agency in society is central to these diverse films. The mundane nature of both white- and blue-collar work in the organized system, the necessity of gong outside of the system to have agency and engage in meaningful labor, the need to subvert authority within the system and work against it and alone to seek justice, and even dropping out of the system without a plan for what to do or how to do it are all evidence of a postwar culture that represents discontented and disaffected men as lacking agency and purpose within the system and struggling to find it.

The Graduate is about Benjamin Braddock (Dustin Hoffman), a recent graduate of an elite college who flies home to southern California, where he spends the summer thinking about his future but deciding nothing, much to his parents' chagrin. Mrs. Robinson (Anne Bancroft), the wife of Ben's father's business partner, seduces Ben and they carry on an excruciatingly meaningless affair before Ben reluctantly dates the Robinsons' daughter, Elaine (Katherine Ross), at his father's request. Ben soon decides he loves Elaine. The problem is that Mrs. Robinson doesn't want

Ben to date her daughter. She doesn't think Ben is good enough for Elaine, so she threatens to tell her about their affair unless Ben stops seeing Elaine. Ben tells Elaine about the affair before her mother can. Shocked, Elaine returns to Berkeley, where she continues her college education and becomes engaged to another man, a medical student named Carl Smith (Brian Avery). Ben decides he wants to marry Elaine and drives to Berkeley to tell her. Elaine meets with Ben several times, they talk, and Ben asks her to marry him. But Elaine believes she can't have a relationship with Ben because he slept with her mother. She goes through with her plan to marry Carl in Santa Barbara, but Ben drives to the wedding and Elaine flees with him. They run from the church, jump on a public bus, and stare blankly into the camera in the final scene.[8]

Beyond this love story, the film is a cultural critique of postwar affluence and the limits associated with the upper–middle-class life depicted by the Braddocks and their friends. But *The Graduate* is not literally a countercultural film because it presents no alternative values or social practices, only those espoused by Ben's parents, which limit the choices he is supposed to make regarding his future. The film critiques the dominant values and social practices of postwar affluent society in a world without apparent alternatives. And that is Ben Braddock's problem. He knows he wants his life to be "different," but he has no alternative values to potentially adopt, no other lifestyle to possibly live. He appears to be as trapped by the circumstances of his upper–middle-class upbringing as much as Melville's Bartleby is by the conditions created by his lawyer-employer in the tale the author penned more than a century earlier. Indeed, of all the movie characters I discuss in this book, Ben Braddock reminds me most of Melville's Bartleby: isolated even while among others, pained when forced to interact with others, seeking solitude whenever possible (even in scuba gear at the bottom of the Braddock swimming pool), and demonstrating no emotion regarding his own life or in response to others' questions and suggestions about it.

In the first scene of *The Graduate*, Ben sits forlornly on a plane as he returns to his upper–middle-class California home after graduating from college. In the final scene, he looks just as forlorn as he sits with Elaine in the back seat of the bus that carries the couple into an ambiguous future. Ben knows just one thing about his future: he wants it to be "different." Different from what, exactly, and it what way, he never says. It's clear, however, that nothing about the lives of his upper–middle-class parents appeals to him, nor does the prospect of going to work or to graduate school, choices others try to get him to make but which he seems to understand would ensure he lives a monotonous, mind-numbing and uneventful life similar to the lives represented by his parents and their friends. Except for Ben's eventual realization that he wants to marry Elaine Robinson and his determination to do so, he exhibits no affect.

There is not much to say about *The Graduate* in relation to social commentary because we see the world much as Ben sees it, and Ben says little about anything and virtually nothing about society or his place in it. The one thing the film critiques, and that by Director Mike Nichols mere display of it, is the emptiness of a life dedicated to self-absorbed affluence. Ben is a pampered upper–middle-class young man who drives a new Alfa Rome — a graduation present from his parents — while he spends far too much time contemplating his future while doing nothing other than smoke cigarettes, drink beer while floating in the family pool, and have sex with Mrs. Robinson. The cultural critique that exists in the film is the result of Nichols' camera shots of the middle-aged affluent men and women who live mundane lives engaged in inconsequential activities that, we assume, is why Ben wants his life to be "different." We don't know what Ben thinks but we know what he sees. The camera often shows us what life looks like from behind his eyes, and it is not attractive. In the end we are not led to believe that when Ben drives off with Elaine Robinson in the back of a bus he is doing his own thing and answering the questions about his future that plague him throughout the film. Rather, we can easily envision Elaine getting pregnant just like her mother did and Ben becoming the next middle manager at Dow Chemical or some other corporation that makes "plastics." Ben merely rejects his parents' reality before he would most likely begin to endure it himself because he knows nothing else, explores nothing else. In the rapidly changing and turbulent world of the 1960s, Ben appears to have somehow lived a cloistered existence on a college campus, of all places, during years that author Todd Gitlin aptly refers to as "years of hope, days of rage."[9]

Just watching his parents and their friends live the lives they do is too much for Ben. He takes no action, however, to create an alternative realty for himself, and there is no indication that will change if he marries Elaine. Ben is so trapped by his upper-bourgeois upbringing he can't imagine what difference could look like, and we can't imagine either Ben or Elaine participating in any aspect of the counterculture or doing anything other than lead the unimaginative and stultifying lives they already lead. Ben merely wallows in the self-indulgent lifestyle his parents' affluence enables him to live but not enjoy. Although youthful audiences in 1967 may very well have identified with Ben's sense of isolation and his desire for something different, the character is a model for nothing more than depression, inaction, isolation and making compulsive and arguably insignificant — even stupid — decisions.

The degree to which Ben is alienated from his parents' world is so severe, however, that he appears to become physically ill when he is with more than one representative of it at the same time. His alienation and desperate need for isolation and silence is evident in a variety of scenes. When he flies home from college in the first scene, he appears to be in a trance as he sits in his seat on the plane and then as he rides on the people-mover system through the airport while we listen to Simon and Garfunkel's "The Sound of Silence." When he is around people, he appears desperate to hear the silence referred to in the song lyrics. He wears the same blank stare at home and throughout the film that he displays on the plane and in the airport, and he flees from people at every opportunity. The only thing we know for sure that he thinks about these people is that he does not respect them, something he reveals to Mr. Robinson when Robinson confronts Ben about the affair he has with Mrs. Robinson.

In an early scene Ben seems overwhelmed by something as he sits in front of an aquarium in his unlit bedroom when his father, Mr. Braddock (William Daniels), enters, flips on the light and asks, "Hey, what's the matter?" But before Ben has a chance to answer, his father tells him all the guests he and his wife invited to Ben's graduation party are waiting to see him downstairs. Ben's first line is, "Dad, can you explain to them that I have to be alone for a while?" Mr. Braddock can't understand and looks into Ben's blank stare and asks, "What is it, Ben?" Ben says, "I'm just...." He pauses and his father asks, "Worried?" Ben exhales deeply and says, "Well." His father refines his question: "About what?" Ben replies, "I guess about my future." When Mr. Braddock asks what it is he's worried about regarding his future, Ben says, "I don't know. I want it to be...." Mr. Braddock prods Ben, "To be what?" Ben smiles slightly, looks into his father's eyes and answers, "Different." Ben is so affectless his father almost literally has to pull this single word from his son's mouth, and we never learn how Ben wants his life to be different because he never discovers it for himself. No alternatives exist in the cultural universe he occupies. The hegemony of his postwar affluent life is portrayed as total, leaving one without choices beyond the norms associated with that life. This is true even in one of the most turbulent decades of the twentieth century, a time of emergent alter-

Benjamin Braddock (Dustin Hoffman) reveals his lack of affect as he contemplates but does nothing about his future in *The Graduate* (1967) (Photofest).

native values and lifestyles and of laments about declining independence and traditional ways of life in the expanding organized system and American consumer culture. None of these things is even referenced in the film; they're not the concerns of people who occupy the Braddocks' socioeconomic position and traverse the social terrain of their upper-bourgeois cultural landscape.

Ben is repulsed by the lives that his parents and their friends lead, but he does not articulate what it is that repulses him. Their lives are centered on business, affluence and the consumption — nice houses, sports cars, scuba gear, elite college educations — that affluence can afford. But Ben demonstrates no understanding of what he finds repulsive and has no alternative values to embrace. He is not countercultural because he has no values to counter those instilled in him by his parents and the upper-bourgeois society they represent. Consequently, he wanders through that summer and fall wanting something different but never exploring alternatives because he does not have a bone of "difference" in his upper middle-class body. *The Graduate*, then, critiques living one's life devoted to meaningless work and conspicuous consumption, but the film recognizes no values other than those associated with living such a life.

In contrast to Benjamin Braddock, the bikers in *Easy Rider* (1969) search for alternatives and find them. Billy (Dennis Hopper), however, is actually quite mainstream and wants to retire in Florida, while Wyatt (Peter Fonda) is attracted to the mythic independence associated with the American past more than he is to any utopian experiment in communal living or to the militant overthrow of society, a possibility not depicted in the film but definitely articulated by radical groups like the Weathermen in the late sixties.[10]

Unlike forties and fifties films that in some way address the systemic issues related to men's declining independence and agency in the postwar corporate order, even though such cultural critique is veiled in the western and gangster genres of those years, the sixties film *The Graduate* and the more countercultural *Easy Rider* contain protagonists absorbed with trying to discover and do one's own thing. The extreme individualism of these films, in my view, makes them less critical than the forties and fifties films that I argue in chapter two contain veiled criticisms of postwar society and culture. On the other hand, *Dirty Harry* and its sequels feature an avenger hero, "Dirty" Harry Callahan, and are more overtly critical of the system. Harry does not merely display more agency than either Wyatt or Ben Braddock; he acts for reasons that transcend a desire to do his own thing. Harry is a cop who acts in the public interest (as he sees it) and is in constant conflict with a bureaucratic system that rewards mediocrity, conformity and even weakness rather than independent thought and action. Harry's overt hatred of the system he ironically works to protect causes *Dirty Harry* to have more in common with *Easy Rider* than the latter film has in common with *The Graduate*.

Easy Rider is a countercultural film where *The Graduate* clearly is not, and Wyatt and Billy act to change their lives and control their futures where Ben Braddock fails to act to control his future in any way. The only two things Ben decides to do are to allow Mrs. Robinson to seduce him and to then pursue Mrs. Robinson's daughter. Ben never actually does his own thing or even considers alternative things to do. When one does not do his own thing we must ask whose thing he is doing and is expected to do. Although that thing is not stated in *The Graduate*, we know it is associated with Ben's parents' norms, which would entail becoming incorporated into the postwar organized system and culture of affluence, consumption and business associated with that system. Nothing about that system is discussed in either a positive or a negative way, however. It just is; its reality is taken for granted and Ben is expected to integrate into it. There is little in the film to cause us to assume he would not. In contrast, although in *Easy Rider* Wyatt and Billy are not depicted as rebelling against the system by confronting it directly, they break the laws associated with the system in order to earn enough money in an illegal business deal (selling a large quantity of cocaine to a drug dealer) to free themselves from it and from the control over their lives that anyone must relinquish if he submits to it. Separating themselves from the system is symbolized early in the film when Wyatt stops for a minute in the desert before he and Billy begin their road trip.

Wyatt and Billy are on a freedom quest, but in order to be free in America they must have financial independence. Similar to protagonists in the gangster genre, their ability to gain that independence involves illegal activities. Following the successful drug deal and with grins across their faces, Wyatt and Billy mount their customized metallic steeds to begin their journey on America's asphalt trails. But Wyatt — stars and stripes emblazoned on his gas tank, across the back of his leather jacket, and on his helmet, signifying that he is "Captain America" — pauses for a minute before the men hit the road. With the expanse of the American desert behind the two bikers, Wyatt holds up his left wrist and stares at his watch as he sits on his chopper next to Billy astride his bike. Wyatt pulls off the watch and tosses it in the dirt. The camera focuses on the face of the watch lying in the dirt with no one to care about the time that it keeps. Wyatt has liberated himself from the regimented time of organized society as he and Billy begin their new lives of independence. We listen to *Born to Be Wild* (Steppenwolf, 1968) as we watch the two men ride across the desert. The expansive scenery of the American West signifies freedom, release from confinement, and contrasts sharply with the regimented modern life associated with the organized system and represented by the watch that Wyatt leaves ticking on the desert floor. In contrast to fifties films that focus on men who work in the organized system, like *The Man in the Gray Flannel Suit* (1956), and eighties and nineties films like *Lost in America, Office Space, American Beauty, Fight Club* and others, the organized system that Wyatt and Billy reject is represented only by Wyatt's discarded watch.

The two men purchase a large amount of cocaine from a Mexican supplier and then sell it to an American drug dealer. Once they have the money and the deal is done, Steppenwolf's cover version of the Hoyt Axton song *The Pusher* plays as Wyatt and Billy drive across the desert in a truck to the building where they keep their choppers. They stuff the money in tubes, plug the ends of the tubes, and place the tubes into the teardrop gas tank on Wyatt's bike. The two are then identified as Wyatt and Billy (symbols of a romanticized earlier western independence associated with Wyatt Earp and Billy the Kid), men who now have the freedom, thanks to the drug deal, to leave the shackles of organized society behind. The money they make from the deal provides them with the independence to do what they want, which is to ride their choppers on a road trip to discover America while they travel to New Orleans to participate in Mardi Gras.

We learn, however, that Wyatt and Billy do not flee lives in factories or offices but of constant travel as performers in local fairs. When they pull into a small town and fall in line at the end of a parade, they get arrested for parading without a permit. Billy becomes irate when they are incarcerated. "Parading without a permit!" he yells to the jailer. "You've got to be kidding! I mean, do you know who this is? This is 'Captain America.' I'm Billy. Hey, we're headliners, baby. We've played every fair in this part of the country. I mean, for top dollar, too."[11] Although the men had unconventional jobs, they had to perform at the fairs to make a living. The drug deal liberates them from that necessity.

On the day that the men begin their journey they try to get a room at an old motel, but the man who runs the place turns on the "no vacancy" sign when he sees them pull up on their bikes. This is the first in a series of events that reveal people fear Wyatt and Billy, but it is not until later in the film that we get an explanation of what they fear. When the motel manager refuses to rent them a room, the men camp just off the road. At this makeshift campsite we begin to learn that Wyatt is the more cerebral of the two, checking out what's going on around him, taking it all in, while Billy is fixated on getting stoned and finding himself a Mardi Gras woman. As the movie progresses, it becomes apparent that Wyatt, like Benjamin Braddock, wants something different. In contrast to Ben, however, he imagines alternatives and explores them. Billy, on the other hand, wants to be free of responsibility but does not demonstrate that he is searching for a more rewarding and meaningful existence. Billy is quick-tempered, rash and loud, and he wants to do something millions of Americans would like to do: retire in Florida. Wyatt is calm, quiet and contemplative, seeking interesting experiences and searching for meaning.

The next morning they pull up to a small independent farmer-rancher's place and Wyatt asks him if he can fix his flat tire there. The man, shoeing a horse, comments on Wyatt's "good looking machine" and says they can use the barn to repair the tire. This man is the one person in the movie whose life Wyatt clearly idolizes, someone who seems to be living in an earlier time, when a man could "do his own thing" without punching a clock and working for "the man" while getting caught up in the rat race. This independent man invites Wyatt and Billy to eat with him and his Catholic, Mexican wife and their many children. At the meal he thanks Jesus for the food and Wyatt tells him, "Well, you sure got a nice spread here." When the man's wife leaves to get them more coffee, Wyatt looks around and continues, "No, I mean it. You've got a nice place. It's not every man that can live off the land, you know. You do your own thing in your own time. You should be proud."

This icon of the sixties counterculture, "Captain America," searches for a modern version of the independence he believes his ancestors experienced, the idealized independent cowboys who ride into the sunset, and the independent farmers and craftsmen who control what they do and when and how they do it, selling their labor power to no man and to no organization, corporate or otherwise. The juxtaposition of the two modern motorcycle cowboys repairing the flat tire on Wyatt's chopper and the independent rancher shoeing his horse is no accident. Wyatt is the independent cowboy on the asphalt trail, minding his own business and hoping others will mind theirs, doing things in his "own time" rather than corporate time, which he leaves in the desert when he tosses his watch on the ground and he and Billy begin their journey.[12]

Historically it is interesting that this small farmer-rancher represents a lifestyle that can be considered countercultural. He owns his own property, both land and tools, and for that reason he lives a life of independence. We can assume from what we see that he plants and grows crops and raises livestock for his family's consumption and to sell. In other words, he represents what many in the nineteenth century considered to be the American dream. By the late twentieth century, however, he is an anomaly, an icon of the counterculture because he represents a way of life that was all but swept away by the corporate reconstruction of American capitalism in the late nineteenth century and the consolidation of that transformation in the early twentieth, especially following the increased centralization of production facilitated by the Great Depression and World War II.[13] By 1969 it had become countercultural to live a life that in much of the nineteenth century was considered by most and promoted by government officials to be the ideal American experience. Moreover, we can envision this independent American's way of life as one George Bailey in *It's a Wonderful Life* (1946) would spend his days protecting from the property-consolidating corporate interests of a man like Henry F. Potter. By 1969, however, such a man does not exist in society but is distanced from it, an outsider whose lifestyle is idolized and romanticized and represented as being countercultural.

When the men leave the independent farmer-rancher, they drive through mountains filled with evergreen trees and Wyatt picks up a hitchhiker on the side of the road. Wyatt's approximately 30-year-old hippie passenger is on his way back to the commune where he lives. Like the two bikers' time with the farmer-rancher, the days they spend with this hippie serve to represent a lifestyle and values far different from those of the people they leave behind in Los Angeles. Interestingly, when Wyatt and Billy visit the commune in this iconic counterculture film of the 1960s, life there is not represented positively. Except for the possibilities of getting high and getting laid, Billy wants nothing to do with the place and is anxious to get back on the road. But beyond Billy's anxieties about the commune it seems doomed to fail.

The night before the three men arrive at the commune, they set up camp. Their conversation that evening reveals that the hippie made a decision to separate himself from society and to keep his distance from it. The conversation also helps us further understand that Wyatt is at peace with himself even as he explores alternative ways of living. Their conversation simultaneously reinforces the fact that Billy is restless and anxious and is the one of the pair most like the society the bikers flee.

The men camp at an old Native-American adobe dwelling. The hippie tells Wyatt and Billy they are sitting on a sacred burial ground. While they sit around a campfire smoking pot, Billy is anxious about getting to Mardi Gras on time. Wyatt tells him they have a week to get to New Orleans and they will get there in plenty of time. Billy asks the hippie where he is from and the man replies, "A city." Billy gets irritated at the hippie's ambiguous answer and wants more information. The hippie elaborates, "It doesn't make any difference what city; all cities are alike. That's why I'm out here now." Billy asks him why and he says, "'Cause I'm from the city, a long way from the city, and that's where I want to be right now." Although the man offers no specifics about why he wants to be away from the city, we are supposed to know intuitively what he means, but Billy just looks confused and irritated. Wyatt sits quietly and asks, "You ever want to be somebody else?" The hippie says, "I'd like to try Porky Pig." Wyatt takes another hit off his joint, shakes his head slowly, stares into the fire and calmly says, "I never wanted to be anybody else." Wyatt has always been at peace with who he is, and he is not on the road to find himself but to experience life without the constraints of regimented time and the constant need to earn a living by doing things he does not want to do. He's searching for true freedom, not identity.

When they pull into the commune the next day, young children and infants are everywhere, a result of the "free love" practiced at the commune. The hippie they picked up on the road shows them around the commune and introduces them to some of the other members. Unlike the independent farmer-rancher, the communal participants' ability to make their experiment in alternative living succeed is questionable at best. When the hippie they met on the road takes Wyatt and Billy to a dry, dusty field where men scatter seed in the dust and women erect a scarecrow, the men stop their work to smoke pot. Wyatt, expressing some doubt about the communal effort at farming, stands with Billy and the hippie on the hard, dry ground and asks, "Get much rain here, man?" The hippie chuckles and says, "Guess we're going to have to dance for that." Billy tells Wyatt what many viewers surely think: "This is nothin' but sand, man; they ain't gonna make it, man. They ain't gonna grow anything here." Wyatt suggests they will, but the image of the stoned men tossing seeds into the hot dust that covers the earth leaves Billy and the audience with the impression that the seeds will most likely blow away with the next strong wind.[14] The contrast could not be starker: the earlier image of the productive independent farmer-rancher and the hippies' brief moments working the land when they take breaks from free love-making, getting high, singing songs and staging short "gorilla-theatre" skits throughout the day.[15] The type of independence represented by the farmer-rancher, a traditional way of life rooted in the American past, is portrayed as something that works, while the experiment in communal living is depicted as a doubtful proposition.

As Wyatt and Billy interact with the people in the commune, it becomes increasingly clear that Billy and the hippie don't care for each other. Billy irritates the hippie as much as the hippie irritates him. Although the hippie participates in an experiment in communal living, he clearly has an unequaled, hierarchal status in the commune. Perhaps Billy's argumentative personality, his unwillingness to take what the hippie says at face value, cause the hippie to realize that Billy would never fit into his world and would no doubt challenge the authority he has developed in the commune. Billy voices his discomfort to Wyatt when he tells him he has to get out of there. Before they leave they go skinny-dipping with two women and the hippie gives Wyatt some acid, instructing him, "When you get to the right place with the right people, quarter this." The scene with the farmer-rancher and the one at the commune depict alternatives

Wyatt (Peter Fonda), center, and Billy (Dennis Hopper), left, in *Easy Rider* (1969) pick up George Hanson (Jack Nicholson), right, the man who teaches them what it is that people fear about the bikers' freedom and the violence they will perpetrate to keep from being reminded that they are not really free themselves (Photofest).

to mainstream American life, but it is not until the two bikers meet George Hanson (Jack Nicholson) that *Easy Rider* makes the most direct critique of postwar society and culture.

When they hit the road again, Wyatt and Billy pull into the small town where they get arrested for parading without a permit. The jail scene is important because it is where Wyatt and Billy meet fellow prisoner and lawyer George. Nicholson was nominated for best actor in a supporting role and does a superb job portraying an intelligent and insightful alcoholic who teaches Billy — and the audience, if they do not get it themselves — about rednecks, the insecurities associated with white prejudice, what it is that people fear about the kind of freedom Wyatt and Billy represent, and the inadequacies of what George refers to at one point as America's and the world's "antiquated systems."

While they sit in their jail cell, Billy refers to the locals as "weirdo hicks" and we see graffiti scrawled on the walls, Jesus signs, and other paraphernalia decorating the cells. George is hung-over and lying down on a cot in the next cell. In a southern accent he complains about his headache. Billy says, "Hey, man. If you don't shut your mouth, you ain't gonna have a head." The jailer refers to George as Mr. Hanson. We discover that George is a lawyer with a drinking problem who has done a lot of work for the American Civil Liberties Union (ACLU). He tells Wyatt and Billy that the locals don't like long-hairs and try to make everyone look like Yul Brynner by shaving their heads. Billy asks George if he can get them out. George says, "Well, I imagine that I can if you haven't killed anybody, at least nobody white." When they get out and walk to the choppers, George shows them a business card for a whorehouse in New Orleans and says he has started to go to Mardi Gras several times but has never made it there. When he says he sure wishes he were going with them, Wyatt invites him to come along. After he gets his old high-school football helmet to wear, they head for New Orleans with George riding on the back of Wyatt's chopper. The two bikers have their interpreter of white southern culture.

The following scene of the three men smoking pot around their campfire that night is relevant to my analysis because of the story George tells about aliens visiting earth. The purpose of the story is to critique people's lack of agency and independence in society compared to the society of alien beings that George describes. Wyatt convinces George to smoke marijuana for the first time. While George gets high, Billy claims he saw an object in the night sky that was headed in one direction and then abruptly "whizzed off" in another direction. Wyatt tells him, "You're stoned out of your mind, man." George holds smoke in his lungs while Billy tries to convince Wyatt he saw something in the night sky. When George eventually exhales, he tells his story.

"That was a UFO beaming back at ya," he says rapidly. He tells Billy he was in Mexico with someone two weeks earlier and "we seen 40 of 'em, flyin' in formation." He says the aliens have bases all over the world and have been visiting earth since 1946, "when the scientists first started bouncin' radar beams off of the moon. And they have been living and working with us in vast quantities ever since. The government knows all about 'em." Billy, clearly stoned, says "What are ya talkin', man?" "Well," George replies, "they are people just like us, from within our own solar system, except that their society is more highly evolved. I mean, they don't have no wars; they got no monetary system; they don't have any leaders. I mean, because each *man* is a leader. I mean, because of their technology, they are able to feed, clothe, house and transport themselves equally and with no effort." Wyatt exhales the smoke he was holding in his lungs and comments, "Wow." Billy, agitated, says he thinks it is a "crackpot idea" and asks, "If they're so smart, why don't they just reveal themselves to us and get it over with?" George replies, "Why don't they reveal themselves to us is because if they did it would cause a general panic. Now, I mean we still have leaders upon whom we rely for the release of this information. These leaders have decided to repress this information because of the tremendous shock that it would cause to our antiquated systems. Now, the result of this has been that the Venusians have contacted people at all walks of life, all walks of life." When George stops he chuckles and repeats, "It would be a devastating blow to our antiquated systems, so now Venusians are meeting with people in all walks of life in an advisory capacity. For once, man will have a god-like control over his own destiny. He will have a chance to transcend and to evolve with some equality for all." George stops talking and Billy sits looking at and gesturing toward the heavens when Wyatt, aware that George is quite high, smiles and asks, "How's your joint, George?"

Imbedded in George's brief story about aliens visiting earth is a systemic countercultural critique of everything wrong in the world: war, inequality, hierarchal social structures, capitalist economics, poverty and any other negative thing associated with America's and the world's "antiquated systems." Americans and other earthlings live in subordination to the leaders of their "antiquated systems" and have little control of their own lives, so the aliens will teach "man" to "have god-like control over his own destiny" and, therefore, equal power and influence in society. George's fictitious aliens have what Wyatt and Billy believe all people should want and what George soon teaches them some people fear when they see others have it and realize they do not: independence and agency over their own lives.

The next day the three travelers drive through poor rural black areas of the South and then stop at a diner filled with white, male racist rednecks and some high school girls. While the girls sit in their booth they flirt with the bikers, and the rednecks make loud cracks about the men that George defines as "country witticisms." The cracks include comments about putting the men in cages like other animals and charging people to see them, about "refugees from a gorilla love-in," about mating one of the men "up with one of those black winches out there," about whether the bikers are green or white, about how a mother couldn't love such an animal, and about "Yankee queers." One man says loudly enough for the bikers to hear him, "they're not going to make the parish line." This diner scene provides the context for George to later teach Wyatt and Billy what it is that others fear about the freedom they represent.

That night the men from the diner come into the bikers' camp and beat them with clubs while they sleep. They kill George and injure Wyatt and Billy. This camp scene is important because prior to the attack George explains to Billy (and the audience) that men like the ones in the diner are dangerous because they fear not what the bikers look like but the freedom and independence they represent. Before the attack, the three men talk and Billy tells George the whole country is scared of people like Wyatt and himself. They're afraid, he says, that "we're gonna cut their throat or something, man." George corrects him: "Oh, they're not scared of you; they're scared of what you represent to 'em." Billy says, "Hey, man, all we represent to them is somebody who needs a haircut." George replies, "Oh, no. What you represent to them is freedom." Billy says, "What the hell is wrong with freedom, man? That's what it's all about." George continues, "Oh, yeah. That's what it's all about all right. But talkin' about it and bein' it, it's two different things. I mean it's real hard to be free when you are bought and sold in the marketplace. Of course, don't ever tell anybody that they're not free because then they're gonna get real busy killin' and mamin' to prove to you that they are." The rednecks see Wyatt and Billy doing their own thing in their own time, and it makes them realize they don't have that kind of freedom. Rather, they sell their labor and their time in the marketplace for others to use and control, something the southern whites' planter ancestors referred to as northern wage slavery, a condition they claimed to be worse than chattel slavery because planters cared for their property in sickness and in health, in old age and in infancy, where northern factory owners merely paid wages and cared not for the men whose labor they purchased for a short duration of time. In contrast to black slaves who became commodities when white planters took their lives from them and bought and sold them in the marketplace like a hogshead of tobacco or a bale of cotton, free laborers commodify themselves; they sell themselves into wage slavery. To racist, poor southern whites during the first years following passage of the Civil Rights (1964) and Voting Rights (1965) Acts, being made aware that they shackle themselves to others who buy their labor and their time would be no different than calling them "niggers" if not slaves.[16] The rednecks' violent attack on the bikers is an attempt to wipe out the source of that knowledge.

George tells Billy something he and Wyatt already knew and acted on at the beginning of the film but did not conceptualize or articulate as George does. If men are bought and sold, if their labor and their time are commodities they must relinquish control of by selling them to others in order to survive, then they cannot truly be free unless they do not participate as sellers in that market relationship, relinquishing control of their time and what they do and how they do it. Wyatt and Billy gained their freedom when they made an illegal drug deal that enabled them to no longer be "bought and sold in the marketplace" where most men must sell their time and their labor. Wyatt does not become "Captain America" for the audience until he slips on his flag-adorned leather jacket and mounts his red-white-and-blue chopper *after* he becomes financially independent. Freedom in America depends on the economic independence that capital provides, even for this film's countercultural heroes, who acquire it through illicit means. Wyatt and Billy represent a threat to other men who must continue to sell themselves in the marketplace because the bikers' freedom causes others to consider if they are really free. Such men, George lectures Billy, "gonna talk to you and talk to you and talk to you about individual freedom, but they see a free individual, it gonna scare 'em." Billy says, "Well, it don't make 'em runnin' scared." George replies, "No. It makes 'em dangerous." That night the rednecks from the diner prove George's point when they kill George and injure Wyatt and Billy before Billy runs them off with a knife. George's point about men becoming dangerous when they confront others who are free is made again at the end of the film, when two rednecks shoot Wyatt and Billy while they drive on an infrequently used rural road.

Between the murders of George and the two bikers, we watch Wyatt and Billy ride to New Orleans, visit the whorehouse George told them about, and participate in Mardi Gras while they share with two prostitutes the acid that the hippie gave them. The day they leave New Orleans, they ride all day and then set up camp. That night Wyatt is even quieter than usual and appears despondent. Billy laughs loudly and says, "We've done it, we've done it! We're rich, Wyatt!" Remarking on the economic independence that being rich provides them, Billy adds, "We can retire in Florida now, Mr." Billy's lines reveal that he sees independence only in the material sense of the market economy from which they are now liberated. Unlike the farmer-rancher who controls his labor and what he does because he owns his own land and the tools to work it in his own time and in his own way, someone who gets satisfaction from his productive labor and the fact that he controls it, Wyatt and Billy achieve instant freedom like someone who makes a fortune through insider trading or by winning the lottery. They do not have the values of the farmer-rancher. Wyatt's response to Billy is, "You know, Billy, we blew it." Confused, Billy says, "That's what it's all about, man. Like, you know. I mean, you go for the big money, man, and then you're free. Ya dig?" Wyatt repeats, "We blew it." He then rolls over and says, "Good night, man." Although Wyatt's "We blew it" response is open to interpretation, it seems likely that he, the more cerebral and searching of the two, recognizes they could have achieved a more meaningful independence had they valued their labor and what they might achieve by controlling it and applying it to create something positive, like the farmer-rancher. Instead, as Hopper later said, these icons of the counterculture "do a very American thing — we commit a crime, we go for the easy money. That's one of the biggest problems with the country right now: everybody's going for the easy money."[17] Hopper recognized that the two icons are not as countercultural as some viewers would like to believe and as the redneck characters fear. They gain economic independence, but Billy's remarks demonstrate he never breaks free of the values that keep him tethered to the culture associated with the economic system and the society the movie critiques.

The next day they drive on a two-lane country road, presumably on the way to retirement in Florida, and pass two rednecks in a pick-up truck. The rednecks decide to "scare the hell out of 'em." When the man in the passenger seat shouts out the window and asks Billy why he doesn't get a haircut, Billy gives him the finger and the man blasts him with a shotgun. Up ahead, Wyatt hears the gun shot, turns around, discovers Billy severely wounded on the side of the road, and rides to get help. The men in the truck turn back because they realize Wyatt is a witness and they need to kill him, too. Wyatt approaches the on-coming truck and the same man shoots at him and hits the gas tank, which explodes and the bike bursts into flames and sails through the air. The camera pans out to a bird's-eye view of the burning chopper on the side of a southern road, two white men's dreams of independence ended like those of so many black men, women and children, a result of terrorist acts perpetrated by white men who fear the freedom of others.[18]

Captain America and his sidekick are two icons associated with the sixties counterculture that search for the presumed freedom of their American ancestors: the independent cowboys who ride into the sunset, and the idealized independent farmers, ranchers and craftsmen who control what they do and when and how they do it, selling their labor to no man and to no organization, corporate or otherwise. Although Wyatt and Billy visit and watch like voyeurs the communal life associated with one aspect of the counterculture, that life is depicted as lacking and conformist when stacked up against the independent lifestyle of the farmer-rancher, a man who does his own thing in his own time. If these two late twentieth-century cultural icons are central symbols of the counterculture, then the counterculture is so diverse and elastic it incorporates key components of the mainstream culture it supposedly opposes. Rather than embrace an alternative totally antithetical to American culture, Wyatt and Billy lament the loss of and search for the kind of freedom George describes before the rednecks who are not free kill him in his sleep. Although living with that kind of freedom may have been a reality for the few and a dream for the many in much of the nineteenth century, it was not life threatening, unless, of course, one was black or red or yellow or a worker struggling with others to gain some control over the number of hours they worked and the conditions with which they labored.[19]

In *Easy Rider* living free is associated with independence of thought and control over what one does, things that social critic Paul Goodman in the 1950s noted were not compatible with the postwar organized system, that Governor Adlai Stevenson told Smith College women were no longer possible for men, and that characters like Tom Rath had to negotiate in corporate life as it is represented in fifties films like *The Man in the Gray Flannel Suit*. In the early seventies, paradoxically, characters associated with the system sometimes criticize the system, "the establishment" from which characters like Captain America and Benjamin Braddock are estranged. Such films contain anti-countercultural themes and feature protagonists willing to use violence to establish control over their lives and regain influence in society that they believe they once had but have lost. These films also contain anti-establishment themes, however; the main characters critique the establishment while simultaneously representing it. In the late sixties and early seventies, then, films associated with the right and the left ironically critique similar things about the established order: mundane and meaningless work, corporate and government bureaucracies that stifle individuals' decisions and actions, and, sometimes, weak men too fearful to do the right thing if it means risking their personal or professional security.

The gun-wielding protagonists in these films tend to be vigilante private citizens or frustrated cops whose abilities to apprehend criminals are restrained by weak and obtuse bureaucrats and by laws designed to protect suspects' rights rather ensure justice and protect citizens' safety and victims' rights. I include a discussion of such films here because the characters' complaints, the reasons the male protagonists are discontented and disaffected, are similar to those voiced or otherwise displayed in films released earlier and later in the twentieth century: men's declining independence, agency and influence in society. The best examples of such films are *Joe* (1970) and *Dirty Harry* (1971). In contrast to earlier and later films, however, men's discontent, especially in *Joe*, is not only associated with their declining agency in modern corporate and government bureaucracies, although that theme remains central. Representations of men's discontent and declining influence in society in these years of crisis and change become associated in part with countercultural individuals and groups, and with advances made by women, African Americans and other minorities.

In earlier films about discontented and disaffected men's declining agency in society race is largely ignored. It is a non-issue in films such as *It's a Wonderful Life* (1946), *Force of Evil* (1948), *Johnny Guitar* (1954), *The Man in the Gray Flannel Suit* (1956), *The Graduate* (1967) and most others. The white male characters in such films take their race for granted and rarely interact with or talk about characters that represent racial minorities.[20] Many films of the late sixties and early seventies, however, depict characters' reactions to specific historical changes that occurred in those years while they continue to represent the long-term theme of men's declining control and agency that emerged with the corporate reconstruction of American capitalism in the late nineteenth century, continued in the early twentieth, and intensified in the postwar years.

In *Joe*, the character Joe Curran (Peter Boyle) is an overtly militant racist and bigot who uses African Americans, hippies and liberals as scapegoats to explain the country's problems and his declining position in society, while in *Dirty Harry* (1971) protagonist Harry Callahan (Clint Eastwood) is a more complicated figure. Harry is someone other cops associate with bigoted and racist language in the first film of the series, but who rarely uses such language himself. Moreover, he is friends with a black physician and, although he always complains whenever he receives a new partner, he works with a Chicano partner in *Dirty Harry*, a black partner in *Magnum Force* (1973), and a female partner in *The Enforcer* (1976), cops he becomes close to and respects because of their character and the way they do their job. Harry is also complicated because he fervently criticizes the system that he literally defends.

The two main characters in *Joe*, Joe Curran and Bill Compton (Dennis

Patrick), use militant force to exhibit agency in a society that Joe, especially, believes is increasingly controlled by liberals who serve the interests of minorities and hippies and is in decline because it does. Joe leads Bill on a literal hunt for people they believe to be significant sources of society's ills. The men act, but they do so outside of the acceptable parameters of civil society because the institutions and officials that represent civil society protect the people the men believe to be responsible for America's decline. They justify killing drug dealers as acts that serve the public good and that merely help the police do their job.

Where Joe and Bill are private citizens, Harry Callahan is a homicide inspector for the San Francisco Police Department. If there is one thing Harry Callahan doesn't lack, it's agency. Due to the constraints placed on Harry's ability to act, however, he must break the rules in order to get the killers. Bad laws enforced by weak mayors, police chiefs and other officials are represented as restraining Harry's ability to do his job and as protecting criminals and denying justice to victims and their families.

Joe depicts the often virulent attitudes and violent actions associated with the backlash to the successes of the civil rights movement, the counterculture, the emergent struggle for gay rights, the anti-war movement, and any other changes the political right associates with the word "liberal." It is a movie about an extremely and overtly racist, sexist and homophobic working-class white, middle-aged man who discovers he has something in common with an upper–middle-class executive at a major corporation. The two men develop a relationship after the executive, Bill Compton, wanders into a blue-collar bar, the "American Bar & Grill," where Joe sits telling the bartender and everyone within earshot what he thinks is wrong with America and what he would like to do about it. After he listens to Joe blame the country's problems on "niggers," "hippies," "social workers," "liberals" and the welfare system, and then say he would like to kill some of them, Compton confesses to Joe that he just killed a hippie. Although Bill convinces Joe he was kidding when he admitted to the murder, Bill comes to the bar after getting into a physical struggle with and killing his daughter Melissa's (Susan Sarandon) drug-dealing hippie boyfriend, Frank Russo (Patrick McDermott), whom Bill blames for Melissa becoming hooked on drugs. After Joe hears on the evening news a few nights later that the police discovered a young man's body in an apartment near the American Bar & Grill, he looks up Compton's phone number and calls him to arrange a meeting. When they meet, Joe tells Compton he knows

Bill killed Frank but assures him he will not tell anyone. It soon becomes clear that Joe, who owns a collection of guns, wants to go "hunting" with Compton. He gets the opportunity when Melissa runs away after overhearing her parents talk about her father killing Frank. Joe helps Compton try to find Melissa.[21]

The men search the hippie cafes and other hangouts that Melissa frequents, but they don't have any luck. At one, though, Compton reveals to a hippie that he has marijuana in the trunk of his car — he took it from the scene of the crime — and the young man lures them into sharing the pot with him and his friends by promising Joe and Bill the young women will have sex with them. During this evening of pot smoking and group sex, one hippie steals the men's wallets and flees. Joe threatens one of the women and gets her to tell him that the men probably went to a house in the country. Joe and Bill drive to the house and Joe pulls two rifles from the trunk of his car. He throws one to Bill, who catches it and reluctantly carries it into the house. Inside they find the men who took their wallets and Joe shoots some in the back as they try to flee and others as they quiver in a corner begging for their lives. When three more hippies arrive and come in the front door, Joe discovers he is out of ammunition and yells to Bill, "It's your ass now, Compton!" Bill shoots the man and the first woman who comes through the door, but the other woman flees into the front yard. We do not see her face until Bill runs onto the porch and shoots his daughter in the back. We listen to the lyrics "All the wisdom wasted on the young, all the peaceful songs you've sung" as the credits appear on the screen and we see Melissa's bloody body lying in the yard.

In the film, Joe associates his discontent with the state of American society and his declining position in it to the successes of the civil rights movement, the welfare programs of the Great Society, anti-war protesters, hippies, unappreciative and unpatriotic countercultural youth, and anyone who might remotely be considered to be a liberal. He targets the people in these groups rather than the government for what he considers to be the country's decline. It is no coincidence that this World War II veteran and ardent American patriot does his drinking and complaining at the "American Bar & Grill." Joe believes that who he is and how he lives represent America and the people he hates do not. The scene at the bar reveals the depth of his convictions and the extent of his hatred.

Although *Joe* was very popular in the early seventies and launched Peter Boyle's movie career, few people today have seen the film and are shocked by Joe's language and his relentless diatribe against the people he hates.[22] "The niggers, the niggers are getting' all the money," he tells the bartender and everyone else in the room the day Bill Compton walks into the bar after he kills Melissa's boyfriend. He continues his rant: "Why work? You tell me, why the fuck work when you can screw, have babies and get paid for it?" In Joe's mind, workingmen like himself pay taxes so others can engage in welfare schemes. "Welfare!" he continues. "They get all that welfare money. They even get free rubbers. Ya think they use 'em? Hell no. The only way they make money is makin' babies. They sell the rubbers, and then they use the money to buy booze." Compton enters the bar at this point and Joe preaches on: "The social workers, the ones in welfare, how come they're all nigger lovers? Ya ever notice that? All those social workers are nigger lovers. Ya find me a social worker who ain't a nigger lover and I'll massage your ass hole." Immediately after he says that, Compton sits down and Joe exhibits his homophobia when he looks at him and shouts, "I ain't queer!" Compton orders a double scotch and water as Joe rages on: "I sweat my balls off 40 hours a week in front of a fuckin' furnace and they make as much as I do, for nothin'. They've got 'em livin' in hotels at 50 dollars a day, a thousand dollars a month." He goes on to blame African Americans for white kids like his son failing to get into college and for burning cities while collecting welfare checks.

When Bill gets up to use the public telephone to call the doctor caring for Melissa, Joe bashes American youth, hippies and liberals. He complains that young people have no respect for President Nixon and claims that "42 percent of all liberals are queer." He says it's a fact revealed in a poll of liberals' sexual preferences. Joe rants about rich white kids like Bill's daughter, complaining they have orgies during spring break, what he refers to as "Easter 'or-gees.'" The bartender hands Joe a quarter and asks him to play something on the jukebox and give them all a break. But songs listed on the jukebox cause Joe to continue his rant: "Look at this shit music. The goddamn nigger-lovin' hippies, they even fucked up the music. I'd like to get my hands on one of those little bastards." He sounds serious when he says, "I'd kill him. I'd like to kill one of 'em." He walks back to his bar stool next to where Compton sits and continues to let everyone know he would like to kill a hippie. "They're getting away with murder," he complains. "Sex, drugs, pissin' on America, fuckin' up the music! I'd like to kill one of 'em. I would." Compton stares into space thinking about what Joe says and then confesses, "I just did." Joe looks at Bill and says, "Glad to hear it." Bill turns and stares at Joe with a shocked look on his face. Joe says, "Hey, you're serious. You're really serious." Bill realizes he confessed to Joe, looks at his drink, and then implies it was the booze talking. Joe tells Bill he had him believing it. Both men laugh and Joe begins to introduce himself when a man answers the phone and announces it's for William Compton. After he talks to the doctor, Bill rushes out as Joe calls after him, "Hey, Compton, I bought ya a drink. What is this?" But Bill is out the door.

Although Joe blames people for his discontent, the film contains scenes that reveal the drudgery of Joe's life on the job, and others in which Joe and Bill, despite their class differences, discuss what earlier films and many produced in the 1980s and 1990s depict as an increasingly corporate bureaucratic system of meaningless work for both working-class guys like Joe and even for corporate executives like Bill Compton. At one point Bill even explains to Joe that the higher one rises in the corporate hierarchy, the more meaningless his job is and the more useless he becomes even though he earns more money. These scenes are important because they reveal that the source of the men's common complaints is not necessarily the scapegoats Joe creates but a system that reduces them to doing repetitive tasks designed and controlled by others.

In *Joe* (1970), blue-collar Joe Curran (Peter Boyle), right, shows corporate executive Bill Compton (Dennis Patrick), left, his small arsenal of weapons as the men learn that despite their class differences they have common criticisms of meaningless work and the youth culture of the 1960s.

In one scene of Joe on the job sweating in front of the furnace that he toils at every day, we observe the mundane and repetitive nature of his labor and realize the drudgery associated with it. While we watch Joe work and see him walk home from the factory through the snow, we listen to the lyrics in the movie's theme song. The lyrics question the necessity of America's wars while simultaneously reinforcing Joe's patriotism and his hatred of people on welfare: "Hey Joe, don't it make you want to go to war, once more. Hey Joe, why the devil did we go to war, before? What the hell for? We gotta get this country off welfare, back our boys in Vietnam, show this world we'll fight for freedom, or doesn't anybody give a God damn?"

At one point Joe acknowledges the breadth of the class divide that separates him and Bill is more extreme than Joe could have ever imagined, but Joe's need to share his hate with Bill enables him to look beyond their class differences. Despite those differences, each man learns that the other spends his days engaged in meaningless and redundant work under conditions he doesn't control. Joe arranges to meet Bill at the bowling alley where he bowls in a league. Bill arrives and Joe orders them a couple of beers that the men drink while they talk at a small table. Joe's bowling shirt and Bill's business suit signify the cultural and socioeconomic divide. Joe assures Bill that he isn't going to blackmail him and suggests they continue their conversation at one of Joe's favorite restaurants. There it becomes clear to Bill that Joe admires him for being a man of action, someone who actually did what Joe only talks about doing. Joe assures Bill that the man he killed was a drug dealer who made "dope fiends" out of a lot of people's kids and says their parents would think Bill's a hero. Joe's eyes light up and a smile spreads across his face when Bill tells him he has recently experienced feelings of "pleasure" and "satisfaction" when he thinks about killing Frank. Joe tells Bill he knows it's hard for someone like him to talk to a working stiff like Joe and instructs him to just relax and talk to him the way he would talk to the other guys he knows. But Joe's curious about Bill's life and status and wants to exchange information. He reveals that he makes $4.00 an hour and presses Bill to tell him how much he earns. He's shocked when Bill tells him his annual salary is $60,000: "Sixty — thousand — dollars a year! Ya gotta be kiddin'! Only movie stars make that kind of money! The fuckin' president of my union pays himself that kind of money!" Joe tells Bill he bets he has to "kiss a lot of ass" and Compton says he got used to it and doesn't notice it much anymore. Joe says, "Ya think I don't have to kiss ass. Four dollars an hour. The foreman, the shop steward. The guy on the night shift so he don't leave my furnace a mess." Bill sees that Joe is curious about his world and asks, "Joe, you like to see where my kind of animal hangs out?" Joe says "sure" and they head for an upscale bar that Compton frequents.

These scenes of Joe learning about Bill's world are important because Joe sees that even though Bill isn't a working stiff like he is, they share similar, if not common, experiences and complaints about those experiences. Whether one makes $4.00 an hour or $60,000 a year, drinks cheap beer or sips expensive scotch, belongs to a bowling league or a sports club, he is still tethered to a job he does not create, design or control, although one lives in far more material comfort than the other.

When they enter the upscale bar and walk through the crowd Joe comments, "They look like a bunch of fags. Not really fags, but close — gettin' there." Compton bonds further with Joe by making a fool out of another executive who stops to talk to Compton. Despite Joe's working-class clothes and speech, Compton gets the executive to believe Joe is the new vice president their company just hired to work in the man's office. He makes the executive nervous when he says Joe will be getting rid of "a lot of dead wood." Before Joe and Bill leave the building they go to the restroom and we notice that even someone from Bill's upper–middle-class universe was compelled to write "The World Sucks" on a chalkboard hanging over the urinals.

That men in Bill's world might, like the men in Joe's, be discontented with the work they do and their lack of control over it is most apparent when the men leave the bar and walk through the streets of New York. Bill tells Joe to look up at the buildings. The camera pans the skyline and then rotates as if we are seeing through Joe's eyes. Compton tells Joe, "I work in one of them. And you know what they do in those buildings, Joe? They move paper. That's right. They pick it up from one place and they move it to another place. They pass it all around their offices." The illuminated offices in the New York skyscrapers are a stark contrast to the gloomy factory where Joe toils every day. "And the more paper you move," Bill continues, "the more important you are, the more they pay you. And if you want to really show how important you are, what you get away with, you make little paper airplanes and you sail them right up somebody else's ass." Joe, and the audience, learn that Bill Compton's work is not merely redundant but entirely meaningless. That neither man, despite their class differences, controls the work that he does everyday like the independent farmer-rancher in *Easy Rider* is apparent when Joe asks, "Ever get the feeling that everything you do your whole life is one big crock of shit?" Compton sighs and replies, "Yeah." But rather than analyze the systemic nature of his life being "one big crock of shit," Joe's reliance on scapegoats to explain his discontent is evident when he stops walking, turns, looks Compton in the face and says, "I got a great idea. Want to go huntin'?" Compton looks confused and asks, "Huntin'?" Joe says, "Yeah" and refers to hunting deer, but the stage is set for the men's hunt for hippies at the end of the film.

The Joe character is a racist, bigoted and violent cold-blooded killer who has no reservations about murdering people he believes to be society's vermin: minorities and pampered young men and women upon whom he projects his anger about his job, the welfare state, the decline of patriotism, his son's failure to get into the college of his choice, and even what he considers to be bad popular music. The title of the film directs our attention to working-class Joe as the problem and therefore portrays as deviant and class specific the character's anger and his actions. At one point during production, however, the working title of the movie was "The Gap," a reference to the generation gap between Bill and his daughter and, perhaps inadvertently, to the income gap that separates men like Bill from those like Joe. Viewers are not introduced to Joe until almost 30 minutes into the film. Furthermore, while the title directs our attention to Joe, it is Bill who kills first and admits it, and Bill becomes Joe's hero because he takes the kind of action Joe only dreams of taking before he meets the $60,000-a-year executive. Moreover, Bill gets Joe to understand that his work, too, is redundant and unfulfilling even though he earns what to Joe is an exorbitant salary. Despite the film's title, then, it is about two men who develop an inter-class bond that rests on the shared scapegoats they create to explain their discontent and to justify their militant actions. Bill, for example, convinces himself, with Joe's encouragement, that he did society a service by killing Frank.[23]

Peter Boyle was able to make the Joe character believable, in part, because he understood first hand what it was like to do repetitive work designed and controlled completely by others and the frustrations of being treated disrespectfully as a struggling actor. He once earned his bread as a postal worker and meditated each night to prepare mentally for the mundane work he did on the night shift. When he read for the part of Joe, the casting people called Boyle back three times and made him waste his time waiting, so one time he walked out even though he needed the part. "I don't think you should make an actor wait," he noted. "It's a difficult enough existence as it is." Boyle earned a mere $2,520 for playing the part, the minimum union compensation at the time. A major reason Boyle became an actor was because of the potential control over his life and his work that acting could provide him. "I'm an actor because an actor can do what he wants," he said. Comparing the profession to what most people do for a living, people represented by both the Joe Curran and Bill Compton characters, Boyle commented, "That's the terrible thing about other people's lives. Their existences are so truncated. That's what's wrong with Joe," Boyle continued. "He's so cut off. If you're treated like an animal, you're going to act like one."[24]

Joe was successful at the box office in large part because it references so many of the salient social, cultural and political issues familiar to potential moviegoers in the late sixties and early seventies: the nature of work, the declining control most people had over their lives in an increasingly organized society, the white backlash to the successes of the civil rights movement, the youth and countercultures, the increasing violence associated with confrontations between anti-war demonstrators and counter-demonstrators who, like Joe, saw themselves as patriots and applauded Nixon's increased use of violence in southeast Asia and at home as the government made policy the president's 1968 campaign pledge to impose "law and order."[25] An event that became directly related to Joe occurred ten weeks before the film was released. A crime occurred that caused a judge to make the film a criterion for jury selection. The railroad worker Arville Garland drove to Detroit and shot and killed his daughter (a pre-med student at Wayne State University), her boyfriend and two of their friends. The judge at Garland's trial ordered each team of lawyers to view Joe. He then dismissed any potential juror who had seen it. In May of 1970, moreover, anti-war demonstrators were attacked by what The New York Times reported to be "construction workers," but those "hard hats" were joined and in some ways directed by men in suits who worked in corporate offices like the ones Bill Compton points to when he tells Joe that the men in those offices push paper and make paper airplanes all day long.[26] At the same time that some blue-collar and white-collar workers united in their opposition to the anti-war demonstrators, The Times also reported that 1,000 "establishment" lawyers announced they would "join the war protest," revealing that representatives of "the establishment" were not always on the political right. Anxieties about these turbulent years help explain the popularity of a film produced on a mere $106, 000.00 budget but grossed a whopping $19,189, 300.00.[27]

Like Joe, some of the issues represented in *Dirty Harry* (1971) also resonated with viewers in the early seventies. *Dirty Harry* is the first in a series of five detective films starring Clint Eastwood as "Dirty" Harry Callahan, a San Francisco Police Department inspector who works homicide. The film and its four sequels—*Magnum Force* (1973, *The Enforcer* (1976), *Sudden Impact* (1983), and *The Dead Pool* (1988)—depict some of the significant race and gender issues of the late sixties, seventies and eighties. The central theme of the films, however, is associated with the major thesis of this book, for Harry is a discontented, disaffected lawman in an increasingly organized society filled with weak citizens and ineffective government officials. Spineless bureaucrats administer laws designed to protect the rights of criminals rather than enable the police to do their job and ensure that citizens are protected and victims receive justice. Much like Will Wright in *Sixguns and Society* demonstrates about independent lawmen in postwar westerns, the .44 Magnum-wielding detective is an urban gunslinger with a badge, a man who must sometimes behave like the criminals he pursues and skirt the law and disobey his superiors' orders so he can get the bad guys.[28] When Harry finally gets his man at the end of the first film, for example, he does so by ignoring the authority of the mayor and the Police Chief, disobeying orders that would restrain his actions and keep him from getting his man. Moreover, like Will Kane (Gary Cooper) in the classic western *High Noon* (1952) throws his badge in the dust, Harry throws his badge into a pond at the end of the film. Kane is disgusted with the society of weak men who refuse to help him stand up against the Frank Miller (Ian MacDonald) gang and depends instead on the newfound agency of his pacifist Quaker wife Amy (Grace Kelly) to help him use deadly force to defeat Miller and his men. By discarding his badge in the dust, Kane symbolically separates himself from the weak society he risks his life to protect. Harry does likewise in *Dirty Harry* two decades later when he throws his badge into the pond. He can only rid society of the serial killer "Scorpio" by ignoring the restraints that society places on him, so he, too, symbolically separates himself from society.[29]

Harry's disgust with and disrespect for spineless bureaucrats is first evident when Callahan meets with "The Mayor" (John Vernon), Lieutenant Bressler (Harry Guardino), and the Chief of Police (John Larch) in the mayor's office. The scene establishes the tension between independent-minded and quick-to-act Harry and the weak and ineffective bureaucrats who administer the system. The tension between Harry and the bureaucrats is a central theme of the sequels, too, as are the personality traits Harry exhibits.[30]

The men meet to discuss the first murder Scorpio (Andy Robinson) commits. Scorpio uses a high-powered rifle with a scope to shoot a woman while she swims in a rooftop pool. Harry investigates and discovers a note the sniper leaves at the scene of the crime. When Harry meets with the mayor and Lieutenant Bressler, they discuss the note and how to proceed with the investigation. Scorpio threatens to kill another person every day if the mayor fails to put an ad in the *San Francisco Chronicle* stating that he will meet the killer's demand for $100,000. "If I do not hear from you," Scorpio writes, "it will be my next pleasure to kill a Catholic priest or a nigger." When Harry enters, the mayor immediately says, "All right. Let's have it." Harry asks, "Have what?" The mayor replies, "The report. What have you been doing?" Harry's disrespect for the mayor is evident in his reply: "Oh, well, for the past three-quarters of an hour I've been sitting on my ass in your outer office waiting on you." After Harry reports that a dozen men are checking identification files, investigating recently released criminals, and engaged in other standard procedures, he is dumbfounded when the mayor says, "Give the message to the *Chronicle*. We'll agree to pay. We'll tell him we need time to get the money together." The police chief nods affirmatively when the mayor says the city will pay. Harry scowls at these bureaucrats and says, "Wait a minute. Do I get this right? You're going to play this creep's game?" The mayor says, "It will give us more breathing space." Harry notes that it might get someone killed and asks, "Why don't you let me meet with the son-of-a-bitch?" The police chief stands up, shakes his head and says, "None of that. You'll end up with a real bloodbath." The mayor says he agrees with the chief and orders them to proceed as he has instructed. Lieutenant Bressler stands up and commands, "Come on, Callahan. Let's go." Harry starts to follow the lieutenant out the door but the mayor stops him when he shouts, "Callahan!" When Harry turns, the mayor warns him not to act independently as he has in the past. In contrast to a character like Benjamin Braddock who lacks affect, Harry is a man who attempts to act in the interests of the public but is constantly restrained by weak bureaucrats in a system that doesn't tolerate independent thought or action.

Harry Callahan must fight the criminals and what he often refers to as "the system" that restricts his ability to protect San Francisco citizens. Harry, like Will Kane and similar protagonists in postwar westerns, is in society but not of it. The system can corrupt virtuous independent men who risk themselves for the public good. It can make them weak and indecisive. Virtuous men must therefore resist society's influence and break its unjust rules, apparent by the means Harry uses to apprehend Scorpio and by his interactions with officials like the mayor who represent the system. Various scenes portray it to be necessary to skirt the system and disobey authority in order to save lives and seek justice.

Scorpio keeps his promise and murders a 10-year-old African American boy. He then tries to kill a priest, but Harry and his new partner, Chico Gonzalez (Reni Santoni), thwart the attempt when they wait on a rooftop near a Catholic church where they believe Scorpio might strike next. They see Scorpio on the roof and exchange fire, but the killer gets away. When Scorpio then kidnaps a 14-year-old girl, he sends the police a letter with a description of the girl and a tooth that a dentist identifies as one of hers. Scorpio demands $200,000 in ten and twenty dollar bills, blames the police for "double-crossing" him and, consequently, for the girl's fate. Lieutenant Bressler says they need a bagman to deliver the money and asks Harry if he wants the job. Harry, always willing to risk himself for the weaker members of the society it is his duty to protect, volunteers. But the lieutenant won't let Gonzalez go with Harry because Scorpio demands that only one person make the delivery. Gonzalez's comment to the lieutenant reveals how Harry got his nickname: "No wonder they call him Dirty Harry — always gets the shit under the stick." The lieutenant has no plan of his own and yields to the

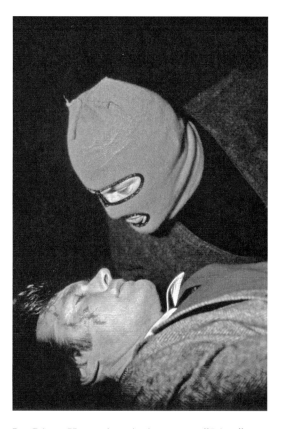

In *Dirty Harry* (1971), inspector "Dirty" Harry Callahan (Clint Eastwood), bottom, is beaten severely by the serial killer Scorpio (Andy Robinson), top, before Harry's partner risks his life to save Harry (Photofest).

criminal's will, creating a situation in which Harry must subvert the system to try to protect himself while he risks his life to try to apprehend Scorpio and save the girl.

Harry and Chico disobey the lieutenant's order and wire Harry so Chico can hear Harry's conversations with Scorpio and meet him at the drop site. After Scorpio sends Harry to a number of public telephones around town to try to ensure that no one follows him to the site, he eventually instructs Harry to meet him at the base of the large concrete cross atop Mount Davidson, the highest elevation in San Francisco. When they meet, Scorpio orders Harry to throw his gun down and turn and face the cross; he then proceeds to beat and kick Harry. He puts his foot on Harry's chest and tells him if he lifts a hand again he won't reveal where the girl is. While Scorpio beats Harry, Gonzalez approaches and shoots just before Scorpio attempts to kill Harry. Scorpio fires back with an automatic rifle and shoots Chico, but not fatally. Harry, on the ground, pulls a knife he has concealed on his body and sticks it into Scorpio's leg. The killer screams and flees with the bag of money.

When a scraped-and-beaten Harry meets with Lieutenant Bressler later, he remains both defiant, independent-minded and self-sacrificing, a stark contrast to the weak-willed and ineffective bureaucrats who run the system. Bressler tells Harry the Chief of Police wants to know why Chico is in the hospital when he ordered Harry to meet Scorpio alone. Harry says he can tell the chief that Gonzalez was obeying an order from a superior, Harry, and that the lieutenant didn't know anything about it. Harry adds that if the chief doesn't like it, he can have Harry's badge. If Chico hadn't followed Harry, Harry would no doubt be dead, justifying his decision to act on his own rather than follow the orders of the weak men who run the system and meet the demands of serial killers.

Harry later meets with Bressler in the lieutenant's office and they get a tip that leads Harry to Scorpio and results in Harry once again breaking the rules to try to save the girl's life before it's too late. Bressler gets a call from an emergency-room doctor who says he just treated a patient with a stab wound in the leg. Harry visits the doctor with detective Frank DiGeorgio (John Mitchum) and discovers that Scorpio is the grounds keeper at a nearby football stadium. When the two detectives go to the stadium, Harry violates the killer's legal rights and tortures him to get him to reveal where he put the girl that he kidnapped. The limping Scorpio tries to run across the football field, but Harry runs after him and yells for him to stop. When DiGeorgio flips a switch that illuminates the stadium lights, the killer stops, turns, and faces Harry. Harry points his gun at Scorpio and shoots him in the leg while the killer stands in the middle of the football field. Scorpio screams and begs Harry not to shoot him again, and DiGeorgio watches from the stands while Harry walks across the field toward the killer, points his gun at him and demands, "The girl. Where is she?" Scorpio says he wants a lawyer and screams repeatedly, "I have rights." While he screams about his rights, Harry asks multiple times "Where's the girl?" He then looks at Scorpio's wounded leg and steps on it until the killer reveals where the girl is. When Harry arrives at the scene, however, it's too late; she's already dead.

With time running out and killer Scorpio's latest victim dying, Harry (Clint Eastwood) resorts to torturing the serial killer to get him to reveal the location of the girl (Photofest).

Harry is as much disgusted with the system as he is with the bureaucrats who run it. He is appalled with what he believes to be the irrationality of the justice system when the District Attorney and a judge who teaches Constitutional Law at the University of California, Berkeley explain why the DA will not prosecute Scorpio. The DA informs Harry that he has been looking at Harry's arrest report and comments, "A very *unusual* piece of police work. Really amazing." Harry says, "Yeah, well, I had some luck." The DA replies sternly, "You're lucky I'm not indicting you for assault with attempt to commit murder." Confused, Harry replies, "What?" The DA lectures him: "Where the hell does it say you have a right to kick down doors, torture suspects, deny medical attention and legal counsel? Where have you been?" The DA mentions the Supreme Court's Miranda decision (1966) and says Harry must have heard of the Fourth Amendment. He continues by reinforcing what the serial killer told Harry: "What I'm saying is that man had rights." Harry replies, "Well, I'm all broken up about that man's rights." "You should be," the DA says. "I've got news for you, Callahan. As soon as he's well enough to leave the hospital, he walks." Harry can't believe it. "What are you talking about?" he asks. The DA shouts, "He's free!" He explains that they have to let Scorpio go because of Harry's illegal tactics. "We can't try him," he says, and informs Harry, "I'm not wasting a half a million dollars of the taxpayers' money on a trial we can't possibly win. The problem is we don't have any evidence." The killer's rifle rests across stacks of files on a desk in the room. Harry points at the weapon and says, "Evidence? What in the hell do you call that?" The DA says, "I call it nothing. Zero!" When Harry asserts that ballistics can match bullets with the weapon, the DA says, "It does not matter what ballistics can do. This rifle might make a nice souvenir, but it's inadmissible as evidence." He tells Harry, "It's the law." Harry replies, "Well, then the law's crazy."

While Harry's conversation with the DA reveals his disgust with a legal system that keeps him from using whatever means necessary to do his job, his conversation with the judge and university professor infuriates him as he learns that the judicial system and the intellectual elites who define it and interpret it value the rights of perpetrators over those of victims. The judge tells them that Harry's search of Scorpio's living quarters at the stadium was illegal, so the rifle and anything else taken from there is inadmissible as evidence in court. He tells Harry he should have gotten a search warrant and Harry replies, "A search warrant? There was a girl dying." Such facts are irrelevant to the system that Harry sees as restraining his ability to do his job in the way he deems necessary given the circumstances of the case. When the DA tells Harry that the girl was already dead, Harry makes it clear he did what he thought to be necessary to find the girl as quickly as he could because he didn't know she was dead. The judge notes, "The court would have to recognize the police officer's legitimate concern for the girl's life. But, there is no way they can possibly condone police torture. All evidence concerning the girl, the suspect's confession, all physical evidence, would have to be excluded." Harry, frustrated, says, "There must be something you can get him on." The judge replies, "Without the evidence of the gun, and the girl? Ha, I couldn't convict him of spitting on the sidewalk." Harry asks who speaks for the victim's rights: "I mean, she's raped and left in a hole to die. Who speaks for her?" Such scenes clearly depict the system and the bureaucrats who run it, "the establishment," as serving the interests of criminals rather than the public good, and as restraining the actions of self-sacrificing men like Harry, who put their lives on the line every day to protect victims like the girl.

The DA informs Harry that his office speaks for the girl but further restricts Harry's ability to act, pushing him to act even more independently and causing him to realize that bureaucrats like the DA do not understand criminals like Scorpio. When the DA tells Harry he has a family and doesn't want Scorpio on the streets either, Harry says the killer won't be on the streets long because "sooner or later he's going to stub his toe and then I'll be right there." But the DA says he won't allow Harry to harass Scorpio. Harry tells him he's crazy if he thinks Scorpio isn't going to kill again. Harry understands something about the killer that the lieutenant, the mayor and other bureaucrats don't. When the DA asks how Harry knows Scorpio will kill again, Harry replies, "Because he likes it." Values that protect the interests of criminals over those of victims, even child victims, have been institutionalized in the legal system and restrain the actions of virtuous men like Harry. But because murderers like Scorpio are protected by the system and victims cannot receive justice within it, Harry is pushed to the point where he must work independently and outside of the system to ensure that justice is served and that Scorpio doesn't kill again.

Harry becomes even more determined to disobey orders and pursue Scorpio on his own after the killer pays another man to beat him. He then claims that Harry beat him and gets the police chief to order Harry to stop following him. When Harry tells the chief he didn't beat Scorpio but has been tailing him on his own time, the chief gives him an order he will have to break: "I don't want anymore surveillance." Harry replies as he turns to leave, "Well, neither does he," implying that the chief is foolish because he's giving the killer exactly what he wants, and that Scorpio knows how to get it by playing the corrupt and ineffective system.

Harry is finally pushed to disobey orders and pursue the killer independently when Scorpio hijacks a school bus full of children and demands that the mayor provide him with a jet, a pilot to fly it, and $200,000, which the mayor says he will arrange because Scorpio threatens to start killing his child hostages. The mayor promises Scorpio, "I guarantee you, you will not be molested in any way. I give you my word of honor on it." The police chief asks Harry if he will take the money to Scorpio, but Harry doesn't think that complying with the killer's demands is effective or that the mayor giving Scorpio his "word of honor" is honorable. Harry says, "When are you people gonna stop messin' around with this guy? He's gotta be stopped now!" The mayor says, "He's got a bus-load of kids and I can't take that chance." Then, yelling, "I gave my word of honor on it, and he will not be molested. Now that's a direct order, Callahan!" While he stares at the mayor in disbelief Harry says, "Well you can just get yourself another delivery boy." Harry's separation from the system and from the weak bureaucrats who run it is almost complete when he walks out the door to pursue Scorpio alone and on his own terms.

When Harry catches up with the bus he jumps from a low bridge onto the roof and causes Scorpio to drive the bus off the road. Scorpio flees on foot and Harry chases him through a rock quarry. The killer grabs a boy he finds fishing in a pond and uses him as a shield when Harry approaches. He tells Harry if he doesn't throw down his gun he'll kill the boy. Harry moves his hand toward the ground as if to release the gun. But as Scorpio laughs insanely, Harry raises his gun quickly and fires over the boy and into Scorpio's left shoulder. The boy runs as the blast thrusts Scorpio backward and onto the ground down a small embankment. Harry walks to where Scorpio was standing and sees the killer lying on a small dock. When Scorpio gets up and reaches for his gun, Harry cocks his .44 Magnum, points it at Scorpio, and speaks his signature lines that he also says to a bank robber earlier in the film:

> I know what you're thinkin', punk. You're thinkin', "has he fired six shots or only five." And to tell ya the truth, I've forgotten myself in all this excitement. But bein' that this is a .44 Magnum, the most powerful handgun in the world, and will blow your head clean off, you can ask yourself a question. "Do I feel lucky?"

Harry then growls through his clinched teeth, "Well, do ya, punk?" As Harry maintains his stern gaze into the killer's eyes, Scorpio grabs the gun and Harry shoots him in the chest. The thrust of the shot pushes Scorpio off the back of the dock and into the pond. His dead body floats in the water as Harry walks to the edge of the dock and holsters his weapon.

While we listen to the sirens of approaching police vehicles, Harry pulls out the black leather case that holds his inspector's badge, removes the badge from the case and holds it in his left hand as he stares at "Inspector 2211 S.F. Police" inscribed on the gold-and-black star. His index finger tightens on one of the star's seven points before he flings it through the air and into the pond. He turns and walks away through the quarry as the camera pans to a bird's-eye view of Harry walking alone, alienated and now separated from a society that tries to keep virtuous men from acting to protect innocent people and elevates criminals' rights above citizens' safety.

When I first conceptualized this book, I created the phrase "fascist-avenger" to refer to late twentieth-century films with strong male characters who take militant action when their agency is curtailed by what Adlai Stevenson in 1955 referred to as the new "collectivism" that led to the decline of "individualism" associated with the postwar "system."[31] I included the Dirty Harry series of movies in this category of films, along with movies like *Death Wish* (1974), *Batman* (1989), and *Fight Club* (1999). Writing about *Dirty Harry*, however, has caused me to realize that although Harry Callahan is clearly an "avenger," it is inappropriate to refer to the character as "fascist."[32] While Harry is alienated from the system and complains about and sometimes defies the restrictions it places on him, and symbolically separates himself from the system at the end of the film, he does not attack the system to try to change it or destroy it. He clearly violates Scorpio's civil rights but is not a fascist on a mission, which is the plot of the second film in the series, *Magnum Force*.

In this sequel Harry defends the system that he hates, and he defends it from four rookie cops who served in the Army Special Forces and a police lieutenant who organizes the rookies into a fascist death squad. These truly fascist cops murder pimps and other common criminals, but they also use a machine gun to shoot in cold blood dozens of counterculture partygoers swimming naked in a backyard pool at a hillside San Francisco home. The lieutenant and the rookies attempt to get Harry to join them, but Harry makes it clear they try to enlist the wrong guy.

One scene with Harry and the rookies and another with the lieutenant and Harry reveal both the rogue cops' plans and Harry's devotion to defending the public and the system whose rules he regularly breaks in order to do his job. When the rookies figure out that Harry has connected them to the murders, they wait for him on their police motorcycles in the parking garage beneath Harry's apartment. One of them notes how difficult it is to prosecute cops, and Harry mentions all the people they have killed that week. When he asks what they will do next week, Officer John Davis (David Soul) replies, "Kill a dozen more." Harry says, "Is that what you guys are all about, being heroes?" One of the other two says, "All our heroes are dead." The leader, Davis, answers for the group: "We're the first generation that's learned to fight. We're simply ridding society of killers that would be caught and sentenced anyway if our courts worked properly. We began with the criminals that the people know, so that our actions would be understood. It's not just a question of whether or not to use violence. There simply is no other way, inspector. You, of all people, should understand that." When the rogue cops tell Harry if he isn't with them he's against them, Harry replies, "I'm afraid you've misjudged me."

When in a later scene Lieutenant Briggs reveals to Harry that he's the one who organized the fascist death squad, Harry asks Briggs why he's involved. Briggs creates a useable past of vigilante justice in the American West to justify his actions. "A hundred years ago in this city," Briggs asserts, "people did the same thing. History justified the vigilantes. We're no different. Anyone who threatens the security of the people will be executed. Evil for evil, Harry — retribution." Harry's reply reveals that he understands where vigilante justice can lead: "That's just fine. But how does murder fit in? You know, when the police start becoming their own executioners, where's it gonna end, huh, Briggs? Pretty soon you start executing people for jay-walking, and executing people for traffic violations; then you end up executing your neighbor because his dog pisses on your lawn." At one point in their conversation Harry tells Briggs, "I'd have upheld the law," to which the lieutenant replies, "What the hell do you know about the law? You're a great cop, Harry. You had a chance to join the team, but you'd rather stick with the system." Harry's response reveals both his disgust for the system and his support of it: "I hate the goddamn system, but until someone comes along with some changes that make sense, I'll stick with it." Their conversation ends when Briggs tells Harry, "You're about to become extinct."

This theme in the Dirty Harry movies about the constraints that the system places on the individual's ability to act pervades the films and is presented as potentially leading to violent, even fascist, solutions — the rookie death squad — and to the possibility of trading victims' rights for those of cold-blooded murderers like Scorpio. Where characters like Benjamin Braddock and Wyatt and Billy critique the system by dropping out, Harry remains in the system to do what he can to protect the public, critiquing it along the way, and subverting it when necessary to prevent crime and ensure that justice is done.

Despite criticisms of the Harry Callahan character being a bigot, a racist and a sexist, the first three films in the Dirty Harry series depict Harry's attitudes about race, ethnicity and gender as ancillary and arguably inconsequential to his frustrations with the system. Harry has a Hispanic partner in the first film, an African-American partner in the second, and a female partner in the third. His relationships with these partners provide opportunities to inject the films with scenes and dialog about the race, ethnicity and gender issues so prominent in the 1970s, issues in the news that resonated with diverse contemporary moviegoers. But these issues do not divert attention from the major emphasis in the films on the individual cop's struggle to do his job in a bureaucratic system staffed with ignorant, ineffective and weak-willed administrators who make decisions that, supposedly, would best be made by street-savvy cops like Harry Callahan. Rather, the issues add realistic content about the integration of the police force in a major American city during years of significant historical change, and they are not portrayed as simplistically as some critics assert.[33]

In *Dirty Harry*, for example, Harry is assigned to work with a new rookie partner, Chico Gonzalez. In a room filled with detectives, Gonzalez asks why other cops call Callahan "Dirty" Harry. Detective DiGeorgio answers, "That's one thing about our Harry; he doesn't play any favorites. Harry hates everybody." The detective then recites a list of derogatory ethnic and racial terms to describe the categories of people Harry supposedly hates, implying that Harry's use of such language and his presumed hatred of such people are what make him "Dirty" Harry. Gonzalez asks, "How's he feel about Mexicans?" DiGeorgio says, "Ask him." Harry answers, "especially spics," just before he winks at the other detective as he walks away. Only when he is asked that question, however, does Callahan use an ethnic slur. DiGeorgio rather than Harry is the source of the comments. Furthermore, Harry's wink demonstrates that he is hazing his new partner, and we learn later that Harry actually became tagged with the nickname "Dirty" because he gets assigned to all of the dirty jobs. Gonzalez himself makes that clear when he questions Lieutenant Bressler's order that Harry deliver the ransom money alone when he meets the killer Scorpio at the cross atop Mount Davidson. Moreover, it becomes apparent throughout the course of the film that Harry respects Gonzalez as a person and a cop, especially after the rookie takes a bullet trying to save Harry's life. We also learn that Harry is a friend of the black emergency-room physician (Marc Hertsens) who sews him up; the doctor grew up in the same working-class neighborhood that Harry did. Race and ethnicity, then, are not factors that cause disrespect and tension in his relationships, especially those with his Hispanic partner in the first film and with the African-American cop, Earlington "Early" Smith (Felton Perry), he works with in the second.

The films deal with gender issues in a similar way, but Harry's inter-actions with women are limited in the first two films to a few short scenes with him talking to other cops' wives. In the third film, *The Enforcer* (1976), however, Harry learns he must partner with a woman, Inspector Kate Moore (Tyne Daly). Harry resists at first but again has no choice in the matter. After making comments about women's inability to do the job and not wanting to risk his life with an unqualified partner, Harry comes to respect Moore as a person and a cop, just as he did with his Mexican partner, Chico Gonzalez, in the original film. At first Tyne Daly rejected the part; she figured the female partner would "be the butt of all the jokes."[34] But Eastwood agreed to allow Daly to help shape her character by reading through the script and making suggestions. Many reviewers referred to Harry's relationship with Moore as the best part of the film. The critic for *The Hollywood Reporter*, Jean Hoelscher, wrote that Eastwood "certainly deserves credit" for "his lack of ego when casting his female leads: He is not afraid to work with excellent women."[35] That willingness extended to the fourth movie in the series, *Sudden Impact* (1983). Here Sondra Locke plays Jennifer Spencer, the strong female perpetrator of numerous murders who, along with her now comatose sister, was brutally gang raped 10 years earlier by the men she now hunts down and kills. In the end, Harry conveniently places Spencer's gun, the murder weapon, on a dead rapist's body, deflecting attention away from the woman victim-turned-vigilante killer. She would be tried for murder in the ineffective system that denied her and her sister justice, so Harry ensures that this strong and, no doubt in his mind, admirable woman walks away.[36]

In films produced in the forties, fifties and early sixties, those in which discontented and disaffected men is a major theme, male characters take for granted they are white and rarely interact with characters that represent minorities. White filmmakers made movies for what they assumed to be predominantly white audiences just as fifties television producers targeted white audiences in the rapidly growing, segregated, and predominantly white suburbs.[37] Given the fact that postwar Hollywood was a bastion of white male economic power, cultural influence, and racist assumptions and hiring practices, films like *It's a Wonderful Life* and *The Man in the Gray Flannel Suit* represent white men negotiating life in a white world. Then, following the civil rights struggle of the fifties and sixties that resulted in the Civil Right Act of 1964, the Voting Rights Act of 1965, and other civil rights legislation, the racist and bigoted character Joe Curran emerges in 1970 and blames minorities and white liberal policy makers and bureaucrats for what he believes to be his declining status, agency and influence in society. We have seen, however, that even a movie like *Joe* contains significant references to the mundane and repetitive nature of work and the declining agency of men — both white collar and blue — in the postwar corporate order, problems that Joe and, to a lesser degree, Bill Compton blame on a host of convenient scapegoats: hippies, African Americans, gays, liberals in general, and anyone associated with the counterculture.

Of course, the emphasis on white male characters creating scapegoats to blame when they feel their status and influence in society are threatened is not new to the late sixties and early seventies. D.W. Griffith's *The Birth of a Nation* (1915), a racist glorification of the Ku Klux Klan as saviors of the American South, demonstrates that. Films with themes about race produced in the fifties and early sixties, however, such as *No Way Out* (1950), *The Blackboard Jungle* (1955) — both featuring the rising African-American star Sidney Poitier — and *To Kill a Mockingbird* (1962), explore injustices associated with prejudice during the years when the civil rights struggle kicked into high gear and not long after Jackie Robinson broke the color line in Major League Baseball (1947) and President Truman desegregated the military (1948). The plots of such films revolve around the issues of race prevalent in postwar American society. In contrast, the plot of *The Man in the Gray Flannel Suit* is about how Tom Rath negotiates his way through corporate life in the organized system filled with and controlled by other white men. Many more films produced in the seventies, eighties and nineties incorporate race as a significant theme; this is especially true of those set in diverse urban environments. It should be evident from my analysis of *Dirty Harry*, however, that while the story is about

Harry pursuing Scorpio, the plot is about him struggling against the system and weak and ineffective bureaucrats, and that both race and gender issues are ancillary to the development of that plot.

Postwar movies about cops and other protagonists set in major urban areas usually contain diverse characters and interracial social situations. Those about upper middle-class men in white suburbs and corporate offices portray a predominantly white world because the movies represent men in a specific social, economic and cultural location in that world. The main characters are white, but the fact that they are white often is not significant to the narratives any more than the fact that the Willy Loman character in Arthur Miller's Toni Award and Pulitzer Prize–wining play *Death of a Salesman* (1949) is white.

Some films produced at the end of the century, such as *American History X* (1998) and *White Men Can't Jump* (1992), focus on racial prejudice and assumptions based on race (the latter film about black men's assumptions of white guys' hoop-shooting abilities). We will see in chapter four, however, that films like *American Beauty* (1999), *Office Space* (1999) and *Fight Club* (1999) continue to feature white male characters, some exclusively. These films focus on men's discontent and disaffection in relation to the nature of work, to men's declining agency in society as a consequence of corporate life, and, increasingly, to a mind-numbing consumer culture. In contrast to earlier films that contain similar critiques of American society and culture, the critiques sometimes become militant.

4
Blowing Up and Dropping Out
Awakenings, Agency and Militancy
at the End of the Century

We have seen that in the early postwar years characters in films like *The Man in the Gray Flannel Suit* (1956) reveal what I refer to as a leery acceptance of corporate life. Traditional ideals such as honesty, integrity, speaking one's mind, and control over one's life and work are increasingly diminished in the corporate order. Characters become gray-suited yes-men who carry out the orders of corporate bureaucrats that manage other men's lives as they run the postwar organized system that Adlai Stevenson proclaimed to be the new reality of American life. But veiled opposition to that system and its values continue to appear in films about gunslingers and gangsters, evident in *Johnny Guitar* (1954) and *Force of Evil* (1948), and such opposition is sometimes associated with female as well as male characters in these films. Dramas produced during the postwar years, how-ever, tend to depict characters negotiating their way in the system rather than confronting the system directly or opposing the values associated with it. Then, in the comedy-drama *The Graduate* (1967) and the counterculture film *Easy Rider* (1969), characters do not oppose the system directly but demonstrate different versions of dropping out as they question the prospect of living their lives in a corporate bureaucracy, like Tom Rath, and their days pondering such mundane things as "plastics," like Benjamin Braddock is advised to do. Characters in many films of the sixties and sev-enties remain discontented and largely disaffected, although those who drop out do act to avoid the otherwise inevitable reality of negotiating their way through life in the organized system whether they work in private or government bureaucracies.

Some characters in seventies' films like *Dirty Harry* (1971) remain in the organized system and demonstrate significant agency as they confront aspects of the system from within. But rather than spend their days in corporate bureaucracies they work in the government bureaucracies of law enforcement. Other characters like the architect Paul Kersey in *Death Wish* (1974) work outside the corrupt system because virtuous real men do not control the system; it works in the interests of criminals, corrupt politicians and businessmen. The urban-avenger heroes in such films take the law into their own hands because the organized system that became a target of social critics like Paul Goodman, William H. Whyte, and C. Wright Mills in the early postwar years does not work. The men who manage it are often corrupt, weak, self-serving bureaucrats, sometimes criminals themselves or serving the interests of criminal businessmen in either mainstream society or the criminal underworld.

More recent super-hero movies like *Batman* (1989) also demonstrate a version of the urban-avenger films in the closing decades of the twentieth century, for these superheroes are in society but not of it, their strength of character, values and power at odds with the weak and often corrupt citizens of cities like Gotham. The western gunslinger of Dodge becomes the .44-Magnum-wielding cop of San Francisco (Harry Callahan), and then the wealthy, self-reliant "Dark Knight" of Gotham whose inherited fortune enables him to be under no man's and no bureaucracy's control, and whose arsenal of weapons Dirty Harry Callahan could not even imagine. These urban-avenger heroes are discontented like characters in earlier films, and they are disaffected in that they are alienated or estranged from society. But they certainly do not lack affect in the psychological sense of the word. Rather, control and power are their hallmarks as they wage war against society's villains in order to save weak and powerless citizens, people who cower in the face of danger and often lie, cheat, steal and manipulate the system to get what they can for themselves.

The superheroes that exhibit this powerful agency are concerned with justice rather than with the oppressive nature of work and the emptiness associated with daily life in the organized system and in American consumer culture. For this reason I acknowledge here the significant agency that the superhero characters demonstrate as they work against the corrupt system, but I focus my attention in this chapter on films that involve regular guys who also exhibit significant agency as they become fed up with the nature of work in the system and, in two of the three films studied here, severely critical of a mind-numbing consumer culture from which they decide they must liberate themselves. Characters that take actions to change their situations appear in dramas and comedies released at the close of the century. Their discontent often becomes associated with anger that leads them to become self-aware and to develop significant agency in their lives, and to sometimes engage in militant, terrorist acts of destruction as they attempt to liberate themselves and others from a society and a culture they come to loathe.

Films released in the closing years of the century such as *Lost in America* (1985), a comedy, and *Falling Down* (1993), a drama, maintain the theme of discontented men that appeared in American literary and then film texts more than a century earlier, albeit in a new and ever-changing historical context. In *Lost in America*, for example, David Howard (Albert Brooks) quits his well-paying job with an advertising agency after he fails to get a promotion and learns that his boss wants him to transfer from the Los Angeles to the New York office. David convinces his wife Linda (Julie Hagerty) to quit her job, too, and the childless couple sets out on the highway like Wyatt and Billy in *Easy Rider* (1969), although the Howards embark in a Winnebago motor home rather than astride two custom-built choppers. The Howards end their road trip quickly after Linda loses their "nest egg" gambling in Las Vegas. It takes capital to be independent in America, so the Howards wind up in New York, where David gets his job back and the couple becomes reincorporated into the system they rejected at the beginning of the film.[1]

In contrast to this comedy, the protagonist in the drama *Falling Down* becomes violent after his car breaks down in Los Angeles traffic while he drives to his ex-wife's house to attend his daughter's birthday party, despite the fact that a judge issued a restraining order to keep him away from his ex-wife and daughter. Frustrated about his family situation and because he recently lost his job, William "D-Fens" Foster (Michael Douglas)— "D-Fens" is on his license plate, he works for a defense contractor, and he defends his vision of America — journeys on foot through Los Angeles after he leaves his stalled Chevette in traffic. Foster's trek provides the context for him to express his anger about what the film depicts as American society's major ills: price-gouging and commercialism, gang violence, racism, greed and selfishness, and the changing nature of an economy that makes hard-working people like Foster obsolete while some people with good, secure jobs — like those on a road crew he comes across — do as little as they can to earn their daily bread.[2] Howard's and Foster's' discontent leads them to act — the former drops out and the latter uses a variety of weapons to attack the things that cause his discontent — and they act almost immediately in reaction to events as the films begin.

In three films produced at the end of the century that represent significantly discontented and disaffected men, the characters lack affect early in the films but develop considerable, sometimes even extreme, agency as the films' narratives unfold. Due to a variety of circumstances, the protagonists become aware that they can wield some control over their lives, that they do not have to submit to the authority of corporate managers or others and, in two of the films, allow their values to be shaped by a mind-numbing consumer culture that causes people to believe happiness can only be achieved through the endless acquisition of material things. Becoming aware that a life lived for consumption is empty empowers the characters to question working at jobs they hate just so they can accumulate more material goods. Although the characters in these films are corporate employees like Tom Rath in *The Man in the Gray Flannel Suit* and are discontented and disaffected for similar reasons as characters in earlier films, these movies contain considerable elements of violence. In two of them, the violence results directly from the characters' discontent with corporate life. Coincidentally, all three films were released in the same year: *American Beauty* (1999), *Office Space* (1999), and *Fight Club* (1999), a drama, a comedy, and a psychodrama, respectively.

Similar to Benjamin Braddock in *The Graduate* and David Howard in *Lost in America,* the protagonist in *American Beauty*, Lester Burnham (Kevin Spacey), turns his back on corporate America and American consumer culture, albeit in his own fashion. Lester complains that he has been a whore for the advertising industry for 14 years, and he thinks his wife Carolyn (Annette Bening) is too materialistic and too fixated on becoming a more successful, wealthy realtor. Lester concludes that he and Carolyn no longer experience life but simply live it, working and consuming and accumulating but not actually enjoying anything, including each other. Although he has what many might consider to be a "good" job as a writer for a magazine, he realizes his work is not creative or fulfilling because he participates in perpetuating the kind of materialism his wife represents and he comes to loath. Lester concludes that happiness is not possible if one spends one's days selling things to others — such as Carolyn's houses and the consumer goods in the ads Lester writes — and wastes personal time and money buying bigger houses and perpetually consuming more and increasingly expensive goods.[3]

Lester spends his days in a cubicle, just like the men in *Office Space* and many other films that portray late twentieth-century white-collar work. Management is in the process of discovering who is "valuable" and who is "expendable." The company hires an "efficiency expert" to do the dirty work of downsizing. Employees are instructed to write reports for the efficiency expert. In their reports, Lester and other employees are supposed to describe what they do and how their jobs are important to the company. During the days when Lester and his colleagues write their reports and schedule meetings with the efficiency expert to discuss them, Lester has his awakening as he begins to speak out about his job, his family, and the values associated with American consumer culture, especially as his wife Carolyn exemplifies those values. Lester does not merely complain about American life and culture, however; he begins to act, thanks in part to the example of the teenage boy, Ricky Fitts (Wes Bently), who lives next door. Prior to this point in Lester's life he did not cause trouble at home or at work by asserting himself with his employer or his wife.

Lester becomes outspoken at work and at home following a banquet for local realtors that he attends with Carolyn. Ricky Fitts works as a busboy at the place where the banquet is held. Ricky notices that Lester is clearly alienated from Carolyn's real estate colleagues, like the smooth talking and successful Buddy Kane (Peter Gallagher), whom Carolyn begins an affair with shortly after the banquet. Ricky sees Lester and asks him if he gets high. Lester gladly accepts the invitation and they go behind the building to smoke a joint. When the manager discovers them and makes it clear that Ricky better stop what he's doing and get back to work or he'll lose his job, Ricky simply tells him he quits and continues smoking the joint with Lester. Lester is inspired by Ricky's action, with the fact that he doesn't fear losing his job. But he is unaware at this point that Ricky's busboy job has been a cover to keep his father, Col. Frank Fitts, USMC (Chris Cooper), from discovering that Ricky sells marijuana so he can afford his expensive hobby. He buys equipment so he can make videos of the "beauty" he sees in the everyday things and people he encounters, including Lester's daughter Jane (Thora Birch).

Following the evening at the realtors' banquet, Lester's control over his life increases rapidly, inspired by Ricky's example and, in part, by Lester's lust for one of Jane's teenage friends, Angela Hayes (Mena Suvari). Lester becomes infatuated with Angela the first time he sees her at a high-school basketball game where Angela and Jane dance with the school drill team. He fantasizes about Angela during the game and throughout the movie, and he starts an exercise regimen when he overhears Angela tell

Jane she thinks he's cute, would be even cuter if he worked out, and would have sex with him. Lester quickly starts running and lifting weights.

Lester is clearly going through a mid-life crisis. But if what he goes through is merely a mid-life crisis, its scope exceeds the crises of other men who just dye their hair, buy sports cars, and try to discover if they're still attractive to members of the opposite sex. "The movie," film critic Roger Ebert notes correctly, "is the story of [Lester's] rebellion."[4] Imbedded in his personal rebellion, however, is a critique of a society and a culture that leaves many people leading desperate, empty lives, alienated from their work and estranged from those they love. Lester's crisis is a vehicle that exposes the mundane nature of work in much of corporate America and the mind-numbing values associated with a consumer culture that promises happiness through the purchase of things but actually leaves people unfulfilled no matter how much they consume. Most men who have mid-life crises have the self-absorbed variety without becoming social and cultural critics. This broader dimension to Lester's crisis is evident in the actions he takes and the ideas he articulates at work and at home.

Lester meets with the efficiency expert, Brad Dupree (Barry Del Sherman), to discuss the report he has written describing what he does for the company. The report and his meeting with Dupree reveal Lester's new-found agency and his willingness to take risks. Brad reads part of Lester's brief report aloud: "My job consists basically of masking my contempt for the ass holes in charge, and at least once a day retiring to the men's room so I can jerk off...." Lester finishes the sentence for him: "...while I fantasize a life that so closely resembles hell." He then says he has been a whore for the advertising industry for 14 years. When Brad tells Lester "management wants you out by the end of the day," Lester asks what kind of severance package management is prepared to offer him given the fact he has information about the boss using company money to pay for whores to live in expensive hotel rooms. The editorial director, Lester tells Brad, "buys pussy with company money." He also notes that some of their advertisers, rival publications, the IRS, and the editorial director's wife would be interested in this information. When Brad asks Lester what he wants, Lester says, "One year's salary with benefits." Brad replies, "That's not going to happen." Lester adds that he can throw in a sexual harassment charge against Brad and asks, "Can you prove you didn't offer to save my job if I let you blow me?" Brad says, "Man, you are one twisted fuck." Lester replies, "Nope, I'm just an ordinary guy with nothin' to lose." Lester wins, packs a box with the things from his cubicle, and walks out a free man. On his way home he applies for and gets a job flipping burgers at a fast-food restaurant called "Smiley's."

When Lester arrives at home, Carolyn and Jane are shocked when they witness his newfound agency and assertiveness. It's evident that Carolyn is the alpha-parent; she has established the rules and controls what occurs in the Burnham home. It seems clear, however, that Carolyn's unbridled agency is not merely a consequence of her more dominant personality, for the control she wields is also a consequence of Lester's passivity. In other words, he has had no say in how things are run because he has said nothing. A scene of the family eating dinner together is important because it reveals that for the first time in his life Lester asserts himself in his domestic as well as his professional life.

At the Burnham's dinner table that evening, Lester and Carolyn argue about him quitting his job, but he is clearly happy, upbeat, glad to be free of a job he hated and reveling in his newfound agency. He's no longer willing to leave Carolyn's complaints unchallenged or accept her control of things like the kind of music they listen to while they eat, something Jane has complained about in the past. He doesn't want to control the music but to have Jane, Carolyn and himself choose the music on alternate evenings. This domestic scene, like the scene at the office, depicts Lester as an agent now shaping his life rather than living a life dictated by others and seemingly shaped by circumstances beyond his influence. When Carolyn complains about Lester quitting his job, he fights back. He is aggressive but doesn't demand his way about things other than his right to quit a job he hated.

Carolyn says he should tell Jane what he did that day. He does so happily and matter-of-factly. "Jane," he begins, "today I quit my job. And then I told my boss to go fuck himself, and then I blackmailed him for almost $60,000. Pass the asparagus." Carolyn responds, "Your father seems to think this kind of behavior is something to be proud of." Lester replies, "And your mother seems to prefer that I go through life like a fucking prisoner while she keeps my dick in a mason jar under the sink." While they argue, he keeps asking if someone will please pass the asparagus; it's at Carolyn's end of the table. He finally stands up and walks over to get the asparagus himself and sits back down. He then looks across the table at Carolyn and says, "I am sick and tired of you treating me like I don't exist." Then to both Carolyn and Jane he says, "You two do whatever you want to do whenever you want to do it, and I don't complain. All I want is the same...." Carolyn interrupts him in mid-sentence and begins yelling and complaining. He responds by throwing the platter of asparagus against the wall, which shocks them and silences Carolyn. He stares at Carolyn and calmly but forcefully says, "Don't interrupt me, *honey*." He sits down, smiling contentedly, and begins eating his asparagus. After a pause he says, "And another thing, from now on we're going to alternate our dinner music because, frankly, and I don't think I'm alone here, I'm really tired of this Lawrence Welk shit." The scene ends as he eats the asparagus dangling on his fork while Jane and Carolyn sit speechless, bewildered by Lester's agency and his demands for equality in the Burnham home.

Lester clearly becomes more self-centered, demanding an equal say about the music the family listens to and willing to sacrifice the Burnhams' material well being so he can be happier. But tied to his discovery of what will make him happy is a criticism of the dominant cultural values that, he believes, have kept him from being happy and keep others from being happy as well. This cultural criticism becomes evident when he tries to get Carolyn to question the values that guide her life. Carolyn's emphasis on material things creates an emotional wall that blocks her ability to be intimate with either Lester or Jane and is a significant cause of her deteriorating relationship with each of them. The quality and number of the things she owns are more precious to her than what should be her most important relationships. In one scene she calls Jane an "ungrateful little brat" and slaps her across the face for, according to Carolyn, failing to appreciate the things her parents provide for her.

The tension that develops between Carolyn and Jane as a consequence of the mother's emphasis on material comfort over emotional and physical closeness becomes the central aspect of the tension between Carolyn and Lester. Over the years, the ability to consume expensive material goods to symbolize their success became the guiding principle of the couple's life together. Lester now rejects that principle. He decides to enjoy what he does rather than spend his days doing what he hates just so he can accumulate material things that do not enhance his quality of life. He experienced an awakening and now questions the cultural assumptions upon which he has based his life and upon which Carolyn bases hers. Like a religious convert, he wants Carolyn to become awakened, too. The tension between them is rooted in Lester's questioning those assumptions and Carolyn's determination to live by them. The tension is not merely the result of a middle-aged man going through a mid-life crisis who wants to forsake his wife and daughter so he can regress into adolescent irresponsibility and physical gratification. He still cares for Carolyn and regrets that they stopped living when they began to focus their lives on making a living, one that would enable them to engage in the insatiable consumption of trophies they could display to symbolize their success. The chasm that now divides them is most apparent in a scene with the two characters in the Burnham living room.

When Carolyn comes home one day she finds Lester sitting in a chair and drinking a bottle of beer. She walks into the room and he looks up at her and asks if she has done something different with herself. She sits down on the couch and he remarks on how great she looks as he moves next to her. He reminds her of when they used to leave parties early and go up on the roof and flash the traffic helicopter and make love. He begins to try to make love to her and she is receptive until she sees his beer bottle tipping and potentially spilling on the couch. She loses it about the beer and then he loses it about her concern for the couch. Her anxiety about the couch ruins the moment, apparently the first such moment they've had in years. He stands up and yells that it's just a couch. She explains that it is not *just* a couch but is a $4,000.00 sofa with Italian silk upholstery. Lester grabs a pillow and hits the sofa with it as he shouts, "It's-just-a-couch!" He then stops and says, "This isn't life." He glances around the room, gesturing at the furniture, and comments, "This is just stuff, and it's become more important to you than living. Well, honey, that's just nuts." Carolyn runs upstairs as Lester calls out, "I'm only trying to help you." He has awakened to the fact that for years he was tethered to a job he hated just so he could purchase material objects that have not created happiness for himself and his family, and he is frustrated because Carolyn continues to live in the spiritual darkness he now associates with the culture of consumption that had determined how he lived and continues to be the center of Carolyn's life.[5]

The most critical statement *American Beauty* makes about the kind of obsession with objects that Lester attempts to "help" Carolyn understand has become more important to her than living is not Lester's criticism of Carolyn. Rather, it's a character: Angela. Angela is a human version of the couch that Carolyn cares so much about, a manufactured product people are supposed to admire purely for its surface beauty, and Angela says she is willing to give herself to any photographer or other man who can help her become the coveted object she so much hopes to be. Angela's obsession with being adored by people in the same way that Carolyn adores her Italian-upholstered couch is evident in every scene that includes her. It is made most apparent, however, near the end of the film, when Ricky —

Lester (Kevin Spacey) and Carolyn (Annette Bening) Burnham in *American Beauty* (1999) just before their conflict over the $4,000 striped Italian-upholstered couch in the foreground that is a symbol of the values that come to divide them (Photofest).

the same character that sparks Lester's awakening — tells Angela the truth about who she is and what she represents.

Jane, Angela, Ricky and Lester are in the Burnham house the night of Lester's murder, and Carolyn and Colonel Fitts are headed to the house as well. All of the main characters are at or on their way to what becomes the crime scene. Ricky asks Jane to go to New York with him and Angela tells Jane she can't go. When Jane asks her why she even cares, Angela says, "Because you're my friend." Ricky tells Angela the truth: "She's not your friend. She's someone you use to feel better about yourself." Ricky recognizes that Angela puts Jane down and hangs out with her because she compares herself to her and feels better about herself by doing so. When Ricky speaks the truth about their relationship, Angela calls him a "psycho" and tells him to "go fuck" himself, which causes Jane to shout, "Shut up, bitch!" Angela responds, "Jane has a freak." Jane says, "Well, then so am I. We'll always be freaks, and we'll never be like other people, and you'll never be a freak because you're just too perfect." Angela says, "Yeah, well, at least I'm not ugly." "Yes, you are," Ricky says softly and calmly as he explains what makes her ugly: "And you're boring. And you're totally ordinary. And you know it." Angela is ordinary because she does not really care about people or the kind of beauty Ricky films in the common things most people take for granted, like a plastic bag swirling in the midst of a group of leaves blowing in the wind on a fall day, or the peaceful expressions some people have on their faces when they die. Angela is just one more object among many; nothing about her stands out and makes her unique. She's merely another ordinary product in a pretty package that will enable her to be bought and sold in the marketplace. Remove the wrapper and there's not much there. Angela, upset by the truth that Ricky speaks, storms out of the room as she gibes, "You two deserve each other."

The climax of the film follows shortly as the main characters converge on the Burnham home. Angela attempts to give herself to Lester downstairs. But when she reveals to him that she's a virgin, he's surprised and the revelation causes him to reach a new stage in his awakening. He sees her for the inexperienced and vulnerable teenage girl that she is and, while she leaves him alone while she goes to the bathroom, he admires old family photos that represent the quality moments the Burnhams once shared. While the kids and Lester are at the house, Carolyn is listening to a motivational tape while she drives home and plans to kill Lester with the new handgun she bought and has been practicing shooting at the local gun club. Likewise, Colonel Fitts removes one of his guns from its display case and heads next door to murder his neighbor. Earlier in the evening Fitts mistakenly thinks he sees Ricky performing oral sex on Lester in the Burnham garage when Ricky is actually leaning over a table and rolling a joint for Lester. Fitts beats Ricky, and his son sarcastically confesses to the act he did not commit before the colonel kicks him out of the house because, as he puts it, "I'd rather see you were dead than be a fucking faggot!" What drives the colonel's anger is his extreme homophobia, which is based on his own repressed homosexual desires, evident when he tries to kiss Lester while Lester lifts weights in his garage. When Lester rejects the colonel, the emotionally disturbed Fitts goes home to get one of his guns and Lester goes into the house, where he runs into Angela. While Angela is in the bathroom following her brief and unconsummated physical encounter with Lester, he looks at an old photograph of his family and says, "Man, oh man." Then the crack of a gunshot shatters the silence and we see blood splattered on the white wall-tile. Ricky and Jane rush downstairs and find Lester lying on the floor, dead. Ricky looks at him and smiles, seeming to know from the expression of "beauty" on Lester's face that he died during a moment of happiness, much like the expression Ricky once saw and filmed on a homeless woman who froze to death.[6] Colonel Fitts shoots Lester before Carolyn has a chance to discover if she could do it. The last thing we hear is Lester's voice say it is hard to be sad when there is so much beauty in the world.

On the surface, *American Beauty* is a movie about the mid-life crisis of an American male at the end of the twentieth century. Lester Burnham is unfulfilled at his job and in his marriage, arguably a sexually frustrated middle-class and middle-aged man who is tired of being a responsible employee, husband and father, a man who romanticizes the freedom he enjoyed in his youth and wants to relive those years by again flipping burgers, driving a hot car, smoking pot, listening to rock music and having sex with teenage girls. Read as an isolated cultural artifact, separated from other such texts and abstracted from time, place and circumstance, this is a legitimate, albeit obvious and simplistic, conclusion to make about *American Beauty*. But Lester Burnham's complaints about his job and his marriage, the apparent reasons for his mid-life crisis, are rooted in what are depicted in the film as larger social and cultural issues. Lester's criticisms of his marriage and his job are part of a broader critique of the normative values endemic to a consumer culture that, as we will see below, the *Fight Club* character Tyler Durden tells discontented and disaffected men has people "working jobs we hate so we can buy shit we don't need."[7] Lester does not blame Carolyn directly for their problems; he blames the consumer culture whose normative values Carolyn has internalized and accepted as natural. When Lester tells Carolyn it's "just nuts" to place so much value on "things" as she runs out of the room, and then yells after her, "I'm only trying to help you," he's clearly trying to get her to do what he has done: reject the normative values that pervade their lives and which Lester himself had promoted for decades working as a whore for the advertising industry.

Most viewers and professional critics who commented on *American Beauty* when it played in theaters for 10 months understood the cultural critique embedded in the film and applauded the movie for that critique. *American Beauty* enjoyed a long run in theaters from September of 1999 to June of 2000, and it won five Academy Awards (Best Picture, Best Director, Best Actor, Best Original Screenplay and Best Cinematography). The film also received overwhelmingly positive reviews and, based on the more than 350, 000 people who have rated it (most in 1999 and 2000) on the Internet Movie Database (IMDb) website, *American Beauty* was a big hit with the general public. Many of the critics and moviegoers understand aspects of the film's social and cultural critique and note the critique in various ways, and many remark on how the themes in the film resonate with their understanding of and experiences with materialism, work, and cultural expectations of conformity. Edward Guthmann of *The San Francisco Chronicle* summed up what many others expressed when he wrote of the film, "a dazzling tale of loneliness, desire and the hollowness of conformity."[8] Many moviegoers who felt compelled to comment on the film echo what one named Ryan says when he refers to some characters' "meaningless existence," although they don't usually proclaim, as he does, that the movie left them with "a cathartic sense of hope." Most don't say they experienced such an awakening, but many see the movie as accurately representing significant realities of American life. One named Mark, for example, comments, "Ahh, suburbia. That manifestation of mediocrity and anonymity in this, our post-industrial society."[9] Academics have analyzed the film in relation to how it deals adroitly with topics like anti-individuation forces (psychology) and religious parables (religious studies).[10] One reduces the film to being a crafty justification for the reassertion of male dominance via a character, Lester, who refuses to take responsibility for his actions and is falsely portrayed as a victim.[11]

The film's relatively few detractors — predominantly religious, academic and lay critics — either do not understand or do not like the film's cultural critique of middle-class suburban life and conspicuous consumption. Kathy Rabin, Vice President of Congregation Gates of Prayer, was asked by her Rabbi to share her criticism of the film with the organizations' Board of Trustees and then published her comments. She complains that there is nothing "beautiful" about *American Beauty*. "The American landscape described in this movie," she writes, "is not beautiful. It shows the destruction of family, the death of the American dream, [sic] it glorifies materialism, infidelity, drug use, guns and violence and accentuates society's obsession with sexuality."[12] Rabin clearly missed what most viewers seem to understand: that the film critiques materialism as the basis for one's existence, reveals the potentially catastrophic consequences associated with the ability to easily buy and readily use firearms, associates infidelity with characters' unhappiness and emptiness rather than with euphoria and fulfillment, and does not depict the death of an American dream of independent homeownership but critiques a dream based on materialism and self-absorbed behavior. Steve Vineberg, on the other hand, a theater professor at the College of the Holly Cross, trashes *American Beauty* and associates it with a string of critical films — *The Graduate* (1967), *Ordinary People* (1980) and *L.A. Confidential* (1997), to name just three — he does not care for that have been released since the late sixties. Neither *American Beauty* nor *The Graduate*, Vineberg writes, "have anything to say about America," and neither do the Pulitzer prize-winning novels and plays written by authors John Updike and Edward Albee, writers whose work critiques various aspects of American life.[13] For some, American culture has been on a downward spiral since the demise of Beaver Cleaver's family when the television show *Leave It Too Beaver* ended in 1963.

As Lester articulates his discontent with his job, with American consumer culture, and with his marriage that these detractors don't appreciate, he becomes critical of Carolyn's obsession with acquiring expensive material things and makes a connection between the unfulfilling work he does and the life as an American consumer he is expected to live. When he sees Ricky quit his job, he admires Ricky's action, the control Ricky has over his life, and Lester follows suit. His discontent reaches a point that he refuses to live with any longer, so he quits his job, blackmails his boss, and begins to assert himself in his marriage. He decides one day that he wants to be free of the control others have over him and to stop being a whore for the advertising industry just so he can earn a paycheck big enough to enable him to consume things like $4,000.00 Italian sofas, empty status symbols that Americans like Carolyn value over all else, including their relationships. Lester's new exercise regimen, the new control he has over his body, is symbolic of the new control he exhibits over his life in general.

Although Lester engages in what is arguably an illegal act when he blackmails his employer, he does not engage in a violent act against anyone in the company or destroy company property, nor does he assault Carolyn or contemplate an act of violence against her. He commits his one act that can be considered to be violent by throwing a plate of asparagus against a wall to get Carolyn and Jane to stop bickering. Carolyn, on the other hand, plans to kill Lester but Colonel Fitts beats her to it. Lester exhibits no evidence that his discontent or his previous lack of agency in his life has festered to the point where he wants to channel his discontent into destructive, violent acts against people or property. Although violence and the potential for violence permeate the film, it doesn't reside in the disaffected protagonist. That is not the case in two culturally significant films about discontented and disaffected men produced at the end of the century.

    In contrast to the non-violent, middle-aged Lester Burnham's mid-
life crisis and personal awakening, the young male protagonists in *Office
Space* (1999) and *Fight Club* (1999) are so numbed and disgruntled by the
tedious, meaningless work they do everyday they become dysfunctional
and need psychological help, although only one of them seeks it. Moreover,
in each film various characters are willing to channel their discontent in
ways the older Lester Burnham never considers. They engage in corporate
sabotage, property destruction and, in *Fight Club*, violence to themselves,
to others, and to American society in general. Real and symbolic acts of
violence and destruction in these films are associated with becoming self
aware and developing agency, the ability to wield control over one's life
by liberating oneself from the control of corporate managers and, in *Fight
Club*, from the normative values of a consumer culture that keeps people
working at jobs they don't like to enable them to purchase goods they don't
need. Where violence and destruction are central to *Fight Club*, they are
limited but clearly evident in *Office Space*.
    Office Space is a comedy based on the Milton series of short comedy
films created by Mike Judge in the early 1990s and aired on *Saturday Night
Live* a few years later. Milton Waddams (Stephen Root) is a character in
Office Space, but the male protagonist is Peter Gibbons (Ron Livingston).
Peter and the men in *Office Space* who work at the high-tech company
Initech face the possibility of being downsized by "The Bobs," two outside
evaluators much like the efficiency expert hired by the magazine where
Lester Burnham works in *American Beauty*. Peter is an extremely discontented and disaffected white-collar worker at Initech. Every day he adjusts
the dates in bank-account software to protect accounts from the year 2000
(Y2K) problem.[14] He has no control over what he does, how he does it, or
whether or not he has to work weekends. Peter fears he could lose his job
if he says "no" to his supervisor, Vice President Bill Lumbergh (Gary Cole),
when Lumbergh orders him to work weekends. Peter never asserts himself
and thinks he is a "pussy" for not being able to say no to his boss. Lumbergh pretty much controls Peter's life and enjoys the power he wields over
Peter and other Initech employees while he strolls through the maze of
office cubicles drinking coffee all day.[15]
    Tedious tasks, working for incompetent and oppressive management,
fear of losing one's job and, consequently, failing to assert oneself with
superiors (being a "pussy") are the major themes defined in *Office Space*
that make the employees unhappy with their jobs and with life generally.
The Bobs must discover which of these discontented workers do essential

tasks and which are expendable. Each employee schedules a meeting with The Bobs. Peter's meeting occurs the day after his first group therapy session with therapist Dr. Swanson (Mike McShane), who uses hypnosis to enable his patients to begin to deal with their problems. Peter starts going to these sessions because, as he tells the group, every day is the worst day of his life because he hates his job so much; each day, he says, only gets worse than the previous one. He asks the therapist, "Is there any way that you could sort of just zonk me out so that I don't know that I'm at work, in here (pointing to his head)? Could I come home and think that I've been fishing all day, or something?" Dr. Swanson tells Peter that treating patients with such mind-altering drugs is not what he does. Instead, he hypnotizes Peter. He instructs Peter to relax from his toes to his fingertips and tells him not to think about work, not to care about his job, and to remain in that state until the therapist snaps his fingers to wake him. But the obese therapist sweats bullets while Peter is going under, places his hand on his chest and falls over, dead from a heart attack. Other group members hopelessly try to revive Dr. Swanson while Peter sits in his chair, oblivious to what is going on around him.

The dead therapist, of course, cannot snap his fingers, so when Peter gets to work the next day he remains in a half-hypnotized state, still following Swanson's instruction not to care about his job. When he meets with The Bobs they ask him what he does at Initech. Peter tells them he doesn't do much. "It's not that I'm lazy," he says, "I just don't care." He tells them he has eight bosses and spends his days trying to avoid being harassed by them. The consultants like his honesty and take what he says as evidence that Peter's supervisors rather than Peter are the ones who are not essential to the company. Due to Peter's honesty and his ability to identify problems, The Bobs decide he is management material. Just before Peter walks out the door at the end of the interview he tells them, "I hope your firings go really well."

Peter is transformed through hypnosis. He is no longer the "pussy" he used to be. He becomes a self-confident and assertive young man who takes control of his life. Without permission, he tears down cubicle walls because he wants more space and a better view. He begins parking in Vice President Lumbergh's parking space. And he brings dead fish to the office and cleans them on reports scattered on his desk. Moreover, he enlists his friend Michael Bolton (David Herman) to help him develop and implement a scheme to siphon money out of company accounts and divert the money into an account the men create. The plan is to take the fractions of pennies in interest that should accumulate in people's accounts and channel those fractions into the new account. The fractions of pennies diverted from individual accounts are so small the men figure the discrepancies will never catch anyone's attention, especially when the company is so busy fixing problems associated with Y2K. If all goes as planed, these funds will enable the men to retire early and never have to work at tedious, boring, mind-numbing jobs again, or for egotistical and incompetent corporate bureaucrats like Bill Lumbergh.

Like Lester Burnham, then, Peter Gibbons has an awakening that transforms his life. The passive, insecure and depressed office worker becomes assertive, confident and content with himself as he takes control of his life and recruits others to work with him to implement a plan that will liberate them all from the mind-numbing and tedious work they must do to be able to pay the bills, and from the mediocre corporate bureaucrats who have had so much control over their lives. Like Wyatt and Billy in *Easy Rider*, Peter develops an illegal scheme that, if successful, could eventually enable him to live in his own time and in his own way.

Michael is willing to develop and implement the plan with Peter after he learns The Bobs decide the work that Michael does is not essential to the company and they will downsize him. The results of The Bobs' research, combined with the fact that Lumberg takes Milton's favorite red stapler, also cause Milton to take even more dramatic action against the company than Peter and Michael decide to take. Although The Bobs' conclusions about Michael and Milton are catalysts for the men's decisions to act, the underlying reasons for their actions have been festering for years in the nature of their work and in the way management has treated them.

The scenes where Michael recruits two of his colleagues and friends to help him implement the scheme reveal the men's animosity toward the company and their total lack of respect for the corporate bureaucrats who control their lives. When Peter first discusses the scheme to divert money with Michael, they talk about how Initech could never check all of the computer code associated with the thousands of accounts. Michael remarks, "Thumbs up their asses, thumbs up their asses." He says the only thing keeping him from helping Peter create the account and diverting the funds is the fact that he has a good job, meaning it is a job that pays the bills, not one that is rewarding in any way and that he looks forward to going to each day. Peter takes Michael to a bar and tells him that Initech is going to let him go. "It's not just about me and my dream of doing nothing," he tells Michael. "It's about all of us together." He continues,

"Michael," he says, "we don't have a lot of time on this earth. We weren't meant to spend it this way. Human beings were not meant to sit in little cubicles staring at computer screens all day, filling out useless forms and listening to eight different bosses drone on about mission statements." Peter reminds his friend that Michael has given five years of his life to the company and "you're going in tomorrow and they're going to throw you out in the street. You know why? So that Bill Lumberg's stock will go up a quarter of a point. Michael," he concludes, "let's make that stock go down. And let's take enough money out of that place so that we never, ever have to sit in a cubicle ever again." Michael tells Peter that he doesn't know the credit union software well enough but that their friend and colleague Samir Nagheenanajar (Ajay Naidu) does. To get Samir on board, Peter appeals to his libido and to the fact that The Bobs have targeted Samir, like Michael, for downsizing.

At first, Samir declines to cooperate for the same reason Michael resisted: he has a job that pays the bills. To combat Samir's resistance, Peter says, "I don't know about you guys, but I'm tired of being pushed around. Aren't you?" Samir replies, "Yes, Peter, but I'm not going to do anything illegal." Peter says, "Samir, this is Amer-ic-a. Come on. Sit down. This isn't Riyadh. You know we're not going to saw your hands off here, all right." Peter then makes the scheme appealing to Samir even if they get caught. "The worst thing they could ever do," Peter tells him, "is they would put you for a couple of months into a white-collar, minimum security resort. Shit, we should be so lucky. You know, they have conjugal visits there." "Really?" Samir asks. "Yes," Michael adds. Samir asks Michael what he thinks and Michael says the scheme is "actually pretty fail safe." Peter says, "Samir, you come here lookin' for a land of opportunity, and this is the knock of that opportunity." Peter then reveals Initech's plans to downsize Samir when he arrives at work in the morning and says Samir has two options: unemployment or early retirement. Peter asks Samir to choose which option he wants. Samir says he has one question: "In these conjugal visits, you can have sex with women?" "Yes," Peter assures him, "you sure can." Samir agrees.

Unaware of Peter's plan, The Bobs promote him when he arrives at work the next morning and assign him employees to supervise, evidence for what Lawrence J. Peter defined as the Peter Principle (the idea that in hierarchal corporate bureaucracies employees tend to get promoted to their levels of incompetency), and, quite likely, the reason Mike Judge chose to name his protagonist Peter. Peter is clearly just the latest in a long line of

Initech employees who have been promoted to positions they are not competent to hold.

How much Peter's animosity toward his employer has festered over the years is perhaps most evident in a scene with his new girlfriend, Joanna (Jennifer Aniston). He tells Joanna about the men's scheme to divert fractions of pennies into the account they created while Peter drives Joanna to meet a former Initech employee, Tom Smykowski (Richard Riehle). (Tom hated his job so much he tried to commit suicide one morning by sitting in his car with the engine running and the garage door closed. When Tom's wife found him sitting in the car he opened the garage door and quickly backed into the street, where another car crashed into him. The accident put him in a wheelchair. But Tom is glad to be disabled because he received a settlement that enabled him to quit his job at Initech.) In his conversation with Joanna, Peter reveals that he thinks corporations wield so much power over their employees, control their lives so thoroughly, that they are no different than Hitler's Nazis. He compares corporations like Initech and the Chotchkie's restaurant where Joanna waits tables to the Nazis because

In *Office Space* (1999), Peter Gibbons (Ron Livingston), left, holds the bat that he and co-workers Michael Bolton (David Herman), center, and Samir Nagheenanajar (Ajay Naidu), right, use to destroy a symbol of the mundane work and oppressive corporate culture at the high-tech company Initech (Photofest).

the corporations dictate what people do and oppress them as much as the Nazis oppressed European Jews before eventually executing them in death camps. When Peter tells Joanna about the scheme she says it sounds like stealing and thinks it's wrong. Peter gets angry and retorts, "It's not wrong! Initech is wrong! Initech is an evil corporation, all right. Chotchkie's is wrong. Doesn't it bother you that you have to get up in the morning and put on a bunch of pieces of flair?" (Joanna and the other Chotchkie waitresses have to wear a variety of pins on their clothes like ornaments on Christmas trees; the more such ornaments they wear, the more management likes them.) She says, "Yeah, but I'm not about to go in and start taking a bunch of money from the register." He says, "Well. Maybe you should. You know, the Nazis had pieces of flair they made the Jews wear." Bewildered, Joanna says, "What?" Upset that she doesn't share the depth of his animosity for corporate America, Peter ends the conversation by saying they don't need to talk about it now.

Despite the hatred and increasing anger that Peter demonstrates for the work he does, for Initech supervisors, and for corporate America in general, the only violent, physical act of destruction that he and his two disgruntled accomplices commit against the company is a symbolic one they engage in after work one day. While the men drive home in Peter's car, Peter tells Samir and Michael that he stole something, "a going away present." He drives to a field, where he parks the car and takes a fax machine and a baseball bat out of the trunk. Peter throws the perpetually malfunctioning fax machine on the ground and the men beat it with the bat, kick it, and even punch it with their bare knuckles, apparently too enraged to feel any pain. While they take out their frustrations and anger on this high-tech symbol of their boring and mundane existence, gangsta-rap music blasts in the background. We learn earlier that Michael listens to the same music when he commutes to and from work every day, and Michael more than the others beats on the machine without restraint and with no thought of the damage he could do to his bare hands. The other men have to pull him off of the machine, but even then he runs back to pound on it some more before they restrain him and usher him back to the car. The scene reveals that the potential for violence associated with the men's repetitive work and lack of agency at the office smolders just beneath the surface, ready to erupt into violent action given the right circumstances. After they destroy the Initech fax machine, the men go to Peter's apartment where they drink beer and dance to more gangsta rap.

Although the act of violence the men participate in that day is symbolic, the one Milton carries out is not, and his degrading experiences at Initech create in him the potential to commit similar acts of violence against other people and other businesses. When the company stops issuing Milton paychecks, and after Lumberg takes his favorite red stapler, Milton carries out a retaliatory act that no one would have anticipated the soft-spoken and mumbling Milton would be capable of committing. But his animosity toward the company has been festering much longer than that of Peter and his friends. How Initech's managers handle Milton's firing exemplifies the way the company has treated Milton for years.

The Bobs discover and tell management that Milton was actually laid off five years ago, but due to a computer glitch he kept receiving regular paychecks and no one ever told him he had been fired. The Bobs say they fixed the glitch but no one needs to bother telling Milton. He will simply stop receiving paychecks and "it will work itself out naturally," as one manager says; it is best to avoid direct confrontations. Like an old dog they no longer want, Initech's managers will simply stop feeding Milton and hope he walks away. Lumberg cannot restrain himself, however. He tells Milton he will need to talk with the people in payroll about the fact that he is no longer receiving paychecks. He also instructs Milton to move his desk, at first back against the cubicle wall and then down to the windowless basement where no one works. Once Milton relocates in the basement, Lumberg, still trying to push Milton out the door, tells him to do something about the cockroach problem employees supposedly discovered in the building. Lumberg says employees have seen cockroaches upstairs and he figures the roaches must be coming from the basement. He tells Milton to get a flashlight and a can of pesticide and use them to find and kill the roaches. Another supervisor enters the scene looking for Lumberg and tells him they need him upstairs because they have discovered "a major glitch in accounting, a lot of money missing." (Peter and his friends put a decimal point in the wrong place and hundreds of thousands of dollars, rather than fractions of pennies, are transferred out of accounts during the first couple of days.) After they leave, Milton sits alone in the dark, mumbling, "Okay, that's the last straw." Burying Milton in the basement and then forcing him to become the company's fictitious-cockroach buster pushes him to engage in militant acts against the corporation and to embrace militancy as a strategy to deal with even minor inconveniences in his life.

When the corporate building burns down along with everything in it at the end of the film, Peter sees Milton walking away from the crowd of people looking at the rubble that is Milton's creation. Peter smiles when he realizes that Milton is responsible for the blaze that destroys Initech and, along with it, any evidence of the scheme that Peter and his friends had designed and implemented. Peter gets a job with his neighbor Lawrence (Diedrich Bader), who works for the construction company that receives the contract to clear away the Initech debris. Peter finds the damaged red stapler that Bill Lumbergh took from Milton. Lawrence says it's beyond repair, but Peter tells him he knows someone who will want it even though it's damaged and burned. Michael and Samir drive up to see if Peter wants to go to lunch. The two men have secured new jobs at another technology company — back to the same monotony at another corporation. Michael offers to get Peter a job there, but Peter says no; he likes working outside doing something that provides him with exercise and allows him to breath the fresh air. After the two men leave, Peter shovels debris with Lawrence and says, "This isn't so bad, huh? Making bucks, gettin' exercise, workin' outside." Lawrence replies, "Fuckin' A." Peter repeats, slowly and with emphasis, "Fuck-in' A."

The significant psychological damage that prolonged employment at Initech causes Milton to destroy the corporation is evident in the final scene, for Milton now considers engaging in terrorist acts when he encounters even minor frustrations. Milton sits in a padded lounge chair at a resort on a beach somewhere in Latin America. He complains to a waiter, mumbling as is his custom, that they never get his drink orders straight. Milton says if it happens again he won't be leaving a tip. As the waiter walks away, Milton mumbles, "I could shut this whole resort down." Especially irritated about the large grains of salt on his Margarita glasses, he mumbles about putting strychnine in the guacamole as the camera moves out to give us a bird's-eye view of Milton lounging on the beach.

Office Space is a comedy designed to get us to laugh at the Initech employees' attitudes about their jobs and at the actions they take as a consequence of their frustrations. The success of the movie since its release, however, demonstrates that the characters' experiences and frustrations resonated with millions of viewers at the end of the century and continue to do so. The movie is often referred to as a cult film. If it is just that, the cult has a lot of members. *Entertainment Weekly* includes the film in the publication's list of the 100 best classic movies produced in the 25 years from 1983 to 2008.[16] In his review of the film, critic Roger Ebert writes that *Office Space* "is a comic cry of rage against the nightmare of modern office life." After he describes what life is like for the characters in the movie, Ebert ends his review by asking, "Reader, who has not felt the same?"[17] In a lengthy news article that appeared in *Entertainment Weekly* in 2003, the author writes, "we office drones depend on Mike Judge's 1999 cubicle comedy to carry us through the pay cycle." This writer notes that one formerly office-bound engineer began to work as a carpenter after seeing the film. Four years after *Office Space* was released it had "evolved into a stealth blockbuster," selling more than 2.6 million copies on DVD and VHS. A spokesperson at Fox Home Entertainment reported that the film was one of the top 30 movies the company ever released on DVD.[18] Of the 96, 451 people who had rated the film on the *IMDb* web site as of November, 2011, just under 72 percent had rated it as an eight or above on a scale of one to ten.[19] A decade after *Office Space* was released, Scott Bowles at *USA Today* noted that writer and director Mike Judge "connects so well with middle America." Why, Bowles explained, is because "His characters look like regular people. They spend their days at tedious jobs and nights sipping beer on their couches."[20] Cultural geographer Shaun Huston analyzes the film in relation to Americans' ambiguous attitudes about suburban landscapes, noting "the alienation, ennui, and emptiness of suburban existence" represented in the film and reinforced in literature and commentary about the suburbs.[21] A tribute to the movie exists at Bullshitjob.com and states, "Although classified as a comedy, it is actually more of a documentary for us here at BullshitJob.com, and quite frankly, an inspiration."[22]

While the characters in *Office Space* perpetrate no violence against people and Peter and his friends commit only a small, largely symbolic act of destruction against company property, the chronic abuse Milton takes from Bill Lumberg and other corporate bureaucrats over the years, combined with the drudgery of his job and his eventual dismissal, cause the mumbling office worker to take control of his life by destroying the company. It is clear, moreover, that Milton, empowered by his successful terrorist act against Initech, gets to the point where he entertains the possibility of committing violent, life-threatening acts against people who merely inconvenience him. If violent acts against property and people permeated *Office Space,* then the film would not be a comedy, for the centrality of such violence should make us think more seriously about its root causes, which are glaringly apparent in the third of these 1999 films, *Fight Club*.

In director David Fincher's film adaptation of author Chuck Palahniuk's novel *Fight Club* (1996), we are introduced to a psychologically disturbed, schizophrenic protagonist (Edward Norton) who leads an empty life of routine, unfulfilling and, arguably, morally reprehensible work. This nameless narrator in both the film and the book (Norton's character often speaks to us as a narrator) crunches numbers all day to figure out if the automaker he works for should recall vehicles with design flaws that cause death and maiming.[23] His job is to estimate how many accidents will occur, the cost of recalling and repairing the vehicles, the damage to life and property and, if the vehicles are not recalled and repaired, how much it will cost the company to settle with the victims' families. If the cost of recalling and repairing the vehicles is greater than that of the potential legal settlements, then the company will send some unknown passengers to their deaths and negotiate out-of-court settlements with the victims' families. This white, male, white-collar, college-educated and well-paid protagonist attempts to fill his meaningless and empty life with consumer goods. Failing to find purpose and happiness in his work or through unrestrained and conspicuous consumption, he attends group meetings for people with terminal diseases, hoping to find what he lacks by interacting with others who face certain death. These people live with the real physical and psychological pain of approaching death but the protagonist does not. Although he experiences for a short time what he refers to as "freedom" by interacting with these people, it does not last.[24]

It is through pain, however, that he finds meaning and direction in his life, if not happiness, and he experiences that pain by organizing and participating in a "fight club" that meets regularly in the basement of a bar. Here he learns that the pain he receives and inflicts through bareknuckled, no-holds-barred street fighting with other disaffected men is something real in a world of falsehoods. The protagonist organizes fight clubs in cities across the country and then enlists the support of the other alienated fight-club members as he transforms the fight clubs into terrorist cells. From these cells the protagonist launches "Project Mayhem," his attempt to destroy the organizations and, in the novel, the institutional history of the corporate-capitalist American society and the consumer culture against which these men rebel.

When we first meet the protagonist, much like Herman Melville's Bartleby character almost 150 years earlier, he carries out his daily routine without questioning what he does. In his case, however, his routine includes sending people to their deaths when his calculations reveal that the company will save money if it does not recall the potentially deadly time bombs masquerading as the company's vehicles traveling on American roads. At one point he euphemistically defines his job as being a "recall campaign coordinator."[25] Unlike Melville's Bartleby, however, and more extreme than any other character we have studied, when the protagonist develops agency at work and in society generally he becomes assertive, aggressive and militant, although his schizophrenia keeps him from realizing the degree to which his agency evolves.

The *Fight Club* protagonist becomes a militant leader of rebellion who, after first organizing the fight clubs and then developing them into gangs of merry pranksters who carry out lurid, humiliating acts against wealthy Americans engaged in decadent displays of conspicuous consumption, transforms the gangs into paramilitary cells. The purpose of these cells is not merely to engage in random acts of terror, but to carry out an organized assault on capitalist institutions and the institutional history of the American society that produced the conspicuous consumers, the immoral auto company, and the meaningless lives of the men who join the fight clubs and become involved in Project Mayhem, the nationwide and secret paramilitary organization under the sole command of the protagonist. The protagonist, through his alter ego Tyler Durden (Brad Pitt), becomes a fascist leader whose consciousness is raised and who then shapes the ideas and values of other disaffected men as they follow his orders without question like mindless drones. It is not surprising, then, that the film has been interpreted as fascist, as well as masochistic and misogynistic. The film and the novel can also be read as anti-capitalist and patriarchal. Author Chuck Palahniuk oversimplified the narrative when he said in an interview "the whole story is just a dark romance."[26]

In both the film and the novel the story is told from the perspective of the white-collar numbers cruncher, who is the schizophrenic protagonist and whose real name we never learn. We only learn the name of his alter ego, Tyler Durden. As the story unfolds, we discover that the protagonist has a condominium he fills with expensive furnishings. He can't distinguish himself from the material possessions that his mundane but well-paying job enables him to purchase. At one point the condo blows up (we later learn that he blows it up himself, as Tyler Durden), and when he talks with the investigating detective he tells the cop that he and his objects were one: "Look, nobody takes this more seriously than me. That condo was my life! Okay? I loved every stick of furniture in that place. That was not just a bunch of stuff that got destroyed. It was me!" In the movie he and the detective are on the phone and Tyler is in the background. At one point Tyler shouts, "Tell him the liberator who destroyed my property has realigned my perceptions." Tyler adds, "We reject the basic assumptions of civilization, especially the importance of material possessions."[27] Like Lester Burnham in *American Beauty*, the protagonist goes through an awakening as he realizes he is not free as long as his desire to acquire more things keeps him incarcerated in an office doing a job he hates.

The protagonist's life, then, is a shallow one centered on the job he hates and the things he owns. He unsuccessfully searches for something more, something meaningful and even spiritual, by trying to connect with other people. He goes to group meetings for people with terminal illnesses: the bowel-cancer people, the brain-parasite people, the melanoma people, the tuberculosis people, the testicular-cancer people. It is at one of these meetings that he meets Marla Singer (Helena Bonham Carter).[28]

Marla, too, is searching, and she is faking it at these meetings — especially the testicular cancer meetings — just like the protagonist. He confronts her, calls her a "tourist," and accuses her of honing in on his terminal-illness meetings. They quarrel about his claim that he somehow owns the rights to these meetings, and they settle the issue by dividing the meetings between them. She gets one; he gets another. He ends up with the testicular cancer group.[29] They divide the bowel cancer meetings; she takes the first and third Sundays of each month.

It quickly becomes evident that Tyler is everything the protagonist is not: tough, unkempt, principled, honest about himself and society, and a staunch critic of the materialistic values associated with the culture of consumption at the center of the protagonist's life. At one point in the novel the protagonist tells Marla what is also evident in the film: that he admires Tyler for his ability to act and his independence, traits the narrator lacks. "I love everything about Tyler Durden," he says, "his courage and his smarts. His nerve. Tyler is funny and charming and forceful and independent, and men look up to him and expect him to change the world. Tyler is capable and free and I am not."[30] Tyler is also an egotistical maniac who arguably sees himself as a god.

In the movie the protagonist believes he meets Tyler when he sits next to him on an airplane.[31] After the flight he arrives at his condominium to discover it has been destroyed. He has no friends or family to call, but he remembers that Tyler gave him his business card and he decides to call him. He arranges to meet Tyler for a drink at a bar. It is at this bar we learn that Tyler believes people have become enslaved by the things they own and that fighting can be a means to release men from being passive consumers of goods rather than active agents who shape their own lives.

The physical pain one encounters while fighting can wake men up and get them to see the reality of their desperate lives. The physical prowess one develops through fighting can cause men to realize they have the power to shape their own lives and society. The basement of the bar becomes the location of the first of a chain of fight clubs that the protagonist, as Tyler Durden, establishes across the country.

While they sit at a table and drink beer, the protagonist tells Tyler about the material possessions he lost in the fire; he emphasizes the loss of a sofa and his wardrobe. He says he had finally arrived at the point in his life where he knew that no matter what else happened he "had that sofa problem handled." (Carolyn Burnham could surely identify.) He adds that he "had a wardrobe that was getting very respectable, close to being complete." Tyler responds, emotionless and sarcastic, "Shit, man. Now it's all gone." Tyler then asks, "Do you know what a duvet is?" The protagonist tells Tyler it's a comforter and Tyler says, "A blanket." He adds, "Now, why do guys like you and I know what a duvet is? Is it essential to our survival in the hunter-gatherer sense of the word? *No.* What are we then?" The protagonist answers, "Consumers?" Tyler says, "Right. We are by-products of a lifestyle of obsession. Murder, crime, poverty: these things don't concern me. What concerns me are celebrity magazines, television with 500 channels, some guy's name on my underwear." The protagonist adds, "Martha Stewart." Tyler says, "Fuck Martha Stewart! Martha's polishing the brass on the Titanic; it's all going down, man." He adds, "I say, never be complete. Stop being perfect. I say, Let's evolve, let the chips fall where they may." The protagonist slips back into worrying about his lost possessions and says the insurance will probably take care of it. Tyler tells him, "The things you own end up owning you. But do what you like, man."

When they walk outside and stand in front of the entrance to the bar, Tyler knows the protagonist wants to ask him if he can stay at his place but is too passive and worried to say it. He tells him to "stop with the foreplay" and just ask. After he finally does, Tyler quickly says "Okay" and then walks out into the parking lot, where he coaxes the protagonist into hitting him. Once he does, the two men begin to fight and the Norton character likes the pain he experiences. It is something real. He could not actually feel the pain, experience the physical and emotional realities, of the people in the terminal-illness groups. But Tyler's kicks and punches begin to peel away the emotional, physical and spiritual numbness that has shrouded his existence as one of the living dead, one of many men working at a job he hates in order to sustain his existence and numb the reality of it with the narcotic of consumption. Tyler and the narrator then establish their first fight club in the basement of the bar. Droves of hopeless, disaffected men living uneventful, meaningless lives and employed at jobs they hate join the fight club. In the novel the narrator says, "You aren't alive anywhere like you're alive at fight club."[32]

As the club's membership grows and as Tyler establishes additional clubs in cities across the country, he molds the men into the nationwide paramilitary organization that the fight club members call Project Mayhem. Project Mayhem is a network of militant terrorist cell groups whose purpose is to destroy society. This is especially evident in the novel, where Palahniuk makes it clear the purpose of Project Mayhem is not merely to blow up the buildings that house America's capitalist institutions but also to destroy history, the institutional memory of the materialistic society of meaningless work and the inebriating consumer ethic that convinces men they need to keep working at unfulfilling jobs in order to be able to buy things they don't need. The members of Project Mayhem blow up skyscrapers that house various corporate headquarters. In the book they also set charges to topple the one-hundred-and-ninety-one-floor fictitious Parker-Morris Building. But Tyler's target is not merely the Parker-Morris building; it's what the building will destroy when it collapses: "the national museum which is Tyler's real target."[33] Tyler wants to destroy the institutional memory of the society he hates so that something new can emerge like a phoenix from the ashes. Although we don't know what shape that phoenix will take, it's clear it is supposed to be untainted by any memory of the society that's destroyed.

The film and the novel end differently, but the endings do not distract readers or viewers from the major themes of the story. The novel ends with the narrator institutionalized; he is incarcerated after killing two people: his boss and someone working for a mayor who is gathering information about the fight clubs so he can shut them down. "God" is the head shrink and people bring him food on trays and his medicine in cups. He says he is not ready to get out, but he hears voices whispering to him: "We miss you Mr. Durden"; "Everything's going according to plan"; "We're going to break up civilization so we can make something better of the world"; and "We look forward to getting you back."[34] Tyler doesn't kill his boss or anyone else directly in the movie, but with all the buildings that crumble in the final scene it is safe to assume that people must die in the rubble. In that scene the Norton character and Marla hold hands as they watch out the window of one skyscraper while the others around it crumble from the blasts planted by the men in Project Mayhem. The film ends when the Norton character — a bloody hole in his cheek created when he puts a gun in his mouth and fires it to try to kill Tyler and keep him from detonating the explosives — says to Marla as they watch the destruction: "You met me at a strange time in my life."

This final scene in the film with Marla and the protagonist holding hands as they watch Tyler's art work has no significance other than to put some kind of closure on their relationship, to let the audience believe that he gets the girl in the end. The important closing scene is the one just before Marla arrives at the top of the building, the scene with the protagonist and Tyler Durden as the protagonist has a conversation with himself about the major themes of the film. Tyler walks around the floor of the building waving a large handgun as the protagonist sits in an office chair with casters that enable Tyler to push him where he wants him to go. He is not restrained in the chair, but Tyler is able to keep him in the chair until the protagonist realizes, aware now that he is Tyler Durden, that he is actually the one with the gun. While the protagonist interacts with his alter ego, Tyler reminds him of how pathetic his life was before he allowed Tyler to take control of it. The Norton character says, "I'm thankful to you for everything you've done for me, but this is too much. I don't want this!" Tyler responds, "What do you want? Want to go back to the shit job, the fuckin' condo world watchin' sitcoms? Fuck you! I won't do it." It was only through the creation of Tyler Durden, only by creating an alternative personality whose values had not been shaped by the consumer ethic, that the protagonist was able to take control of his life and reject the values he had internalized, values that turned him into "IKEA Boy," imprisoned him in "condo world watchin' sit-coms," and worrying about whose name he had on his underwear. And only through his creation of Tyler, the man who is everything the protagonist is not, could the protagonist make a difference in society. As Tyler tells him while they wait for the bombs to explode: "Think of everything we've accomplished, man. Out these windows, we will view the collapse of financial history — one step closer to economic equilibrium." Destroying people's credit records in the blast would cause everyone to start over in the same financial position, a revolutionary prospect that could not be entertained by a man sitting on an IKEA sofa and confined to a condo by a culture that prescribes watching others act on sit-coms as being more rewarding and more important than actually acting in the world.

The closures on these texts, then, and the fact that the protagonist is schizophrenic are inconsequential to understanding the frustrations, anxieties and rage of the men, including the many characters that become Tyler's legion of paramilitary troops for Project Mayhem. Those frustrations and anxieties resonate with a general audience of predominantly young men. Reviewers discuss some of these issues in, for the most part, perfunctory ways. For a few years after the movie was released, people who viewed the film and read the novel addressed the issues on a web site with a chat room where young men, and some women, vented the same kind of rhetorical rage we get in the film and in the novel. Others at the site philosophized about the themes in the movie. These often enraged viewers and organic fight-club philosophers waged a rhetorical battle with each other about the meaning of the film, about American consumer culture, about going to real fight clubs, and about engaging in Project-Mayhem-like activities.[35] The popularity of the film and viewers' devotion to it is evident by the number of people who rate it on the *IMDb* web site. Of the 497, 938 viewers who had rated the 12-year-old movie on or before November 19, 2011, approximately 43 percent gave the film a 10. Just four

The affectless narrator's alter ego, Tyler Durden (Brad Pitt), center, in *Fight Club* (1999) watches with fight-club members and future Project Mayhem Space Monkeys as two other men develop consciousness and agency through the brutal fighting that club membership requires.

days later, the number of people who had rated *Fight Club* jumped to 499,518, evidence of the daily increasing number of fans. On that date 85.8 percent of viewers had rated the film at or above an eight on the site's one-to-ten scale.[36]

The themes in the film and the novel that resonate with many viewers and readers and elicit the rage that leads to violence include regimented, mundane and unappreciated work; individuals' lack of control over their lives; the spiritual emptiness and inequality in materialistic, capitalist society; a critique of a disintegrating patriarchal family structure but not of patriarchy itself, for women in the texts are objects and threatening and, according to Tyler Durden, not the answer to men's problems; and a sense of being disconnected from history and, therefore, in no way responsible for correcting the problems created by earlier generations.

The solution to the personal and social problems associated with these themes is violence against other individuals and against society. The thread that holds the texts together is violence as it is manifested in individual fights and in terrorist acts against society, and the rage that leads to violence. This rage and violence and the pain associated with the violence are liberating. It is important to note, however, that neither Palahniuk in the novel nor Fincher in the film presents a positive picture of the men who are supposed to be liberated by the violence. Tyler Durden makes some positive comments about the men's virtues, but they are portrayed as drones that merely do the will of their master, Tyler Durden. When the men become part of Project Mayhem Tyler calls them "space monkeys" because they do whatever they are supposed to do, whatever they are told, just like the actual space monkeys directed by Mission Control at NAASA. Moreover, in his attempt to destroy society and to stamp out all historical memory of it, Tyler treats his men like Henry Clay Frick, Henry Ford and other early captains of industry treated their employees: he efficiently and relentlessly utilizes the exploitative business principles and the regimented labor practices of the society he condemns.[37]

Although some of the men who join fight clubs are well-paid, white-collar workers like the narrator, most hold other, even less appealing service-sector jobs. In various scenes Palahniuk and Fincher depict the attitudes of both the server (worker) and the served (consumer or customer) associated with this type of work and reveal the potential rage smoldering in the service workers. At one point in the novel, and in a short scene in the film, Tyler gets the narrator a night job in the service sector working evenings at a hotel. Tyler tells him, "The job will stoke your class hatred."[38]

The narrator later comments on his work with Tyler at the hotel banquets: "Tyler and me, we've turned into the guerrilla terrorists of the service industry. Dinner party saboteurs."[39] In one scene Tyler tries to urinate in the soup before they serve it to the people dining at the hotel. The narrator tells Tyler to "go already." Tyler says he can't, and the narrator reminds him, "if the soup gets cold, they'll send it back."[40] Referring to the diners as "giants" the narrator explains,

> The giants, they'll send something back to the kitchen for no reason at all. They just want to see you run around for their money. A dinner like this, these banquet parties, they know the tip is already included in the bill so they treat you like dirt. We don't really take anything back to the kitchen. Move the Pommes Parisienne and the Asperges Hollandaise around the plate a little, serve it to someone else, and all of a sudden it's fine.[41]

Because the tip for the banquet is included in the cost of the dinner, the narrator notes that the "giants" attending the event "know they can't threaten you with the tip, to them you're just a cockroach."[42]

This overt class animosity is evident in the dialog in a number of scenes, perhaps most starkly in a later scene when the narrator and an assault team of "space monkeys" are on a mission to cut off the "steaming testicles" of the Seattle Police Commissioner because the Commissioner has begun to crack down on the fight clubs in his city. In the movie the scene takes place in the men's bathroom of a hotel where the Commissioner is attending a banquet. In the novel the space monkeys know the commissioner walks his dog in the park every night and they attack him there. The dialog is essentially the same. In the film Tyler waits for the Commissioner in the bathroom and takes him down from behind. The space monkeys hold him on the floor, pull down his pants, and wrap a rubber band around his testicles while other men watch the door. Tyler tells him to call off his investigation and issue a public statement stating there's no underground terrorist group. "Or," Tyler says, "these guys are going to take your balls. They're going to send one to the *New York Times* and one to the *L.A. Times*, press release style." We look at and listen to Tyler from the perspective of the Commissioner lying on his back on the floor and staring up into Tyler's face as Tyler threatens the Commissioner and lectures him about the fact that the men he is investigating are the ones who do everything necessary for society to function. Pressing his face up against the Commissioner's (up against the camera lens for the audience) Tyler says, "Look, the people you are after are the people you depend on. We cook your meals. We haul your trash. We connect your calls. We drive your ambulances. We guard you while you sleep. Do-Not-Fuck-With-Us!" The Commissioner nods his head in agreement and one of the men quickly slices the rubber band but leaves his testicles in place.

The nature and status of service-sector work is one of two major reasons in these texts for what Tyler refers to as the spiritual depression of the men. The other major reason for this spiritual depression is the rampant materialism and insatiable consumer ethic associated with it. In *Fight Club,* spiritual awareness is realized through brute force, force against others and against the corporate bureaucracies that make life so meaningless and not worth living. Those who possess some kind of connection to others, who are not wallowing in a sea of selfish and empty materialism based on relationships to objects rather than relationships with people, are those who face death by disease. It is not a coincidence that the terminal-illness group members come to the narrator's aid at the end of the novel when they learn he is schizophrenic and institutionalized; they can empathize with his disease, with his psychological pain. Many of the healthy members of the fight clubs, on the other hand, find some kind of transcendent meaning in the physical pain that results from their fights, and they simultaneously achieve momentary control over their world by inflicting excruciating pain on their opponents, controlling the outcomes of the fights.

They can also rise above the mundane, material existence of others by having "near-life experiences," by placing themselves in potentially deadly situations and showing no fear of death.[43] The fight club member referred to as the "mechanic" in the novel does this when he takes the narrator and three space monkeys for a joy ride in a Cadillac he hot-wires. Tyler drives the car in the movie. He drives against traffic on the wrong side of the freeway, willing to look death in the face and enjoy the thrill, not of defying death but of embracing the emotional truth found in it. Just like the physical and emotional pain of dying from cancer is real, just like the physical pain that results from fighting is real, facing the potential of dying in a head-on collision is real. It is something true in a world of falsehoods associated with the mind-numbing effects of American consumer culture. When Tyler drives against traffic and eventually takes his hands off the wheel, instructing the Ed Norton character to just let go, the car eventually veers off the road and crashes. Tyler sits on the ground in the rain with the injured Norton character on his lap and says, laughing, "We just had a near-life experience."

The most scathing critique of an American consumer culture that keeps people from really experiencing life is related to Tyler's business making soap. He manufactures soap out of human fat. He steals the fat from trash bins behind hospitals where doctors do plastic surgery. He sells the soap to upscale department stores. The purchasing agents for the cosmetic counters at these stores tell him their customers can't get enough of the soap, which is exactly the point. The customers live in a materialistic society in which the normative values they have internalized cause them to believe that happiness is tied to unlimited consumption, to never satiating their desires while they perpetually try to do just that. These consumers eat as much as they want to eat and they get fat. They pay expensive medical bills to have surgeons remove the fat so they can continue to consume, to eat as much as they want, which is never enough. Tyler then reprocesses their fat and sells it back to them in the form of soap they use to clean their skin. In the film the protagonist accompanies Tyler on one of these fat-finding missions one night. At one point in the novel the character known as the mechanic contemplates the fat they will harvest at a medical waste incinerator: "liposuctioned fat sucked out of the richest thighs in America. The richest, fattest thighs in the world." The narrator comments, "our goal is the big red bags of liposuctioned fat we'll haul back to Paper Street and render and mix with lye and rosemary and sell back to the very people who paid to have it sucked out." "At twenty bucks a bar," he explains, "these are the only folks who can afford it."[44]

Once the fat is collected, teams of Project Mayhem space monkeys make the soap for the Paper Street Soap Company, Tyler's business venture and a source of working capital for Project Mayhem. Working at Paper Street is no experiment in humanitarian labor practices, however, as the men work tediously and without question under Tyler's authoritarian industrial production. We view the process in the film but Palahniuk uses the narrator to describe it for us in the novel. The narrator comes home one day to discover "the house is filled with strangers that Tyler has accepted. All of them working. The whole first floor turns into a kitchen and a soap factory."[45] One night Tyler realizes the narrator is home and has seen the space monkeys making soap. Tyler enters his bedroom and tells him, "Don't bother them. They all know what to do. It's part of Project Mayhem. No one guy understands the whole plan, but each guy is trained to do one simple task perfectly."[46] The guys do not need to understand the entirety of the production process or the "whole plan" of Project Mayhem, for, the narrator tells us, "The rule in Project Mayhem is you have to trust Tyler."[47] Tyler's space-monkey laborers would be the envy of early twentieth-century scientific-management guru Frederick Taylor as they labor efficiently at individual tasks, mass-producing bars of soap for the greater good of Project Mayhem. The conditions designed by Tyler that the narrator describes and we view in the film could compete with those on the assembly line where Charlie Chaplin's character works drudgingly in the Depression-era film *Modern Times* (1936). The narrator explains:

> Teams of Project Mayhem guys render fat all day.... All night I hear other teams mix the lye and cut the bars and bake the bars of soap on cookie sheets, then wrap each bar in tissue and seal it with the Paper Street Soap Company label....
>
> I hug the walls, being a mouse trapped in this clockwork of silent men with the energy of trained monkeys, cooking and working and sleeping in teams. Pull a lever. Push a button. A team of space monkeys cooks meals all day, and all day, teams of space monkeys are eating out of the plastic bowls they brought with them.[48]

Paradoxically, then, in order for the space monkeys to be liberated from the monotony of American economic life and from the spiritual decadence associated with American consumer culture, they must be controlled by Tyler Durden. They must work tediously for and without questioning him. He must assign them tasks in the soap factory and in Project Mayhem, and they must carry out his orders without question. In their present psychological and physical condition they are merely clay to be shaped by the master sculptor. Tyler must shape their minds and their bodies. Only then will they experience spiritual liberation. The space monkeys and others have been indoctrinated with the wrong values. They are free only to consume and are shackled by the values of the consumer culture and to their mundane and meaningless jobs, the unfulfilling employment they must have in order to be able to consume. They are afraid to live without the materialism that corporate capitalism offers. Consequently, the mechanic asserts in the novel, "We have to show these men and women freedom by enslaving them, and show them courage by frightening them." "Imagine," he continues, "when we call a strike and everyone refuses to work until we redistribute the wealth of the world."[49]

In the novel the mechanic character speaks pure Tyler Durden dogma, illustrating the ideological indoctrination the space monkeys go through as they become members of Project Mayhem. Tyler speaks many of these lines himself in the film, usually defining his own dogma about work, the consumer ethic, weak families with absent fathers and, therefore, the decline of the patriarchal family structure. In a scene in the bathroom at

Tyler's dilapidated house, Tyler takes a bath while he talks with the Norton character, who sits on the floor against the wall. Tyler asks, "If you could fight anyone, who would you fight? The protagonist answers, "I'd fight my boss, probably." Tyler says, "I'd fight my dad." The protagonist says he doesn't know his father, that his dad left when he was six, married another woman, had more kids and followed the same routine about every six years in a new city. Tyler says it sounds like starting a business franchise. He then tells the protagonist that his father did not go to college and he insisted that Tyler go, so he did. When he graduated he called his father and asked him what he should do next. Tyler recalls that his father said, "I don't know. Get married." Tyler comments, "We're a generation raised by women. I'm not sure another woman is really the answer we need." The problem with women is they cannot raise men appropriately. The problem with men is they are not involved enough in raising their sons.

Tyler's simultaneous critique and reinforcement of patriarchy in the novel extends to his heavenly as well as his biological father. The mechanic tells the narrator, "If you're male and you're Christian and living in America, your father is your model for God. And if you never know your father, if your father bails out or dies or is never at home, what do you believe about God?"[50] The answer, the mechanic asserts, "is you spend your life searching for a father and God."[51] The problem, the narrator explains, is that "We are God's middle children, according to Tyler Durden, with no special place in history and no special attention."[52] Like a child who engages in unacceptable behavior in order to get the attention of a parent who otherwise ignores him, even though it will be negative attention for misbehaving, Tyler still tries to get his father's attention and the negative attention of God the Father. The narrator elaborates: "How Tyler saw it was that getting God's attention for being bad was better than getting no attention at all. Maybe because God's hate is better than His indifference."[53] Like the prodigal son, the narrator reflects, "The lower you fall, the higher you'll fly. The farther you run, the more God wants you back."[54] But the narrator's alter ego becomes a god-like figure himself in this twisted tale of discontented and disaffected men. Near the end of the novel we discover that Tyler desires to be the omnipotent father figure. He walks into a fight club at the Armory Bar, aware now that he is Tyler Durden, and tells us, "the crowds part zipper style when I walk in. To everybody there, I am Tyler Durden the Great and Powerful. God and father."[55]

Fathers, mothers, corporate capitalism and the consumer culture necessary for the system to continue are responsible for the problems that

Tyler's generation experiences, problems seemingly insurmountable for anyone other than a god-like figure with the power to destroy the system and free people from the cultural prison within which they are trapped. Tyler's generation is not responsible for fixing the problems because they did not create them. Rather, their responsibility is to destroy the system so a new one can be built from scratch.

In one scene in the film Tyler tells the fight club members gathered in the basement of the bar that his generation of men lives at a different historical moment than previous generations and that they are mad about the world their ancestors have created for them. As he paces the floor of the basement Tyler lectures, "I see in fight club the strongest and smartest men who ever lived. I see all this potential, and I see us squandering it." His anger mounting, Tyler continues: "God damn it, an entire generation pumping gas, waiting tables, slaves with white collars. Advertising has us chasing cars and clothes, working jobs we hate so we can buy shit we don't need." The men remain fixated on Tyler as he walks among them and defines their historical situation while also justifying and nurturing their anger. "We're the middle children of history, man. No purpose or place. We have no Great War, no Great Depression. Our Great War is a spiritual war. Our Great Depression is our lives." The men are not responsible for creating their situation but will be responsible for remaining in it now that they are learning the truth about it and about the false ideology associated with it. "We've all been raised on television," Tyler continues, "to believe that one day we'd all be millionaires and movie gods and rock stars. But we won't, and we're slowly learning that fact. And now we're *very, very* pissed off."

The wrath the men have for the state of the world extends beyond humanity and society and is also vented at nature, evident in a scene when the Ed Norton character beats another young man so severely he puts him in the hospital and disfigures him for life. When he beats the man to a literal bloody pulp we learn that he is not thinking about the man but about the environmental disasters his generation of men inherited from their ancestors. While he beat the man, he recalls later, "I felt like putting a bullet between the eyes of every panda that wouldn't screw to save its species. I wanted to open the dump valves on oil tankers and smother all those French beaches I'd never see. I wanted to breathe smoke." In the novel he adds, "What Tyler says about being the crap and the slaves of history, that's how I felt. I wanted to destroy everything beautiful I'd never have. Burn the Amazon rain forests. Pump chlorofluorocarbons straight up to gobble the ozone."[56] Rather than attempt to fix the problems his generation inherited, the narrator concludes that the young men must start fresh: "For thousands of years, human beings had screwed up and trashed and crapped on this planet, and now history expected me to clean up after everyone. I have to wash out and flatten my soup cans. And account for every drop of used motor oil."[57] Moreover, he continues, "I have to foot the bill for nuclear waste and buried gasoline tanks and landfilled toxic sludge dumped a generation before I was born."[58] While he beat the angel-faced kid until the kid's skin "turned black," the narrator remembers thinking of how "Birds and deer are a silly luxury, and all the fish should be floating." He recalls that he "wanted to burn the Louvre. I'd do the Elgin Marbles with a sledgehammer and wipe my ass with the *Mona Lisa*. This is my world, now." He then informs us, "It was at breakfast that morning that Tyler invented Project Mayhem." Why? Because, "We wanted to blast the world free of history."[59]

The cultural and economic context within which the protagonist's relationship with Marla Singer develops and unfolds; Tyler's consistent critiques of American consumer culture and of mundane and unappreciated labor; the purpose of Project Mayhem to destroy not only the buildings and institutions of American corporate-capitalist society but, in the novel, also to obliterate the institutional memory of that society by destroying the museums where that history is housed: these are the central themes of the *Fight Club* texts. That the novel ends with the narrator institutionalized and the film with Marla Singer and the Ed Norton character holding hands while they watch Tyler's mass destruction of the city from the top of a skyscraper take little if anything from the meaning of the story. The story is about the conditions in the protagonist's and the other men's lives, their lack of agency at work and in society generally, and the failure of the con-sumer ethic to fill the void created by their meaningless jobs and their inability to act. Consumption is a narcotic that, according to Tyler, keeps the men enslaved to an organized system controlled by corporate bureau-crats.

What these three films share is a focus on the experiences of the young and middle-aged male characters in relation to the social and economic history of the late twentieth century. They all work at jobs they hate and, in the beginning, demonstrate little or no control over their lives at work and in society generally. As the protagonists in the three films discover and develop their agency, they assert themselves at work and take control of their private lives. Together the films, the reviews, and the commentaries and blogs about the films demonstrate how central the issue of men's agency was in American society and culture at the end of the twentieth century. Although the films tell stories about individuals, the issues those individuals confront are shared by other characters in the films, and the issues resonate with many of the people who view the films. Lester Burnham, Peter Gibbons and Chuck Palahniuk's nameless protagonist are not alone, evinced clearly in the texts themselves, especially in *Office Space* and *Fight Club*, where the shared experiences of the discontented and disaffected men are central to the narratives. As Peter Gibbons takes control of his life, he enlists his discontented colleagues to join him in a joint effort to free the men from the control that Initech and its managers wield over them. Other employees, represented by characters like Milton and Tom, develop their own agency and take different and more radical steps to try to liberate themselves from their depressing existence at the company. Tom attempts suicide but is happy to be disabled in exchange for his freedom from Initech and its managers. Milton becomes militant, destroying the company and contemplating additional militant acts to deal with even the most minor frustrations of everyday life. The *Fight Club* protagonist develops an alternative personality who exercises total control of his own life and liberates himself from the control others have over him at work and from the normative values of a consumer culture that keeps him working at a job he hates in order to buy shit he doesn't need. But Tyler is not alone as he also wields dictatorial control over a growing mass of other discontented and disaffected men across the country, men whom he is supposedly liberating. Although we encounter Lester Burnham on a more individual basis at work and at home, his experiences on the job and with American consumer culture are similar to those of characters in the other films.

Conclusion

Disaffected Men and Resistance in American Culture

In the introduction I discuss why I chose not to make *Soured on the System* a book about whiteness (race) or masculinity (gender). It is important here, then, to make some final comments about gender and race in relation to my analysis of the films before I draw some conclusions about cultural representations of discontented and disaffected men in relation to agency, work, culture and society more generally.

Gender is significant in these films because the male characters have relationships with female characters, and those relationships are represented within the changing historical circumstances in which the films were produced. Where Betsy Rath is confined to the sphere of home and family in 1956, she is not the contented wife that Adlai Stevenson promoted in his 1955 commencement address to Smith College women. Rather, she displays signs of what a few years later Betty Friedan would define as someone suffering from the "feminine mystique." Betsy is frustrated with the responsibilities and the limits associated with being a traditional wife and mother, but she creates an entrepreneurial opportunity for herself and her husband even though she is confined to the home. Moreover, Betsy is the source of Tom's willingness to take risks and assert himself with Ralph Hopkins. A decade after the release of *The Man in the Gray Flannel Suit*, Mrs. Robinson pays with her happiness for conforming to the culturally prescribed role of affluent spouse and mother, trading her interests and her independence for upper–middle-class stability and respectability, the things that 30 years later Lester Burnham realizes he and his career-minded and success-oriented wife Carolyn likewise have been trading their happiness to achieve. Male characters often argue with the women in their lives, and their relationships sometimes add significantly to their frustrations. But those frustrations are subordinated to the major themes in the films' narratives that are associated with adjusting to or choosing to reject the work, lifestyle and values depicted as representing middle-class or upper–middle-class respectability. Single male characters like Peter Gibbons in *Office Space* and the *Fight Club* narrator have relationships with women — the latter relationship an interesting and complicated one deserving an article on the subject — but the male characters' discontent and disaffection are rooted in their work and, in *Fight Club* as in *American Beauty*, in the cultural norms about achieving happiness through consumption that the men come to reject.

In some cases, moreover, where men channel their discontent into direct and even militant acts that can be defined as "masculine," emphasizing masculinity as an abstract but primary historical force motivating and even determining men's actions can distract our attention from the evidence regarding the conditions that elicit the aggression and the militancy; it can also keep us from realizing that female as well as male characters, especially in postwar films, also sometimes engage in aggressive and militant acts when they are expected to continually submit to the often patriarchal authority in their personal relationships but also to the institutional authority of mid-level corporate bureaucrats who deny them agency on the job. Betsy Rath is more assertive than Tom, Carolyn Burnham more so than Lester prior to the latter's awakening. And women are represented as assertive but not masculine in films as diverse as *Adam's Rib* (1949), *Johnny Guitar* (1954), *Giant* (1956), *Norma Rae* (1979), *9 to 5* (1980), *Sudden Impact* (the fourth in the Dirty Harry series, 1983), *Thelma and Louise* (1991), *Panic Room* (2002) and *The Brave One* (2007), to name a mere handful.

Race is not as central as gender to the films studied here because the characters, for the most part, are placed in homogeneous white environments, and the characters' whiteness is not associated with their discontent or their disaffection, with the exception of Joe Curran, any more than the race of Melville's Bartleby contributes to the character's discontent and disaffection in 1853. Race is portrayed as a significant issue in *Dirty Harry* and *Joe* as a consequence of historical changes propelling integration and white reactions to it in the 1960s and early 1970s. In neither of those films, however, is race the central theme, despite Joe's rants against African Americans, the integration of his neighborhood, and "liberals" who are "queers" and "nigger lovers." The scapegoats in the film that become Joe's and Bill's targets are the white youth who are members of the counterculture. These young men and women choose not to spend their days engaged in the kind of tedious labor Joe must do each day so he can pay the bills, nor do they choose to push paper as Bill does, producing nothing of use but receiving what to blue-collar Joe is an unfathomable salary. *Dirty Harry* and its sequels incorporate themes associated with race into their narratives, but the major theme is Harry's struggle against the restrictive government bureaucracies that are the public equivalent of the private corporate bureaucracies that a character like Tom Rath must negotiate at the United Broadcasting Corporation and that Peter Gibbons and his friends deal with at Initech more than 40 years later. Race and race relations are central themes in a variety of films I do not discuss, such as *Shaft* (1971) and other blaxploitation films of the 1970s, *Mississippi Burning* (1988), *Do the Right Thing* (1989), *White Men Can't Jump* (1992), *Crash* (2004) and many other films released in recent decades, just as race is the subject of earlier postwar films such as *No Way Out* (1950), *The Blackboard Jungle* (1955), *To Kill a Mockingbird* (1962), and *Guess Who's Coming to Dinner* (1967). Issues related to race are significant in most of the films studied here, however, only by their absence: by the exclusion of minority characters in the corporations and in the neighborhoods where, despite a half century of historical change, white characters like Tom Rath, Benjamin Braddock and Lester Burnham spend their days interacting only with other white characters. The characters' whiteness, then, is not associated with their discontent and disaffection. Rather, the nature of everyday life and culture and men's lack of agency and independence in society result in the men's discontent and disaffection even though the characters represent privileged, white middle-class men. These disaffected characters become non-conformists and, in the late twentieth century, more willing to take militant actions as a result of their discontent.

While I was finishing *Soured on the System*, over the course of several months in 2011, men and women throughout the world demonstrated their discontent with corrupt, bureaucratic and often oppressive political systems. They believed these systems, even the "democratic" ones, served the personal and career interests of the officials who administered them and the economic interests of those with the means and the connections to most influence the officials. Throughout the world people participated in protest movements against authoritarian governments in various Arab countries, against the corrupt and undemocratic political practices of Vladimir Putin and his United Russia party, against austerity measures imposed on average citizens in European countries for problems they did not create, and against the connections between Wall Street and Washington that enabled corporate executives at financial institutions deemed "too big to fail" to destroy their companies and the security of their employees, average investors, and independent home owners while they continued to earn obscene bonuses. For these reasons *Time Magazine* named "The Protestor" the publication's Person of the Year for 2011. The magazine cover reads: "The Protester: From the Arab Spring to Athens, from Occupy Wall Street to Moscow." This discontent has not lain dormant in the United States or elsewhere. The only people who may have been asleep are those who take for granted the compliance of others over whom they have authority. The potential protesters are always thinking and stirring even when they are not storming the barricades or occupying Wall or some other street in another city.[1]

The preceding pages are devoted to an analysis of cultural representations of discontented and predominantly white middle-class men in the United States — not the folks most people think about when they hear or read the word "protester." And, indeed, none of the characters studied here represent the kind of organized public protesters recognized by *Time*, not even the ones in a counterculture film like *Easy Rider*. For the most part, the characters' protests are personal and individual. The Space Monkeys in *Fight Club* are organized into the arguably fascist cells associated with Tyler Durden's Project Mayhem, but these are tightly controlled and militant armies of destruction rather than peaceful protesters. White middle-class men have participated in the occupy Wall Street protests, however, and in the various "occupy" demonstrations in American cities and in various other countries. While the "occupy" protests are associated with the political left, middle-class men have also participated in the Tea Party movement associated with a libertarian strain of American conservatism on the political right. Although these actual discontented men on both the left and the right of the American political spectrum might argue about various themes in the films studied here, most would no doubt be sympathetic to the theme of declining independence and individual control in an increasingly organized society and in a culture that values conformity and dependence rather than individualism and independence. These films reveal cultural manifestations of discontent and disaffection associated with declining independence and growing corporate and government bureaucracies endemic to American society and culture since the late nineteenth century and expressed in a variety of ways and associated with particular and changing historical circumstances.

I argue in chapter three that films like *Dirty Harry* and *Joe* and *The Graduate* and *Easy Rider* represent similar complaints but dissimilar solutions as to what to do about those complaints. Benjamin Braddock and Wyatt and Billy drop out because they reject the inevitability of making Tom Rath's decision to be "9-to-5 and home and family" in the postwar corporate order. Harry Callahan hates "the system" and despises the local government bureaucrats who administer it and the federal officials who enact laws that protect criminals' rights and restrain Harry from doing what he believes he must to protect the citizens of San Francisco from serial killers like Scorpio. Harry is the exception because, unlike most characters studied here, he deals with inefficient government bureaucrats and laws that restrain his ability to act, where most characters exist in the private sector; they adapt to the assumed inevitabilities of everyday life in the postwar corporate order and American consumer culture or reject the idea that their options are naturally limited by that order and that culture. Harry's solution is not to drop out like the affectless Benjamin Braddock, but to take direct and independent action. Joe Curran and Bill Compton do likewise but as private citizens, and they target the scapegoats they blame for what Joe defines as the decline of American society and culture. Militancy in later films like *Office Space* and *Fight Club* is directed at the corporate order itself rather than at Joe Curran's scapegoats.

While the objects of these male characters' frustrations change in the second half of the twentieth century in relation to relatively short-term historical developments, the sources of their discontent are in large part rooted in the significant social and structural changes that began in the nineteenth century. At that time most of America's emerging corporate elite would have agreed with John D. Rockefeller when he remarked, approvingly, that the interests and influence of corporations like his own Standard Oil had supplanted those of individual citizens and, sounding a lot like the character Joe Morse talking to his brother Leo in *Force of Evil*, announced, "The day of combination is here to stay. Individualism has gone, never to return."[2] Implied in Rockefeller's statement is the assumption that individuals in the new corporate order that he and other captains of industry and finance were creating would out of necessity submit to the increasingly centralized authority of men like himself, authority that became embedded in the corporate and public institutions associated with modern life, accelerated by the Great Depression and World War II, and represented in postwar films by characters like Henry F. Potter and Ralph Hopkins.[3]

   The male characters studied here that refuse to accept the inevitability and the necessity of devoting one's life to mundane and unfulfilling labor, the consumption of goods as material and psychological compensation for that labor, and the idea that they must submit to the centralized and bureaucratic authority associated with the modern corporate order engage in individual protests, even if, like Bartleby in the 1850s and Benjamin Braddock in the 1960s, their protests begin when they merely "prefer not" to participate. Characters are represented as responding to events and conditions endemic to American society and culture at the moments when the films were created. I demonstrate in the introduction, however, and in my analysis of postwar films during decades of significant historical change, that characters' resistance to the necessity of selling themselves as commodities in a labor market, to conspicuous consumption as a way of life, and to the conformity associated with corporate life have deep roots in American culture.[4]

   Recall that in *Easy Rider* it is the independent farmer-rancher that Wyatt speaks of approvingly for doing his own thing in his own time. Likewise, significant elements of what in the sixties people began to refer to as the counterculture are, paradoxically, central elements of American culture represented not only in counterculture films like *Easy Rider* and later movies like *Fight Club* and *American Beauty*, but in the nonfictional works of Herman Melville's nineteenth-century contemporary Henry David Thoreau. In the context of the rapidly industrializing economy that Melville and Thoreau experienced, with the spread of wage labor, centralized production in factories, and the expansion of commercial agriculture and the railroad that caused Thoreau to complain "we don't ride on the railroad; it rides upon us," this icon of American letters preached the gospel of economy in individuals' lives. Foreshadowing *Fight Club's* Tyler Durden character 150 years later, Thoreau argued that unnecessary consumption keeps one from actually living, which he defined not as mere biological existence but as emotionally fulfilling and even spiritual. Living, for Thoreau, involved spending as much time as possible engaged in more rewarding and fulfilling activities than working for the purpose of acquiring money to buy things rather than for personal satisfaction. He therefore preferred not to drink coffee or tea and other such luxuries. Thoreau told his hardworking Irish neighbor that he could be more independent if he practiced the kind of economy that Thoreau himself embraced. Thoreau informed the Irish immigrant he could build a "tight, light and clean house," a "palace" like Thoreau's small cabin at Walden for about what the man was paying in annual rent for the "ruin" he currently occupied. As part of his recipe for independent and fulfilling living Thoreau recalls instructing the man, "I did not use tea, nor coffee, nor butter, nor milk, nor fresh meat, and so did not have to work to get them; again, as I did not work hard, I did not have to eat hard, and it cost me but a trifle for my food; but as he began with tea, and coffee, and butter, and milk, and beef, he had to work hard to pay for them, and when he had worked hard he had to eat hard again to repair the waste of his system..., for he was discontented and wasted his life into the bargain." Thoreau argued that "the only true America is that country where you are at liberty to pursue such a mode of life as may enable you to do without these" things.[5]

If this icon of American letters experienced one day of modern corporate life he would surely be glad that he lived when he did. Thoreau and his neighbor had far more control over what they did and how they did it than exists in the modern corporate bureaucracies represented in films like *The Man in the Gray Flannel Suit*, *Office Space* and *Fight Club*. The physical labor that both Thoreau and his neighbor did inherently involves more independence and individual control over the labor process than the regimented and organized labor designed and directed by the managerial class depicted in such films. At the end of *Office Space,* Peter Gibbons trades corporate life in a cubicle for the more backbreaking labor on a construction site, but he is glad to make the trade because, although he is not an independent artisan, he can talk with his friend while he works and does not have to be on the lookout for the corporate-cubicle Gestapo (to use Peter's Nazi analogy) masquerading as managers who roam the isles and halls at Initech.

In his recent book *Shop Class as Soulcraft: an Inquiry into the Value of Work,* the political philosopher Matthew Crawford writes that representations of modern white-collar work in American popular culture resonate with the employees who have little input into what they do and how they do it. "The popularity of *Dilbert*, *The Office*, and any number of other pop-culture windows on cubicle life," he asserts, "attests to the dark absurdism with which many Americans have come to view their white-collar work."[6] Crawford analyzes the sociological and psychological literature on office work and notes that, as Tom Rath discovers in *The Man in the Gray Flannel Suit*, independent thought and action are the last things managers want. Consequently, Crawford writes, "it is the office rather than the job site that has seen the advent of speech codes, diversity workshops, and other forms of higher regulation."[7] In such environments authority rests not with individuals but with that abstract entity the corporation: "something that can sustain the kind of moral demands normally associated with culture."[8] Crawford notes that independence disappears as people submit to the kind of "soft authority" that the nineteenth-century French student of American democracy, Alexis de Tocqueville, warned could happen in the United States if people came to see the democratic state, rather than themselves, as the source of authority in their lives and then willingly submitted to that authority. Evidence pervades American popular culture that causes me to agree with Crawford when he asserts, "a case could be made that it is now outsized corporations, more than government, that exercise this peculiarly enervating form of authority in our lives, through work."[9] Although Inspector "Dirty" Harry Callahan struggles with local government bureaucrats, far more often in American culture we find representations of people dissatisfied with the nature of their work and with the control that corporate, rather than government, bureaucrats wield over them.

This study of cultural representations of discontented and disaffected men reveals a significant irony endemic to American culture. Henry David Thoreau is an icon of American letters because of his emphasis on independence and his insistence that the best government is the one that governs least, supposedly enabling people by the absence of government to be free and independent. But surely if the radically independent Thoreau had lived in the late twentieth century he would have recognized that the kind of "soft authority" about which his contemporary Alexis de Tocqueville warned became associated with corporate institutions as much as and if not more than government institutions. Captains of industry like John D. Rockefeller, not government officials, acknowledged and applauded the decline of individualism and independence that they promoted as they created corporate combinations they controlled and as they subordinated individuals to the managerial structures they designed. The irony lies in the fact that American political rhetoric continues to associate declining individualism and independence with increasing government authority and influence when even the men who created corporate behemoths like Standard Oil acknowledged the declining individualism and independence that resulted from their increasing control of people's lives on the job and their influence in society generally.[10]

In the films studied here, "Dirty" Harry Callahan confronts government bureaucracies because he works for them and takes his orders from the government bureaucrats who manage him. Tom Rath, Lester Burnham and other characters, however, confront corporate rather than government bureaucracies because they work for corporations and take their orders from the corporate bureaucrats who manage them. Ironically, while corporate authority and people's *dependence on corporations* increased in the twentieth century, political rhetoric warning about citizens' *dependence on government* and about the virtues of corporate capitalism increased, and this rhetorical change occurred in the context of the developing cold war with the Soviet Union.

This anti-government, pro-corporate rhetoric served to infuse corporate interests into American political ideology. Traditional rhetoric about freeing people from the power of corporations (a.k.a. "the trusts" represented by Woodrow Wilson's New Freedom speeches) and about using government to subordinate private, corporate interests to public needs (represented by Theodore Roosevelt's New Nationalism speeches) increasingly became marginalized and associated with the political Left as politicians like Adlai Stevenson and Harry Truman became anti-communist corporate liberals and shed the old Progressive label that Franklin Roosevelt's Vice President Henry Wallace adopted, like Theodore Roosevelt in 1912, as a third-party candidate in 1948. In addition to the two major parties, this changing political rhetoric became institutionalized in the Screen Actors Guild (SAG), whose president and friendly HUAC witness would later become president of the United States. Guild President (1947–1952 and 1959) Ronald Reagan, whom the FBI gave the code name Confidential Informant T-10, led the charge for SAG to adopt as official language a statement that declared the Hollywood union rejected communism and embraced capitalism. Although prominent actors such as Humphrey Bogart, Lauren Bacall, Katharine Hepburn, Danny Kay, John Garfield, Lucille Ball and Groucho Marx, among others, opposed having SAG adopt the statement and formed the Committee for the First Amendment, Reagan's group won the battle within SAG.[11] In addition to SAG and the two major political parties, the anti-communist and pro-corporate political culture of the early postwar years also became institutionalized in law and in corporations' relationships with organized labor, evident, for example, in the non-communist affidavits required by the Taft Hartley Act (1947). In this context, which included the very real possibility of writers, actors and directors showing up on a Hollywood blacklist, men's problems with work and corporate power were increasingly represented as individual problems associated with negotiating corporate life as in *The Man in the Gray Flannel Suit* rather than as structural problems related to corporate power and influence veiled in a postwar gangster film like

Force of Evil or evident in earlier films such as *The Grapes of Wrath* in 1940 or even in *It's a Wonderful Life* as late as 1946.[12]

While democracy became indelibly fused with corporate capitalism in postwar political ideology, postwar films reveal significant anxieties about corporate authority, far more so than government authority, in people's lives. In 1955, Adlai Stevenson emphasized to Smith College women that men had to adapt to their lack of independence in the postwar corporate order and that women's role was to create a refuge for men in the American home, a place where men could be rejuvenated in order to go forth and negotiate corporate life another day, submitting to the authority of corporate managers and corporate culture rather than asserting their own independent thoughts and taking their own independent actions. On the big screen just a decade earlier, George Bailey and his father Peter are represented in *It's a Wonderful Life* as confronting and opposing Henry F. Potter's attempts to combine all financial interests in his hands and subordinate Bedfod Falls' citizens to his authority. But one year after Stevenson spoke at Smith, a discontented Tom Rath is portrayed in *The Man in the Gray Flannel Suit* as leerily negotiating his way within a corporate culture that demands conformity of thought and behavior, and he is disaffected because of it. Veiled in the gunslinger and gangster films of the politically charged anti-communist culture of these years, characters and coalitions of characters continue to confront and oppose the influence and authority that representatives of the postwar corporate order have over their lives, much like George Bailey is depicted as confronting and opposing Potter in the first year following World War II. Male characters in films of the fifties and sixties follow Tom Rath's lead. But by the late sixties and early seventies direct critiques of the lack of independence associated with accepting and submitting to corporate authority and to consumption as just compensation for that acceptance and that submission become increasingly evident in American films. This theme continues in the last decades of the twentieth century and intensifies in films like *American Beauty*, *Office Space* and *Fight Club*. The popularity of such films reveals that many Americans, if no longer their politicians, understand that corporate control of their lives at work and corporate influence in society and culture generally can be as or more detrimental to their independence and their liberties as government control and influence can. Perhaps politicians' approval ratings would go up if they watched more movies and realized that Americans would like their politicians, as well as themselves, to be more independent of such influence.[13]

Chapter Notes

Introduction

1. Herman Melville, "Bartleby, the Scrivener: A Story of Wall Street," in Norman Foerster and Robert P. Falk, eds., *Eight American Writers: An Anthology of American Literature* (New York: W.W. Norton & Company, Inc., 1963), 808–839; *The Graduate*, Mike Nichols, director (Embassy Pictures Corporation, 1967, DVD); Chuck Palahniuk, *Fight Club* (New York: Henry Holt and Company, LLC, 1996); *Fight Club,* David Fincher, director (Twentieth Century–Fox, 1999, DVD).

2. For a discussion of these early social problem films see Kay Sloan, "Silent Cinema as Social Criticism: Front Page Movies," in Steven Mintz and Randy W. Roberts, eds., *Hollywood's America: Twentieth-Century America Through Film*, 4th ed. (West Sussex, UK: Wiley-Blackwell, 2010), 31–42.

3. On Depression-era rhetorical themes see Robert S. McElvaine, *The Great Depression: America, 1929–1941* (New York: Times Books, 1993), 196–223. For abridged copies of relevant Theodore Roosevelt and Woodrow Wilson speeches, see Leon Fink, ed., *Major Problems in the Gilded Age and the Progressive Era* (New York: Houghton Mifflin Company, 2011), 392–395. A copy of the entire Roosevelt speech can be accessed on the TeachingAmericanHistory.org website at the following URL: http://teachingamericanhistory.org/library/index.asp? document=501. Wilson's entire speech can be accessed at the following page of the same web site: http://teachingamericanhistory. org/library/index.asp?document=165.

4. Adlai Stevenson, "A Purpose for Modern Woman," reprinted in *Woman's Home Companion* (September, 1955): 29–31. Paul Goodman, *Growing Up Absurd: Problems of Youth in the Organized System* (New York: Random House, 1956); C. Wright Mills, *The Power*

Elite (New York: Oxford University Press, 1956); Mills, *White Collar: The American Middle Classes* (New York: Oxford University Press, 1951); David Riesman, *The Lonely Crowd: A Study of the Changing American Character* (New Haven: Yale University Press, 1950); and William H. Whyte, Jr., *The Organization Man* (New York: Simon & Schuster, 1956).

5. On Hollywood's role in promoting a culture of consumption beginning in the 1920s see Lary May, *Screening Out the Past: the Birth of Mass Culture and the Motion Picture Industry* (Chicago: University of Chicago Press, 1980), 197–236. On the expansion of consumption and its impact on postwar social and political life, see Lizabeth Cohen, *A Consumer' Republic: The Politics of Mass Consumption in Postwar America* (New York: Alfred A, Knopf, 2003).

6. For discussions of films as significant historical, cultural and sociological texts consult the following sources: Mintz and Roberts, *Hollywood's America*, x–xi, and John Bodnar, *Blue-Collar Hollywood: Liberalism, Democracy, and Working People in American Film* (Baltimore: The Johns Hopkins University Press, 2003), xv–xxxiv.

7. On the key tenets of manhood and masculinity see Michael S. Kimmel, *Manhood in America: A Cultural History*, 2nd ed. (New York: Oxford University Press, 2006), 5, 6, 81–82, 218, and Sally Robinson, *Marked Men: White Masculinity in Crisis* (New York: Columbia University Press, 2000), 30–31.

8. Kimmel, 5, 6, 81–82, and 218. While Kimmel writes that his "book is a history of the Self-Made Man" (6), he also states that "American manhood is many histories at once" (5), evidence of the problem associated with an over-generalized concept of either manhood or masculinity.

9. Ibid., 5. At one point Kimmel discusses homophobia in relation to the concept of mas-

culinity and states that homophobia is not about an actual fear of homosexuals. He quotes positively David Leverenz, who claims, "The word 'faggot' has nothing to do with homosexual experience or even with fears of homosexuals." Rather, "It comes out of the depths of manhood: a label of ultimate contempt for anyone who seems sissy, untough, uncool." (See Kimmel, 5 and Leverenz, "Manhood, Humiliation and Public Life: Some Stories," *Southwest Review* 71 (Fall 1986), 455. We will see that when insecure men and the characters who represent them in a film like *American Beauty* (1999) use such terms it can have everything to do with fears of homosexuality, especially when a homophobic man must confront the reality that he has homosexual tendencies himself, and those fears can have violent and tragic consequences.

10. Kimmel, 218.

11. This is more the case with Sally Robinson's work on the 1970s and 1980s than it is with Michael Kimmel's. Robinson notes her disagreements with historian Gail Bederman regarding the issue of white masculinity in crisis. In her book *Manliness and Civilization: a Cultural History of Gender and Race in the United States, 1880–1917* (Chicago: University of Chicago Press, 1995), Bederman does not see white masculinity "in crisis" at the turn of the century despite significant threats to men's status due in large part to the changing corporate-capitalist society, changing women's roles, the successes of black athletes like boxer Jack Johnson and other factors. But white masculinity was not in crisis because white men never gave up on the idea that they should maintain a privileged position of power in American civilization. Clearly, evidence in Robinson's own work demonstrates that many men in the late twentieth century still held to that same belief. In contrast to Bederman, Robinson's study of American culture from the late sixties through the eighties emphasizes that cultural representations of white men are images of men "wounded." She consequently asks, "Why is it that when dominant masculinity becomes visible, it becomes visible as *wounded*?" (Italics in the original, 12.) Although she writes that the "question of whether dominant masculinity is 'really' in crisis is, in my view, moot," she uses much of the introduction of *Marked Men* to argue that crisis is central to our understanding of white masculinity, especially after 1968, and asserts that "the rhetoric of crisis is flexible enough to accommodate a range of narratives driven by competing investments and intentions" (11).

For Robinson, then, white masculinity itself

is not the central theme that drives her narrative. Rather, white-masculinity "in crisis" is the protagonist in the narrative. A problem with Robinson's crisis scenario — evident in her disagreement with Bederman — and, more specifically, with her idea that masculinity only becomes visible when "wounded," when actual men who think they are wounded create novels, films and other cultural artifacts in which they reveal their wounds, is that men, even white men, have felt wounded and displayed wounds of various sorts throughout history. Robinson assumes that some groups are "authentically disempowered" and "visibly wounded" and representations of them as such are "legitimate," but representations of others — e. g., white males — as in some ways disempowered and in some ways wounded are cultural fabrications rather than cultural representations of actual wounds and actual disempowerment. (For Robinson's discussion of Bederman see *Marked Men*, 9–10.)

We cannot assume that all white men are created equal and are represented as such, and that cultural representations of them are some kind of anthropomorphized totality, a force with identifiable human agency negotiating with other such forces in a cultural marketplace for representations of authentic disempowerment and for the most visible and legitimate wounds. It is indisputable that white men have been in privileged, institutionalized positions of power throughout American history, but other white men with less privilege — sometimes just as racist and just as sexist but sometimes not — have often done battle, shed blood, and died in events like labor conflicts and anti-war protests in which they challenged the privileges and power of their white-male counterparts. Too much focus on one relatively short historical period can cause us to elevate the significance of those years over others that may be equally revealing and demonstrate continuity as well as change. Kimmel, for example, writes of manhood and masculinity over a span of two centuries, and he has "visible" evidence of men acting in relation to the values associated with the concepts.

Whites in general and white men in particular have held and do hold positions of significant privilege in education, business, politics and other areas of American life, and they sometimes may not even be aware of their privileged positions. But evidence in the cultural texts analyzed in *Soured on the System* reveals that with the corporate reconstruction of American capitalism that took place in the late nineteenth century and accelerated throughout the twentieth, white men are depicted as losing power on the job and as losing influence in society, not just to women and minorities in the late twentieth century, but to the system itself, a system that has shaped the lives of all Americans and American culture. That system is not an anthropomorphized entity like "white masculinity," for the corporate bureaucrats who manage the system are real people wielding real influence over public policymakers and over the real people they manage on the job.

12. See Robinson, for example, but also Fred Pfeil, *White Guys: Studies in Postmodern Domination and Difference* (New York: Verso, 1995). Two books that focus on the post-civil rights and post-women's movement years but are not confined by the concept of white masculinity as Robinson's work is are Susan Faludi, *Stiffed: The Betrayal of the American Man* (New York: Perennial Harper Collins, 2000), and Faludi, *Backlash: The Undeclared War against American Women* (Crown Publishers, 1991).

13. Pfeil, 257; Robinson, 14.

14. Robinson, 14. Although I disagree with his emphasis on the concepts of manhood and masculinity acting in society, Kimmel's work demonstrates that the concept of white masculinity existed well before the successes of the civil rights and women's movements of the late twentieth century.

15. This is also the reason that *Soured on the System* is not a study of the more general concept of whiteness, neither the historical construction of whiteness, nor white Americans' "possessive investment in whiteness," nor whiteness as it is represented in Hollywood films. For monographs on these subjects see the following works: David R. Roediger, *The Wages of Whiteness: Race and the Making of the American Working Class* (London and New York: Verso, 1991); George Lipsitz, *The Possessive Investment in Whiteness: How White People Profit from Identity Politics* (Philadelphia: Temple University Press, 1998); Daniel Bernardi, ed., *The Birth of Whiteness: Race and the Emergence of U.S. Cinema* (New Brunswick, Rutgers University Press, 1996); and Daniel Bernardi, editor, *Classic Hollywood, Classic Whiteness* (Minneapolis and London: University of Minnesota Press, 2001).

16. *Clockwatchers*, directed by Jill Sprecher (Goldcrest Films International, 1997, DVD), and *Office Space*, directed by Mike Judge (Twentieth Century–Fox, 1999, DVD). Only one small act of Luddite-like behavior occurs in *Clockwatchers*: a character uses paper clips to sabotage a copy machine; although another

character defaces the top of her desk, it would be a stretch to refer to carving words in the top of a desk as "Luddite-like." In *Office Space* one employee steals a fax machine that always breaks down and he and his co-workers beat it with a baseball bat and their fists and feet in an open field; another disgruntled employee destroys the office building by burning it to the ground at the end of the film.

17. Melville, "Bartleby," in Foerster and Falk, 814–820.

18. Ibid., 818 and 815.

19. Ibid., 808.

20. Ibid., 820.

21. For discussions and interpretations of realism and naturalism consult the following works: Eric J. Sundquist, ed., *American Realism: New Essays* (Baltimore: Johns Hopkins University Press, 1982); Donald Pizer, ed., *Documents of American Realism and Naturalism* (Carbondale: Southern Illinois University Press, 1998); Pizer, *Twentieth-Century American Literary Naturalism: An Interpretation* (Carbondale: Southern Illinois University Press, 1982); Amy Kaplan, *The Social Construction of American Realism* (Chicago: University of Chicago Press, 1988).

22. Pizer, ed., *Documents of American Realism and Naturalism*, 167–174; William E. Cain, "Presence and Power in *McTeague*," in Sundquist ed., *American Realism*, 199–214.

23. Eileen Bowser, *The Transformation of Cinema, 1907–1915*, *History of the American Cinema*, vol. 2, Charles Harpole, general ed. (Berkeley: University of California Press, 1994), 121–136; Steven J. Ross, *Working-Class Hollywood: Silent Film and the Shaping of Class in* America (Princeton: Princeton University Press, 1998, 30–33; May, *Screening Out the Past*, 43–59.

24. Sloan, "Silent Cinema as Social Criticism," 31–42.

25. Rockefeller is quoted in Alan Trachtenberg, *The Incorporation of America: Culture and Society in the Gilded Age* (New York: Hill and Wang, 1982), 86; for events that influenced Howells and others see 191–193. Trachtenberg writes of realism, "On the whole, realism portrayed the old American credo of a community of autonomous natural beings as a sad illusion" (202).

26. Ibid., 201. Richard Hofstadter, *The Age of Reform: from Bryan to F.D.R.* (New York: Vintage Books, 1954).

27. For Roosevelt and Wilson see Fink, ed., 392–395, http://teachingamericanhistory.org /library/index.asp?document=501. And http:// teachingamericanhistory.org/library/index. asp?document=165. For a copy of Debs' 1912

speech "Capitalism and Socialism," see the following URL at the *Eugene V. Debs Internet Archive*: http://www.marxists.org/archive/debs/works/1912/appeal.htm.

28. On declining illiteracy rates see http://nces.ed.gov/naal/lit_history.asp

29. William Dean Howells, *A Traveler from Altruria* (New York: Sagamore Press, 1957).

30. Edward Bellamy, *Looking Backward: 2000–1887* (New York: Signet Classic, 2000).

31. A collection of essays on *Looking Backward* is Daphne Patai, editor, *Looking Backward, 1988–1888: Essays on Edward Bellamy* (Amherst: University of Massachusetts Press, 1988). On the novel's popular appeal Csaba Toth writes the following: "*Looking Backward* sold half a million copies by 1900 and became the second largest selling book in nineteenth-century America. Translated into countless languages, it reached hundreds of thousands more in Germany, England, Hungary, Russia, Japan, Indonesia, New Zealand, and many other countries. A utopia of cross-class appeal, *Looking Backward* not only converted workers to socialism but also mobilized middle-class reformers to face the 'social question' and spawned a cross-class movement demanding change." See Toth, "Utopianism as Americanism," *American Quarterly*, vol. 45, No. 4 (December 1993): 649–658; for the quotation see 653. On Bellamy's influence on European utopianism see Toth, "The Transatlantic Dialogue: 19th-Century American Utopianism and Europe," dissertation (University of Minnesota, 1992), 217 pages.

32. David Montgomery, *Workers Control in America: Studies in the History of Work, Technology, and Labor Struggles* (Cambridge: Cambridge University Press, 1979); Walter Licht, *Industrializing America: the Nineteenth Century* (Baltimore: Johns Hopkins University Press, 1995); Leon Fink, *Workingmen's Democracy: the Knights of Labor and American Democracy* (Urbana: University of Illinois Press, 1983).

33. See the following web sites on the committee and for a sample of the testimony that the committee solicited and heard: http://www.archives.gov/legislative/guide/house/chapter-09-labor.html; http://www.archives.gov/legislative/guide/house/chapter-09-labor.html; http://historymatters.gmu.edu/d/27/mule spinner; accessed on November 23, 2011.

34. Christopher P. Wilson, *White Collar Fictions: Class and Social Representation in American Literature, 1885–1925* (Athens and London: University of Georgia Press, 1992), 2.

35. Sinclair Lewis, *Babbitt* (New York: Harcourt, Brace and Company, 1922).

36. Sherwood Anderson, *Winesburg, Ohio* (New York: Bantam classic, 1995).

37. Ross, 3–10; for quotations see 7.

38. Sloan, "Silent Cinema as Social Criticism," 31–42; Robert Sklar, *Movie-Made America: A Cultural History of American Movies* (New York: Vintage Books, 1976), 141–157; Douglas Gomery, "U.S. Film Exhibition: the Formation of a Big Business," in Tino Balio, editor, *The American Film Industry*, rev. ed. (Madison: University of Wisconsin Press, 1985), 218–228.

39. I agree with Robert Sklar when he notes that while we should be skeptical of industry insiders' assertions that consumer demand decides film content, there is some truth to those assertions. See Sklar, *Movie-Made America*, 148. I would add that while production companies might understand that the public will pay to see movies about particular events or social situations, the companies can meet that demand without necessarily allowing writers and directors to tell the stories in ways the companies disapprove of.

40. Gregory W. Bush, "Like 'A Drop of Water in the Stream of Life': Moving Images of Mass Man from Griffith to Vidor," *Journal of American Studies*, Vol. 25, No. 2 (August, 1991): 213–234. Bush relates *The Crowd* to elements of both realism and romanticism.

41. William Leuchtenburg, *The Perils of Prosperity, 1914–1932*, 2nd edition (Chicago: University of Chicago Press, 1993). For information on the postwar strike wave, conditions for steel workers, and general strife in 1919, consult John Whiteclay Chambers, *The Tyranny of Change: America in the Progressive Era, 1890–1920*, 268–273.

42. May, *Screening Out the Past*, 200–236. For May's discussion of *The Affairs of Anatol* see 210–211; for his discussion of *Forbidden Fruit* see 213.

43. *The Crowd*, directed by King Vidor (Metro-Goldwyn Mayer, 1928, VHS).

44. For a general discussion of movies and values during the Depression see McElvaine, *The Great Depression*, 196–223.

45. Michael E. Parrish, *Anxious Decades: America in Prosperity and Depression, 1920–1941* (New York: W. W. Norton, 1994), 71–93.

46. Quoted in McElvaine, *The Great Depression*, 212.

47. Ibid.

48. John Steinbeck, *The Grapes of Wrath* (New York: Penguin Books, 1976), 40–50.

49. On the impact of local strikes see Robert T. Schultz, *Conflict and Change: Min-*

neapolis *Truck Drivers Make a Dent in the New Deal* (Prospect Heights, Illinois: Waveland Press, 2000). On opposition to the New Deal generally see McElvaine, *The Great Depression,* 224–249.

50. *Our Daily Bread,* directed by King Vidor (King W. Vidor Productions, 1934, VHS); also see McElvaine's short discussion of the film in *The Great Depression,* 209.

51. On the merger movement at the turn of the century see Chambers, *Tyranny of Change,* 54–56.

52. Godfrey Hodgson, *America in our Time: from World War II to Nixon—What Happened and Why* (Princeton: Princeton University Press, 2005), 67–98.

53. Steven J. Whitfield, *The Culture of the Cold War* (Baltimore: The Johns Hopkins University Press, 1991); see particularly the chapter, "Reeling: The Politics of Film," 127–151.

54. Jonathan Munby, *Public Enemies, Public Heroes: Screening the Gangster from Little Caesar to Touch of Evil* (Chicago: University of Chicago Press, 1999), 132.

55. Ibid., 133.

56. On the significance of Vietnam see Richard Slotkin, *Gunfighter Nation: The Myth of the Frontier in Twentieth-Century America* (Norman: University of Oklahoma Press, 1998), 489–623; and Randy Roberts and David Welky, "Coming to Terms with the Vietnam War: A Sacred Mission: Oliver Stone and Vietnam," in Mintz and Roberts, 281–300. An excellent book on the impact of the cold war on a variety of popular cultural artifacts is Tom Engelhardt, *The End of Victory Culture: Cold War America and the Disillusioning of a Generation* (Amherst: University of Massachusetts Press, 1995).

Chapter 1

1. John Patrick Diggins, *Proud Decades: America in War and Peace, 1941–1960* (New York: W.W. Norton & Company, 1988); Arthur M. Schlesinger, Jr., *The Vital Center: the Politics of Freedom* (Boston: Houghton Mifflin, 1949); Godfrey Hodgson, *America in Our Time* (Garden City, New York: Doubleday, 1976); David W. Noble, *Death of a Nation: American Culture and the End of Exceptionalism* (Minneapolis: University of Minnesota Press, 2002), and *The End of American History: Democracy, Capitalism, and the Metaphor of Two Worlds in Anglo-American Historical Writing, 1880–1980* (Minneapolis: University of Minnesota Press, 1985); Lary May, ed., *Recasting America: Cul-*

ture and Politics in the Age of Cold War (Chicago: University of Chicago Press, 1989), and *The Big Tomorrow: Hollywood and the Politics of the American Way* (Chicago: University of Chicago Press, 2000); George Lipsitz, *A Rainbow at Midnight: Labor and Culture in the 1940s* (Urban: University of Illinois, 1994); Steven Whitfield, *The Culture of the Cold War* (Baltimore: Johns Hopkins, 1991); Walter LaFeber, *America, Russia and the Cold War, 1945–1966* (New York: Wiley, 1967); Robert T. Schultz, "Illusions of Consensus and Conformity in Postwar America," *American History,* ABC-CLIO, 2011, Web; accessed December 5, 2011.

2. On women and gender in these years see the various essays in Joanne Meyerowitz, ed., *Not June Cleaver: Women and Gender in Postwar America, 1945–1960* (Philadelphia: Temple University Press, 1994). On film see the following: John Belton, *American Cinema/ American Culture* (New York: McGraw Hill, 1994), 184–204; Whitfield, 127–152; and Robert T. Schultz, "Celluloid History: Postwar Society in Postwar Popular Culture," *American Studies* 31 (spring, 1990): 41–63. Essays on a variety of cultural fronts are collected in Lary May, ed., *Recasting America.*

3. John Milton Cooper, *Pivotal Decades: The United States, 1900–1920* (New York: W. W. Norton & Company, 1990), 169–189.

4. Sloan Wilson, *The Man in the Gray Flannel Suit* (New York: Simon & Schuster, 1955); Adlai Stevenson, "A Purpose for Modern Woman," reprinted in *Woman's Home Companion* (September, 1955): 29–31.

5. Paul Goodman, *Growing Up Absurd: Problems of Youth in the Organized System* (New York: Random House, 1956). For an analysis of masculinity and politics during these years and examples of the vocabulary associated with masculinity that politicians used, see K. A. Cuordileone, "'Politics in an Age of Anxiety': Cold War Political Culture and the Crisis in American Masculinity, 1949–1960," *The Journal of American History,* 87 (September 2000): 515–545. On the postwar culture of domestic "containment" see Elaine Tyler May, *Homeward Bound: American Families in the Cold War Era* (New York: Basic Books, 1988). May describes the various sources of official and general propaganda designed to try to contain women in the domestic sphere during these years just as the United States government tried to contain communism abroad.

6. Joanne Meyerowitz discusses how the author of *The Feminine Mystique,* Betty Friedan, emphasized the constraints on women in the postwar years. Although this emphasis served

the necessary purpose of drawing attention to a domestic ideology that limited women's roles, it led to misconceptions about a homogeneous experience for American women. Later thoughtful, informed and needed studies on the extent of the domestic ideology reveal how pervasive it was, while other excellent studies reveal the cracks in the ideology and the diversity of women's experiences and values in the 1940s and 1950s. Betty Friedan, *The Feminine Mystique* (New York: W.W. Norton, 1963). See Meyerowitz, ed., *Not June Cleaver*, 1–16, for a discussion of the historiography on this issue. The best monograph on the pervasiveness of the domestic ideology is Elaine May, *Homeward Bound*. See the multiple essays in *Not June Cleaver* that demonstrate the diversity of women's activities outside of the domestic sphere.

7. In *The American Dream and the Popular Novel* (Boston: Routledge & K. Paul, 1985), Elizabeth Long recognizes in her study of popular literature that a narrative transformation occurs in postwar fiction. The individual hero no longer conquers the world but becomes integrated into the postwar corporate order. Long writes, "The individual becomes dependent — on others for happiness, on an organization for a job." Long defines "the 'corporate-suburban' model, in which the hero's saga is less one of conquest than one of integration of a set of disparate tasks and roles." She continues, "Work is described as a fragmented and abstract process rather than as the creation of a product, and the hero's search for a sphere of mastery draws him increasingly into the private world of domestic and affective ties." I agree with Long that a narrative transformation occurs and is represented in Sloan's novel and in the film. I would disagree, however, that the domestic sphere is one of potential mastery for Tom, for he continually negotiates with Betsy in that sphere just as he negotiates with managers at UBC. If a master exists in the Rath home, it is arguably Betsy, who argues aggressively and effectively with Tom about where they should live, where he should work, and how he should behave in relation to the other gray-suits, even with the business empire builder, Mr. Hopkins. For quotation see page 82.

8. Friedan.

9. Stevenson, 29–31.

10. Ibid.

11. Goodman, ix.

12. Ibid., 3.

13. Ibid., 14. Other monograph-length critiques of postwar society and culture published in these years include William H.

Whyte, Jr., *The Organization Man* (New York: Simon & Schuster, 1956); C. Wright Mills, *The Power Elite* (New York: Oxford University Press, 1956); C. Wright Mills, *White Collar: The American Middle Classes* (New York: Oxford University Press, 1951); and David Riesman, *The Lonely Crowd: A Study of the Changing American Character* (New Haven: Yale University Press, 1950).

14. Gail Bederman, *Manliness and Civilization: A Cultural History of Gender and Race in the United States, 1880–1917* (Chicago: University of Chicago Press, 1995).

15. On the social problem films of the Progressive era see Kay Sloan, "Silent Cinema as Social Criticism: Front Page Movies," in Steven Mintz and Randy W. Roberts, eds., *Hollywood's America: Twentieth-Century America through Film* (West Sussex: Wiley Blackwell, UK, 2010). On Progressive-era Presidents Roosevelt and Wilson see Cooper, 31–219. On the changing nature of Franklin Roosevelt's political rhetoric over the course of the Depression, and on Long and Sinclair and various Depression-era films, see Robert S. McElvaine, *The Great Depression: America, 1929–1941* (New York: Random House, 1993), 196–263. On the changing political economy and World War II, see the various primary documents collected in Colin Gordon, ed., *Major Problems in American History, 1920–1945* (Boston: Houghton Mifflin, 1999), 429–436; in the same volume also see the essays by Michael Sherry, "Mobilization and Militarization," 436–443, and Alan Brinkley, "World War II and American Liberalism," 443–451.

16. Frank Capra, *The Name Above the Title: An Autobiography* (New York, 1971), 383.

17. *Variety Film Reviews, 1943–1948*, 7 (New York, 1983), December 25, 1946.

18. *Time*, December 23, 1946, 54.

19. Capra, 401.

20. Ibid., 383–384; on *It's a Wonderful Life* see Schultz, "Celluloid History," 41–63.

21. *It's a Wonderful Life*, Frank Capra, director (Liberty Films, 1946, DVD); all dialog and scene descriptions are taken from this film.

22. Raymond Carney, *American Vision: The Films of Frank Capra* (Hanover, New Hampshire: University Press of New England, 1986), 381.

23. Ibid., 388.

24. *The Man in the Gray Flannel Suit*, Nunnally Johnson, director (Twentieth Century–Fox, 1956, DVD); all dialog and scene descriptions are taken from this film.

25. The fact that these values reside in Betsy and that she is the staunchest advocate

of them reveals that the values are not associated only with concepts of manhood and masculinity.

26. On the origins of the concept of true womanhood see Barbara Welter, "The Cult of True Womanhood, 1820–1860," *American Quarterly* 18 (1966): 151–174; Kathryn Kish Sklar, *Catharine Beecher: A Study in American Domesticity* (New Haven: Yale University Press, 1973); and Nancy Cott, *The Bonds of Womanhood: "Woman's Sphere" in New England, 1780–1835*, 2nd ed. (New Haven: Yale University Press, 1997). Two primary sources that reveal some elite men's defense of the ideology in the late nineteenth and early twentieth centuries are Grover Cleveland, "Woman's Mission and Woman's Clubs," *Ladies Home Journal*, vol. 22 (May, 1905), and George G. Vest, "Remarks," *Congressional Record*, 49th Congress, 2nd Sess., 25 January 25, 1887, 986.

27. Bederman, 170–216.

28. Goodman, 14.

29. Wilson, 159–166.

30. Scenes like this one and the earlier one when Betsy tells Tom she is "ashamed" of him caused the reviewer for *Variety* to criticize Jennifer Jones' portrayal of Betsy. The reviewer wanted Jones to demonstrate more love for Tom, commenting, "She alternates between being the nagging wife and the frustrated lover, except that she rarely conveys the impression of being in love with her husband in the first place." Betsy's husband demonstrates no initiative to better their lot in life, no imagination about what to do with the estate he inherits, and reveals to Betsy that he had an extended affair with a young Italian woman and fathered a child with her during the war while Betsy waited loyally and patiently at home. But the *Variety* reviewer wanted Betsy to express more love to her almost emotionless husband. See the review in *Variety*, April 4, 1956, 6. For a review with a more positive take on Jennifer Jones' work see Bosley Crowther, "Screen: Mature, Tender and Touching," *New York Times*, April 13, 1956, 21; accessed with Proquest Historical Newspapers. Male reviewers in the fifties often expressed dissatisfaction with female characters that did not meet their expectations of what those characters should be and how they should act. This will become glaringly apparent in reviews of *Johnny Guitar* (1954) in chapter two, a western with two women in traditionally male roles.

31. Crowther, 21.

32. Mae Tinee, "'Man in Gray Flannel Suit' Is Delightful," *Chicago Daily Tribune*, April 5, 1956, C10; accessed with ProQuest Historical Newspapers.

33. David Seed, "The Flight from the Good Life: *Fahrenheit 451* in the Context of Postwar American Dystopias," *Journal of American Studies*, vol. 28, No. 2 (August, 1994): 225–240, especially 225–227.

34. On some of the new spheres and many aspects of American life that many men found threatening see the following sources: Kathy Peis, *Cheap Amusements: Working Women and Leisure in Turn-of-the-Century New York* (Philadelphia: Temple University Press, 1986); Nan Enstad, *Ladies of Labor, Girls of Adventure: Working Women, Popular Culture, and Labor Politics at the Turn of the Twentieth Century* (New York: Columbia University Press, 1999); Susan A. Glenn, *Female Spectacle: The Theatrical Roots of Modern Feminism* (Cambridge: Harvard University Press, 2000); and Maureen E. Montgomery, *Displaying Women: Spectacles of Leisure in Edith Wharton's New York* (New York: Routledge, 1998).

35. Sophia Smith wanted the fortune she inherited to be used to found a women's college. Smith College was founded in the 1870s after Sophia died. She noted in her will, "I hereby make the following provisions for the establishment and maintenance of an Institution for the higher education of young women, with the design to furnish for my own sex means and facilities for education equal to those which are afforded now in our colleges to young men." See the Smith College web site: http://www.smith.edu/about_smithtradition.php

36. In addition to the secondary sources authored by Welter, Sklar and Cott (see note 26 above), two primary sources that reveal some elite men's defense of the ideology in the late nineteenth and early twentieth centuries are Grover Cleveland, "Woman's Mission and Woman's Clubs," *Ladies Home Journal*, vol. 22 (May, 1905), and George G. Vest, "Remarks," *Congressional Record*, 49th Congress, 2nd Sess., 25 January 25, 1887, 986.

37. How different people surely viewed the Raths' relationship, each character's role, and how Betsy's role did or did not accurately represent that of American women is perhaps best represented in the debate one professional woman had with Sloan Wilson in the pages of the *New York Times*. See Sloan Wilson, "The Woman in the Gray Flannel Suit," *New York Times*, January 15, 1956, SM8; and Bernice Fitz-Gibbon, "Woman in the Gray Flannel Suit," *New York Times*, January 29, 1956, I96; accessed via Pro Quest Historical Newspapers.

38. Two documentaries on war and postwar propaganda and women's experiences are *The Life and Times of Rosie the Riveter*, Connie

Field, director (Clarity Films, 2007, DVD); and "Seeds of the Sixties," David Hoffman, director, episode one, *Making Sense of the Sixties* (WETA, 1991, VHS); also see May, *Homeward Bound*. For a survey of women's experiences in these years see Ellen Carol DuBois and Lynn Dumenil, *Through Women's Eyes: An American History with Documents*, 2nd ed. (Boston: Bedford/St. Martin's, 2009), 588–663. For discussions of women who accepted the domestic ideal but engaged in various types of activism outside of the home see the following essays in Meyerowitz, *Not June Cleaver*: Harriet Hyman Alonso, "Mayhem and Moderation: Women Peace Activists during the McCarthy Era," 128–150; Deborah A. Gerson, "'Is Family Devotion Somehow Subversive?' Familialism against McCarthyism," 151–176; Margaret Rose, "Gender and Civic Activism in Mexican American Barrios in California: The Community Service Organization, 1947–1962," 177–200; and Dee Garrison, "'Our Skirts Gave Them Courage': The Civil Defense Protest Movement in New York City, 1955–1961," 201–228.

Chapter 2

1. Some examples of films released during these postwar years that depict corporate life as something that must be negotiated ignobly and deceitfully for the sake of survival, and dishonestly manipulated in order to advance within it include, in addition to *The Man in the Gray Flannel Suit*, Henry Koster, dir., *The Power and the Prize* (1956); Frank Tashin, dir., *Will Success Spoil Rock Hunter* (1957); and Fielder Cook, dir., *Patterns* (1956).

2. In *Sixguns and Society: A Structural Analysis of the American Western* (Berkeley: University of California Press, 1975), Will Wright discusses how the structure of the Western changes over time, noting that heroes increasingly cannot be directly tied to society because such ties would cause the heroes to be corrupted by society. My analysis of films representing a variety of genres reveals that Wright's observation is true of heroes in films other than westerns as well, especially in the final decades of the twentieth century. See 154–184.

3. Steven J. Whitfield, *The Culture of the Cold War* (Baltimore: Johns Hopkins, 1991), 127.

4. Ibid., 127–151, especially 127–131 for the information on Rand and the Motion Picture Alliance.

5. *Citizen Kane*, Orson Welles, director (RKO Pictures, 1941, DVD).

6. *The Fountainhead*, King Vidor, director (Warner Bros., 1949, DVD).

7. On women and gender in these years see the various essays in Joanne Meyerowitz, ed., *Not June Cleaver: Women and Gender in Postwar America, 1945–1960* (Philadelphia: Temple University Press, 1994); Elaine Tyler May, *Homeward Bound: American Families in the Cold War Era* (New York: Basic Books, 1988).

8. John Steinbeck, *The Grapes of Wrath* (New York: Penguin Books, 1976), 40–50.

9. *Force of Evil*, Abraham Polonsky, director (MGM, 1948, DVD); all dialog and scene descriptions are taken from this film.

10. See the Polonsky interview in Patrick McGilligan and Paul Buhle, eds., *Tender Comrades: A Backstory of the Hollywood Blacklist* (New York: St. Martin's Press, 1997), 481–494; for quotation see 483.

11. Paul Buhle notes that the film is clearly about "crime and capitalism" (not just crime), and quotes director Martin Scorsese as referring to it as "a political as well as an existential drama." See Buhle, "Abraham Lincoln Polonsky's America," *American Quarterly* 49, no. 4 (December 1997): 874–881; for quotations see 874 and 877 respectively.

12. In her otherwise informative analysis of the politics in the movie, Christine Noll Brinckmann notes, "the film did not receive proper publicity. It was distributed by MGM in an inexpensive, listless way and advertised as another gangster thriller. Although a few critics mentioned it favorably, *Force of Evil* soon disappeared from the screen." The film actually played in theaters for months. See Brinckmann's article, "The Politics of *Force of Evil*: An Analysis of Abraham Polonsky's Preblacklist Film," *Prospects* 6 (1981): 357–386; for quotations see 360.

13. The first review I found appeared in *Variety*, December 29, 1948, and the last in the *Chicago Daily Tribune*, April 8, 1949, A8. A New York theater advertised the film as late as April 1, 1949; see *New York Times*, April 1, 1949, 30.

14. "*Force of Evil* Is Film That's Sadly Amiss," *Chicago Daily Tribune*, April 8, 1949, A8. For information about the National Film Registry see the web site for the National Film Preservation Board at http://www.loc.gov/film/filmnfr.html.

15. "Whimsical Mouthpiece," *Newsweek*, January 3, 1949, 57–58.

16. *Variety*, December 29, 1948. An excellent source for reviews that appeared in *Variety* is *Variety Film Reviews*, 1907–1980, vols. 1–16 (New York: Garland Publishing, 1983). The citations for *Variety* reviews cited in these

notes that I read in this multi-volume set do not include page numbers because the reviews are listed only by dates; numbers do not appear on the pages. Reviews read in the trade journal itself include page numbers.

17. *Good Housekeeping*, January, 1949, 11 and 100.

18. On the Breen Office and *Force of Evil* see Robert Sklar, *City Boys: Cagney, Bogart, Garfield* (Princeton: Princeton University Press, 1992), 207–210.

19. *Wall Street*, Oliver Stone, director (20th Century–Fox, 1987, DVD).

20. Sklar., 209.

21. Ibid., 207–210.

22. Ibid., 210.

23. Paul Goodman, *Growing Up Absurd: Problems of Youth in the Organized System* (New York: Random House, 1956); C. Wright Mills, *The Power Elite* (New York: Oxford University Press, 1956); Mills, *White Collar: The American Middle Classes* (New York: Oxford University Press, 1951); David Riesman, *The Lonely Crowd: A Study of the Changing American Character* (New Haven: Yale University Press, 1950); and William H. Whyte, Jr., *The Organization Man* (New York: Simon & Schuster, 1956).

24. Concerning the slump in ticket sales, *Variety* blamed the extended 1954 winter as a factor keeping many Americans at home and out of movie theaters. The trade journal also noted, "Too many holdovers and extended runs plus an increase in [the] number of reissues are proving handicaps to any extensive improvement at the tickets this stanza." See *Variety*, May 12, 1954, 3. The film was often ranked first or second in ticket sales in major metropolitan areas. See *Motion Picture Herald*, May 29, 1954, 30, and *Variety*, May 26, 1954, 8. On the rising competition between movies and television see John Belton, *American Cinema/American Culture* (New York: McGraw Hill, 1994), 257–273.

25. *Variety*, May 26, 1954, 8.

26. *Variety*, June 6, 1954, 2.

27. *Time*, June 14, 1954, 106–110.

28. *Variety*, May 5, 1954; *The New Yorker*, June 5, 1954, 63; *Newsweek*, June 14, 1954, 104.

29. *Johnny Guitar*, Nicholas Ray, director (Republic Pictures, 1954, DVD); all dialog and scene descriptions are taken from this film.

30. Elaine May, *Homeward Bound*. May points out that many middle-class and upper-class women who gave up careers for full-time roles in the home said they preferred marriage and even viewed the change as a change of ca-

reers. See page 29, for example. The female characters in *Johnny Guitar* break the social norms of many of May's women. The production and popular reception of this film demonstrates the deep tensions in the culture over these social prescriptions. Due to the necessity of multi-income family economies for many working-class Americans, working-class women could not have accepted such prescriptions so readily.

31. George Lipsitz, *Class and Culture in Cold War America: "A Rainbow at Midnight"* (New York: Praeger, 1981), 232–238.

32. Elaine May demonstrates that, among other things, experts presumed that "An essential ingredient to winning the cold war was presumably the rearing of strong and able offspring." To achieve that goal, these experts assumed women would need to be contained in the traditional family structure. See May's article, "Explosive Issues: Sex, Women, and the Bomb," in Lary May, ed., *Recasting America: Culture and Politics in the Age of Cold War* (Chicago: University of Chicago Press, 1988), 154–170; for quotation see 157.

33. May, "Explosive Issues," 163. In this essay and more thoroughly in *Homeward Bound*, May makes some interesting cultural connections between the idea of the need to contain the Soviets in American foreign policy and the idea of a need to contain women in traditional family roles in order to facilitate a moral front in the cold war at home. See *Homeward Bound*, 92–134.

34. *The New Yorker*, June 5, 1954, 63.

35. *Time*, June 14, 1954, 106–110.

36. *Newsweek*, June 14, 1954, 104.

37. Wright, 154–184.

38. See Victor S. Navasky, *Naming Names* (New York: Viking Press, 1980).

39. Raymond Carney, *American Vision: The Films of Frank Capra* (Hanover, New Hampshire: University Press of New England, 1986).

40. Peter Biskind, "Rebel Without A Cause: Nicholas Ray in the Fifties," *Film Quarterly*, 28 (Fall 1974): 33.

41. Michael Wilmington, "Nicholas Ray's *Johnny Guitar*," *Velvet Light Trap* 12 (Spring 1974): 21.

42. Biskind, 32.

43. Ibid.

44. Wilmington, 22.

Chapter 3

1. On local attempts in the early twentieth century to control what moviegoers could

view, see Lary May, *Screening out the Past: the Birth of Mass Culture and the Motion Picture Industry* (Chicago: University of Chicago Press, 1980), 41–59; on the origins of the code see Stephen Vaughn, "Morality and Entertainment: the Origins of the Motion Picture Production Code," *The Journal of American History* 77, no. 1 (June 1990): 39–65; for a concise discussion of the replacement of the code with the rating system see Paul Monoco, *The Sixties, 1960–1969*, History of American Cinema series, Charles Harpole, General editor (Berkeley: University of California Press, 2001), 60–62; for copies of the code and the rating system that replaced it, see Steven Mintz and Randy W. Roberts, eds., *Hollywood's America: Twentieth-Century America Through Film*, 4th ed. (West Sussex, UK: Wiley-Blackwell, 2010), 119–128 and 301–303, respectively.

2. For an abbreviated copy of the Supreme Court ruling see *United States v. Paramount Pictures., Inc.* (1947), in Steven Mintz and Randy W. Roberts, eds., *Hollywood's America: Twentieth-Century America Through Film,* 4th ed. (Oxford: Wiley-Blackwell, 2010), 234; also see Robert Sklar, *Movie-Made America: A Cultural History of American Movies* (New York: Vintage Books, 1976), 272–274. For the Hopper and Lucas quotations see Peter Biskind, *Easy Riders, Raging Bulls: How the Sex-Drugs-and-Rock 'n' Roll Generation Saved Hollywood* (New York: Simon & Schuster, 1998), 75.

3. Dr. Martin Luther King, Jr., "A Time to Break Silence," in James M. Washington, ed., *A Testament of Hope: The Essential Writings and Speeches of Martin Luther King, Jr.* (New York: HarperCollins Publishers, 1986), 233. King delivered the speech at Manhattan's Riverside Church, April 4, 1967. The speech can also be accessed at *American Rhetoric Online Speech Bank*: http://www.american-rhetoric.com/speeches/mlkatimetobreaksilence.htm.

4. In Jonathan Munby's scholarship on the gangster genre, he makes it clear that "Regardless of the poetic and ideological license gangster fictions take with the very real socio-historical problems of the ethnic poor, the central conflict which informs these narratives remains the question of social, economic, and cultural exclusion." As he aptly puts it, "Gangsters want in — they want to 'go ligit'— yet find themselves always positioned on the outside looking in." See Munby, "'Manhattan Melodrama's'"Art of the Weak': Telling History from the Other Side in the 1930s Talking Gangster Film," *Journal of American Studies* 30, no. 1 (April 1996): 101–118; for quotation

see 101–102. Also see his, *Public Enemies, Public Heroes: Screening the Gangster from Little Caesar to Touch of Evil* (Chicago: University of Chicago Press, 1999).

5. For example, in the Vietnam War film *The Green Berets* (Warner Bros., 1968, DVD), directed by and staring John Wayne, the George Beckworth character (David Janssen) is a reporter who asks critical questions about the war and comes off as a communist sympathizer. Wayne wrote a letter to President Lyndon Johnson to inform him that he wanted to make a pro-war, anti-communist film. For an analysis of the film in relation to other films about the war and in relation to the historical context see James W. Davidson and Mark H. Lytle, "Where Trouble Comes: History and Myth in the Films of Vietnam," in Davidson and Lytle, *After the Fact: The Art of Historical Detection,* 6th ed. (McGraw-Hill, 2009), 420–447. In his letter to Johnson, Wayne wrote that he wanted the film to "help our cause throughout the world." He continued, "We want to tell the story of our fighting men in Vietnam with reason, emotion, characterization and action. We want to do it in a manner that inspires a patriotic attitude on the part of our fellow Americans — a feeling which we have always had in this country in the past during times of stress and trouble" (426).

6. Terry H. Anderson, *The Sixties,* 3rd. ed. (New York: Pearson/Longman, 2007), 131.

7. In addition to Anderson's *The Sixties,* author, academic and sixties activist Todd Gitlin's well researched and autobiographical *The Sixties: Years of Hope, Days of Rage* (New York: Bantam Books, 1987), reveals in nearly every chapter the many disparate groups, actions and cultural expressions that many label countercultural.

8. *The Graduate,* Mike Nichols, director (Embassy Pictures, 1967, DVD); all dialog and scene descriptions are taken from this film.

9. Gitlin, *The Sixties.*

10. Ibid., especially 377–408.

11. *Easy Rider,* Dennis Hopper, director (Columbia Pictures DVD, 1969); all dialog and scene descriptions are taken from this film.

12. For an interesting analysis of some similarities "counterculture" shares with the "Cowboy Code," see Michael Allen, "'I Just Want to Be a Cosmic Cowboy': Hippies, Cowboy Code, and the Culture of a Counterculture," *Western Historical Quarterly* 36, no. 3 (Autumn, 2005): 275–299. I agree with Allen's conclusion that "Although by most historical accounts the sixties hippies supposedly aimed to 'counter' the dominant 'culture,' they

in fact adopted some of the fundamental tenets and values of that culture" (296). Although the communal hippies represented in *Easy Rider* do not, the countercultural icon bikers certainly do, both in their independence on the road and in Wyatt's quest to do his own thing in his own time, an attribute he admires in the western farmer-rancher.

13. Stanley Aronowitz, *False Promises: the Shaping of American Working-Class Consciousness* (Durham: Duke University Press, 1992), 267–282; George Lipsitz, *Rainbow at Midnight: Labor and Culture in the 1940s* (Urbana: University of Illinois Press, 1994), 19–20, 56–62; William H. Chafe, *The Unfinished Journey: America Since World War II*, 3rd. ed. (Oxford: Oxford University Press, 1995), 7–8.

14. Wyatt's line is "They're gonna make it," a line Fonda later said he regretted was in the script: "I really don't like that line in the commune sequence.... [I] would have preferred saying nothing at all." Quoted in Gene Siskel's review, *Chicago Tribune*, September 25, 1969, B16; accessed ProQuest Historical Newspapers.

15. The sign in the film reads "gorilla" rather than "guerrilla."

16. On the interconnectedness of race, class and psychology see David R. Roediger, *The Wages of Whiteness: Race and the Making of the American Working Class* (London: Verso, 1991). Also see Bryant Simon, "Race Reactions: African American Organizing, Liberalism, and White Working-Class Politics in Postwar South Carolina, " in Jane Dailey, Glenda Elizabeth Gilmore and Bryant Simon, eds., *Jumpin' Jim Crow: Southern Politics from Civil War to Civil Rights* (Princeton: Princeton University Press, 2000), 239–259. For a southern apologist of slavery and criticism of northern wage slavery see George Fithugh, C. Vann Woodward, editor, *Cannibals All! Or, Slaves without Masters* (Cambridge: Belknap Press of Harvard University, 1960).

17. For an interpretation of *Easy Rider* as merely reinforcing the ideology of the dominant culture associated with the economic system that, I believe, the film paradoxically critiques and reinforces simultaneously, see Donald P. Costello, "From Counterculture to Anticulture," *The Review of Politics* 34, no. 4 (October, 1972): 187–193, especially, 88–90; on the ambiguity of Wyatt's "we blew it" comment, see Biskind 74 and 77.

18. Hopper and Fonda may have been thinking about a sequel because it's not certain that the two characters die. Wyatt's chopper rather than Wyatt is hit and he is not on the bike when it sails through the air, so he could have been thrown clear. And it is left possible that someone may have driven by and found the men before Hopper bled to death.

19. David Montgomery, *Workers' Control in America: Studies in the History of Work, Technology, and Labor Struggles* (Cambridge: Cambridge University Press, 1979).

20. The significant exceptions would be westerns like *The Searchers* (1956), films with southern themes like *To Kill a Mockingbird* (1962), and those set in urban environments like *The Blackboard Jungle* (1955).

21. *Joe*, John G. Avildsen, director (Cannon Films, 1970, MGM DVD); all dialog and scene descriptions are taken from this film.

22. *Chicago Tribune* critic Gene Siskel gave the movie three-and-a-half stars and recognized "its timeliness is responsible for a large portion of its success." See *Chicago Tribune*, August 21, 1970, B15; accessed through ProQuest Historical Newspapers. Peter Boyle told one interviewer that people shouted "Hey, Joe!" to him whenever he went out; see interview with Mary Daniels, "He's More than a Good 'Joe,'" *Chicago Tribune*, August 28, 1970, B15; accessed through ProQuest Historical Newspapers. One Hollywood union used a picture of Joe carrying a rifle and an American flag in its advertising campaign; see the ad in Derek Nystrom, "Hard Hats and Movie Brats: Auteurism and the Class Politics of the New Hollywood," *Cinema Journal* 43, no. 3 (spring, 2004): 18–41 (ad appears on 29).

23. Nystrom, 18–41.

24. Mary Daniels interview with Peter Boyle.

25. Chafe, *The Unfinished Journey*, 383–388. Although *Joe* makes no direct reference to unemployment, the rate increased from 3.5 percent in 1969 to as high as 8.5 percent in 1975; these years were ones that found Americans increasingly anxious about if they would have jobs as well as the nature of the work they were doing. Unemployment statistics can be accessed at the following URL: www.ct.gov/ecd/LIB/ecd/20/14/md0006-08.pdf (accessed on December 10, 2011).

26. Homer Bigart, "War Foes Here Attacked by Construction Workers," *The New York Times*, May 9, 1970, p.1; Derek Nystrom discusses this clash between antiwar demonstrators and counter-demonstrators in "Hard Hats and Movie Brats," 23–25; Thomas Brady, "1,000 Establishment Lawyers Join War Protest, *The New York Times*, May 15, 1970, p. 21; newspapers accessed through ProQuest Historical Newspapers.

27. Statistic available at the Internet Movie Database (IMDb) site: http://www.imdb.com/title/tt0065916/.

28. Will Wright, *Sixguns and Society: A Structural Study of the Western* (Berkeley, University of California Press, 1975). Wright analyzes how the plot in the western genre changes over time to reflect the diminishing role of the individual in the increasingly organized corporate capitalist society of the twentieth century. Aspects of his argument are pertinent to our understanding of urban cop characters like Harry Callahan whose agency is restricted by modern bureaucracies.

29. *High Noon*, Fred Zinneman, director (United Artists, 1952, DVD).

30. *Dirty Harry*, Don Siegel, director (Warner Bros., 1971, DVD); all dialog and scene descriptions are taken from this film.

31. Adlai Stevenson, "A Purpose for Modern Woman," reprinted in *Woman's Home Companion* (September, 1956), 29–31.

32. Clint Eastwood Playboy interview, "Eastwood Talks Dirty Harry," February, 1974; a copy of the interview is available at http://www.the-dirtiest.com/playboy.htm (accessed October 20, 2011); Roger Ebert, review of *Dirty Harry*, *Chicago Sun Times*, January 1, 1971, available at http://rogerebert.sun times.com/apps/pbcs.dll/article?AID=/197101 01/REVIEWS/101010307; accessed on October 20, 2011.

33. In their short survey of movies released from 1967–1971, Michael Ryan and Douglas Kelner refer to *Dirty Harry* as "one of the most notorious films of the period." See their "Films of the Late 1960s and Early 1970s: from Counterculture to Counterrevolution, 1967–1971," in Mintz and Roberts, eds., *Hollywood's America*, 255–263; for quotation see 260. If one googles the words "dirty harry" with others words such as "race" or "gender" or "fascist," a plethora of current and historical articles and blogs emerge written by people who either defend or attack the film in relation to contemporary issues related to immigration, race and ethnicity. One wonders if most of these writers and bloggers have ever seen the film. Regardless, they debate it ardently. See, for example, "More 'Racism' and that Racist Dirty Harry" at http://www.asterling.com/ 2010/06/ more-racism-and-that-racist-dirty-harry.html, and Dr. Clarence Spigner, "Racist Cops on Screen: Cinema Imitates Life or Vise Versa?" at http://www.blackpast.org/?q=blog/ clarence/ racist-cops-on-screen-cinema-imi tates-life-or-vice-versa; both accessed on October 20, 2011.

34. Patrick McGilligan, *Clint: The Life and Legend* (New York: St. Martin's Press, 1999), 277–278.

35. Quoted in Ibid.

36. For information on the casting of Tyne Daly and her input on the script see Ibid., 274–278.

37. On how fifties sit-coms propagated the mythic image of a homogeneous white, middle-class suburban culture see Stephanie Coontz, *The Way We Never Were: American Families and the Nostalgia Trap* (New York: Basic Books, 1992), 23–41.

Chapter 4

1. *Lost in America*, Albert Brooks, director (Warner Bros., 1985, DVD).

2. *Falling Down*, Joel Schumacher, director (Warner Bros., 1993, DVD).

3. *American Beauty*, Sam Mendes, director (DreamWorks Pictures, 1999, DVD). All dialog and scene descriptions are taken from this film.

4. Roger Ebert, "*American Beauty*," September 24, 1999 available at http://rogerebe rt.suntimes.com/apps/pbcs.dll/article?AID=/1 9990924/REVIEWS/909240301/10. The multiple reviews of *American Beauty* at the popular site rottentomatoes.com are overwhelmingly favorable, but I tend to agree with the reviewer for BBC Home Entertainment Film who writes the following: "But most of us know that America is on the verge of imploding and characters, such as Lester, who find themselves in stagnant lives have only one, predictable response: rebellion. A film like *Fight Club* takes a far more original response to social conformity, and *American Beauty* is less imaginative." This BBC review is available at http://www. bbc.co.uk/films/2000/12/11/american_beauty _2000_review.shtmlhttp://www.bbc.co.uk/fil ms/2000/12/11/american_beauty_2000_re view.shtml; accessed on 11/20/11.

5. I use the term "spiritual" darkness here in a way broadly enough to associate with viewers of a variety of religious and non-religious persuasions. I do not use the term in relation to religion in general or Christianity or another religion specifically. Rather, some viewers might associate "spiritual" with a lack of human spirit when people merely work and consume like programmed automatons without ever reflecting on what they are doing and why they are doing it. Religious viewers, on the other hand, surely will and have read the film from religious perspectives and see the focus on materialism as being associated with a more divine spiritual emptiness. For an excellent reading of both *American Beauty* and *Fight Club* "as contemporary religious parables," see Christopher Deacy's excellent essay,

"Integration and Rebirth through Confrontation: *Fight Club* and *American Beauty* as Contemporary Religious Parables," *Journal of Contemporary Religion* 17, no. 1 (2002): 61–73.

6. Jane and Ricky get to know each other and enjoy each other's company. They walk down a street together and see a funeral procession. He tells her he once filmed a homeless woman who froze to death. She asks why and he says, "because it was amazing." She asks, "What's amazing about it?" He answers, "When you see something like that, it's like God is looking right at you, just for a second, and if you're careful, you can look right back." She says, "And what do you see?" He replies, softly, in almost a whisper, "Beauty."

7. *Fight Club*, David Fincher, director (20th Century–Fox, 1999, DVD); all dialog and scene descriptions are taken from this film.

8. Edward Guthmann, "Breathtaking 'Beauty,'" *San Francisco Chronicle*, September 17, 1999, *Internet Movie Database* (*IMDb*), http://www.sfgate.com/cgibin/ article.cgi?f=/c/a/ 1999/09/17/DD106066.DT; accessed on 11/20/11. Of the 362, 797 viewers who rated *American Beauty* on a scale of one ("awful") to ten ("excellent"), 32.4 percent gave it a ten, 27.1 percent a nine, 20.3 percent an eight, 9.7 percent a seven, 3.8 percent a six, 1.9 percent a five, 1.0 percent a four, 0.8 percent a three, 0.7 percent a two, and 2.2 percent a one. See the statistics at http://www.imdb.com/title/tt0169547/ratings; accessed on 11/19/11.

9. *IMDb.* For viewers' comments see http://www.imdb.com/title/ tt0169547/ reviews; accessed on 11/20/11.

10. David Hewison, "'Oh Rose, thou art sick!' Anti-individuation Forces in the Film *American Beauty*," *Journal of Analytical Psychology* 48 (2003): 683–704; Deacy, "Integration and Rebirth through Confrontation."

11. Erica Arthur, "Where Lester Burnham Falls Down: Exposing the Façade of Victimhood in American Beauty," *Men and Masculinities* 7, no. 2 (2004): 127–143.

12. Kathy Rabin, "American Beauty???" *Journal of Family Social Work* 6, no. 1 (2001): 97–99.

13. Steve Vineberg, "'American Beauty': No Joy in the Gilded Suburbs," *Chronicle of Higher Education* 46, no. 10 (October 29, 1999): B10.

14. The Y2K problem was related to software that had been programmed with only the last two digits of the four-digit years in twentieth-century dates. For example, 1999 was programmed as just 99. No one knew what computers would do when the year 2000 ar-

rived and a new century began; time would potentially be read as passing in 100-year cycles, beginning anew at 1900.

15. *Office Space*, Mike Judge, director (20th Century–Fox, 1999, DVD); all dialog and scene descriptions are taken from this film.

16. The *Entertainment Weekly* article is available at the following site: http://www.ew.com/ew/article/0,,20207063,00.html; accessed on 11/20/11.

17. Roger Ebert, *Chicago Sun Times*, February 19, 1999, available at http://www.ew.com/ew/article/0,,20207063,00.html; accessed on 11/20/11.

18. "The Fax of Life," *Entertainment Weekly*, May 23, 2003, available at http://www.ew.com/ew/article/0,,452194_2,00.html; accessed on 11/20/11.

19. *IMDb.* http://www.imdb.com/title/tt0 151804/ratings; accessed on 11/23/11. Of those who rated the film, 23.8 percent gave it a ten, 20.6 percent a nine, 27.6 percent an eight, 16.2 percent a seven, 6.6 percent a six, 2.6 percent a five, 1.1 percent a four, 0.6 percent a three, 0.4 percent a two, and 0.6 percent a one.

20. Scott Bowles, "Mike Judge: Back on the Grind with 'Extract,'" *USA Today*, September 9, 2009, section Life, 8.

21. Shaun Huston, "Filming Postbourgeois Suburbia: *Office Space* and the New American Suburb," *The Journal of Popular Culture* 42, no. 3 (June 2009): 497–514; see 497–493.

22. *Bullshit Job.com*, http://www.bullshit job.com/officespace/; accessed on 11/23/11.

23. Although some people believe the protagonist's name is "Jack," to attach a name to the character seems to be something imposed on the story by some viewers and readers rather than a clear name that the author created and the director followed. The name "Jack" comes from a scene in the dilapidated house that the protagonist occupies with his alter ego. He discovers an extensive library of old books and periodicals there. One day he finds and reads a series of stories told from the perspective of various organs belonging to a character named "Jack." At no time, however, is a direct relationship made between the name of the character in these stories and the name of the protagonist. Moreover, there are similar stories told from the perspective of organs belonging to a character named "Joe." "There's a whole series of these," the protagonist says as he talks to Tyler Durden, who is riding a bike throughout the house: "I am Joe's nipple. I am Jack's colon." The protagonist also refers to "Jack" in a scene when he goes to his boss's office to blackmail him, much like Lester Burnham does in *American Beauty*. In this

scene his boss tells him he is being reviewed and the protagonist replies, "I am Jack's complete lack of surprise" and then describes the information he has about the company that he will reveal to the authorities if he does not get what he wants. The fact that the character says this line does not demonstrate emphatically, in my opinion, that his name is Jack. Rather, it demonstrates that he has been reading the stories he found in the house. Also, when he calls Tyler Durden after his condo blows up, Tyler asks who it is and he never says his name. He pauses and just says that he is the "clever" guy that Tyler gave his business card to and sat next to on the plane. As the story develops we learn that no one in the fight clubs has a name, and even the one character whose name we know because the protagonist met him at a terminal-illness meeting, Robert Paulson, becomes nameless when he becomes a Fight Club member but regains his name when he dies. If Chuck Palahniuk meant for the narrator's name to be Jack, he left that fact too ambiguous to matter one way or another.

24. Chuck Palahniuk, *Fight Club* (New York: Henry Holt and Company, LLC, 1996); Fincher, *Fight Club*. I include information from the novel at various places because author Palahniuk's narrator sometimes describes with relevant dialog scenes that director Fincher creates in the film. Moreover, the dialog in the novel sometimes contributes to our understanding of particular scenes and themes and demonstrates that Fincher sometimes restrained the cultural critique in his adaptation of the book.

25. Palahniuk, 31.

26. In the same online question-and-answer session with readers and filmgoers throughout the world, Palahniuk answered a question about his inspiration for the book by stating "Fight Club is just a collection of stories told to me by my friends and the people I worked with." These questions and the author's responses are available at the following site: http://abcnews.go.com/ onair/DailyNews/chat_palahniuk991116.html; accessed on 11/23/11. Roger Ebert refers to the film as "fascist" in his review. Ebert's review is available at the following site: http://rogerebert.suntimes.com/apps/ pbcs.dll/article?AID=/199910 15/REVIEWS/910150302; accessed on 11/23/ 11. Ebert calls the film "the most frankly and cheerfully fascist big-star movie since 'Death Wish.'"

27. In the novel Palahniuk gets more specific: "I loved every stick of furniture. That was my whole life. Everything, the lamps, the chairs, the rugs were me. The dishes in the cabinets were me. The plants were me. It was me that blew up." See Palahniuk, 110–111.

28. Also see Ibid., 16–24 and 34–49.

29. Also see Ibid., 38–39.

30. Ibid., 174.

31. In the novel they meet at a nude beach. They are the only two people on the beach, and Tyler asks the Narrator what time it is. They talk about the logs Tyler has stacked so the shadow they cast looks like a giant hand, but only at exactly 4:30, a single minute of perfection, which, according to Tyler, is enough. See Palahniuk, 32–33.

32. Also see Ibid., 51–55; for quotation see 51.

33. Ibid., 14.

34. Palahniuk, 206–208.

35. The URL for this site is http://www.project-mayhem.ndo.co.uk/images.htm. Unfortunately, since I first began research on this project the information is no longer available at that address and I cannot find it elsewhere. A researcher who goes to the site today will be informed that the site "has been suspended." I have a printed copy of some of the contributions to the site in my possession. Numerous other "Fight Club" and "Project Mayhem" sites now exist and can be accessed by using those terms in any search engine. Various sites include but are by no means limited to the following: http://chuckpalahniuk.net/books/fight-club; http://www.fightclubquotes.net/. The creators of the last site (http://www.fightclubquotes.net/) definitely see the movie and the novel as models for reality, texts upon which they want to model their behavior and from which they adopt their values and question and critique American society and culture. The "welcome" statement on the site reads as follows: "Gentlemen — Welcome to Fight Club. It's time for change. We have to stop living a boring, robotic life where everything is a copy of a copy of a copy — as Tyler says. We have to wake the fuck up and understand that life is not what they're telling us. Society is feeding us a lie, and that lie has to stop, today — now. There's no more time for bullshit, no more time and no more tolerance for mind washing. We want the truth, we want freedom — not slavery." For a humorous, three-minute fight-club video based on the works of Jane Austin see the following YouTube video: http://mashable.com/2010/07/25/jane-austens-fight-club/; accessed on 11/23/11.

36. *IMDb*, http://www.imdb.com/title/tt0137523/ratings; accessed on 11/19/11 and 11/23/11. On November 23, 2011, 42.9 percent of viewers gave the film a ten, 27.4 percent a

nine, 15.5 percent an eight, 6.6 percent a seven, 2.7 percent a six, 1.4 percent a five, 0.8 percent a four, 0.6 percent a three, 0.5 percent a two, and 1.6 percent a one.

37. *The Richest Man in the World: Andrew Carnegie,* Austin Hoyt, director (WGBH Educational Foundation, 1997, VHS), and *The Great Depression,* episode one, "A Job at Ford's, John Else, Lyn Goldfarb and Stephen Stept, directors (Boston: WGBH, Blackside Productions, 1993, VHS).

38. See Fincher, but the quotes here are taken from Palahniuk, 65.

39. Palahniuk, 81.

40. Ibid., 80; the scene in the film is similar, only Tyler says he can't urinate with the protagonist watching.

41. Palahniuk, 80.

42. Ibid., 81.

43. For the scene in the novel see Ibid., 148–150.

44. Palahniuk, 150.

45. Ibid., 130.

46. Ibid.

47. Ibid.

48. Ibid.

49. Ibid., 149.

50. Ibid., 141.

51. Ibid.

52. Ibid.

53. Ibid.

54. Ibid.

55. Ibid., 199.

56. Ibid., 123.

57. Ibid., 124.

58. Ibid.

59. Ibid.

Conclusion

1. *Time Magazine,* December 26, 2011, vol. 178, no. 25; Gretchen Morgenson and Joshua Rosner, *Reckless Endangerment: How Outsized Ambition, Greed, and Corruption Led to Economic Armageddon* (New York: Times Books, 2011).

2. Alan Trachtenberg, *The Incorporation of America: Culture and Society in the Gilded Age* (New York: Hill and Wang, 1982), 86.

3. On these structural and institutional changes see Gabriel Kolko, *The Triumph of Conservatism: A Reinterpretation of American History, 1900–1916* (New York: The Free Press, 1963), and Martin J. Sklar, *The Corporate Reconstruction of American Capitalism, 1890– 1916: The Market, The Law, and Politics* (Cambridge: Cambridge University Press, 1988); see especially Sklar's discussion of "the market and

the law," 42–178, and "the corporate-liberal solution," 324–332.

4. Although he has his critics, an excellent discussion of the social consequences of living in a culture in which individuals must constantly be marketing their personalities to others is Christopher Lasch, *The Culture of Narcissism: American Life in an Age of Diminishing Expectations* (New York: W. W. Norton & Company, 1979). A comprehensive analysis and criticism of Lasch's application of psychoanalytical theory to American culture generally is Jesse F. Battan, "The 'New Narcissism' In 20th-Century America: The Shadow and Substance of Social Change," *Journal of Social History* 17, no. 2 (Winter: 1983): 199–221, especially 200–203 and 199–211.

5. Henry David Thoreau, *Walden and Other Writings by Henry David Thoreau,* Joseph Wood Krutch, ed. (New York: Bantam Classics, 1981); see 174 for railroad quotation and 257 for quoted material from Thoreau's discussion with his Irish neighbor.

6. Matthew B. Crawford, *Shop Class as Soulcraft: an Inquiry into the Value of Work* (New York: The Penguin Press, 2009), 126.

7. Ibid., 157.

8. Ibid., 153.

9. Ibid., 155. Of particular interest in de Tocqueville's writings is his essay "What Sort of Despotism Democratic Nations Have to Fear," in Alexis de Tocqueville, *Democracy in America,* vol. II, Phillips Bradley edition (New York: Vintage Books, 1945), 334–339. On the problem of such "soft authority" de Tocqueville writes, "The will of man is not shattered, but softened, bent, and guided; men are seldom forced by it to act, but they are constantly restrained from acting. Such a power does not destroy, but it prevents existence; it does not tyrannize, but it compresses, enervates, extinguishes, and stupefies a people, till each nation is reduced to nothing better than a flock of timid and industrious animals, of which the government is the shepherd" (337). Replace the word "government" near the end of the sentence with "corporation" and the point is clear.

10. In *Supercapitalism: The Transformation of Business, Democracy, and Everyday Life* (New York: Vintage Books edition, 2008), Robert B. Reich demonstrates how since the late nineteenth century, especially since the 1970s, American democracy has increasingly served corporations' rather than citizens' interests, providing us with evidence of citizens' declining influence in the political system and, consequently, their rising disaffection in relation to politics. For Reich's discussion of the his-

torical antecedents, see 3–87; for his discussion of corporate influence and contemporary democracy, see 168–208.

11. Steven J. Whitfield, *The Culture of the Cold War* (Baltimore: The Johns Hopkins University Press, 1991), 142; Michael Paul Rogin, *Ronald Reagan, The Movie: and Other Episodes in Political Demonology* (Berkeley: University of California Press, 1987), 29–32; Victor S. Navasky, *Naming Names*, 3rd ed. (New York: Hill and Wang, 2003), 80, 83, 146.

12. For an analysis of this ideological shift among American intellectuals, see David W. Noble, *The End of American History: Democracy, Capitalism, and the Metaphor of Two Worlds in Anglo-American Historical Writing, 1880–1980* (Minneapolis: University of Minnesota Press, 1985), especially his discussion of Charles Beard, Reinhold Niebuhr and Richard Hofstadter, 41–114. Also see Lary May, *The Big Tomorrow: Hollywood and the Politics of the American Way* (Chicago: University of Chicago Press, 2000). On Hollywood and the anti-communist culture of the cold war see Whitfield, 127–151. For abridged copies of relevant Theodore Roosevelt and Woodrow Wilson speeches, see Leon Fink, ed., *Major Problems in the Gilded Age and the Progressive Era* (New York: Houghton Mifflin Company, 2011), 392–395. A copy of the entire Roosevelt speech can be accessed on the TeachingAmericanHistory.org website at the following URL address: http://teachingamericanhistory.org/library/index.asp?document=501. Wilson's entire speech can be accessed on the same web site but at the following URL address: http://teachingamericanhistory.org/library/index.asp?document=165. Speeches accessed on 12/31/11.

13. Increasing people's dependence on corporations was discussed among business leaders in the 1920s and became known as "welfare capitalism," a system where corporate employers promoted loyalty to the company by providing benefits to employees. For a short discussion of employers' interests in developing welfare capitalism in the 1920s, see Michael E. Parrish, *Anxious Decades: America in Prosperity and Depression, 1920–1941* (New York: W. W. Norton & Company, 1992), 88–93. Employers' views are also evident in a publication of the Industrial Union Conference Board in 1925, portions of which are reprinted as "The Employers' Case for Welfare Capitalism, 1925," in Colin Gordon, ed., *Major Problems in American History, 1920–1945: Documents and Essays* (Boston: Houghton Mifflin Company, 1999), 60–61. In the postwar years, historian Eric F. Goldman notes, "conservative groups often talked a formula that was decades old but now had a fresh significance and a new name, 'welfare capitalism.' Industry itself, the formula ran, should protect the welfare of its employees to such an extent that social legislation, and perhaps unions, would lose their appeal." See Goldman, *The Crucial Decade—And After: America, 1945–1960* (New York: Vintage Books, 1960), 9. It is interesting that in the recent health-care debate Democrats, led by President Obama, did not advocate or discuss that a single-payer national health-care system would enable more Americans to become independent entrepreneurs by freeing them from the benefits provided by their employers. People are tied to corporate benefits that cause many to avoid beginning independent entrepreneurial ventures because they cannot risk losing the benefits for themselves and their families that are provided by corporate employers. This is one example where government could facilitate independence, entrepreneurship and economic growth by liberating people from the corporate paternalism that keeps them from becoming entrepreneurial risk takers. Interestingly, in response to a question following a speech he gave at Illinois Wesleyan University on March 23, 2011, Illinois' senior United States Senator Dick Durbin noted that he believes the United States will eventually adopt a health care system like Germany's. The debate over alternatives is restricted, however, due to the influence of corporate lobbying interests and, therefore, as Durbin mentioned, the American system will probably experience a significant crisis before such a change is made.

Bibliography

Allen, Michael. "'I Just Want to Be a Cosmic Cowboy': Hippies, Cowboy Code, and the Culture of a Counterculture." *Western Historical Quarterly* 36, no. 3 (Autumn 2005): 275–299.

American Beauty. DVD. Directed by Sam Mendes. DreamWorks Pictures, 1999.

American Rhetoric Online Speech Bank: http://www.americanrhetoric.com/speeches/mlkatimetobreaksilence.htm.

Anderson, Sherwood. *Winesburg, Ohio*. New York: Bantam Classics, 1995.

Anderson, Terry H. *The Sixties*. 3rd. ed. New York: Pearson/Longman, 2007.

Arnold, Gordon. *The Afterlife of America's War in Vietnam: Changing Visions in Politics and on Screen*. Jefferson, NC: McFarland, 2006.

Aronowitz, Stanley. *False Promises: the Shaping of American Working-Class Consciousness*. Durham, NC: Duke University Press, 1992.

Arthur, Erica. "Where Lester Burnham Falls Down: Exposing the Façade of Victimhood in American Beauty." *Men and Masculinities* 7, no. 2 (2004): 127–143.

Balio, Tino, ed. *The American Film Industry*. Rev. ed. Madison: University of Wisconsin Press, 1985.

_____. *Grand Design: Hollywood as a Modern Business Enterprise, 1930–1939*. Vol. 5 of *History of the American Cinema*. Berkeley: University of California Press, 1995.

Bapis, Elaine M. *Camera and Action: American Film as Agent of Social Change, 1965–1975*. Jefferson, NC: McFarland, 2008.

Battan, Jesse F. "The 'New Narcissism' in 20th-Century America: The Shadow and Substance of Social Change." *Journal of Social History* 17, no. 2 (Winter: 1983): 199–221.

Bederman, Gail. *Manliness and Civilization: a Cultural History of Gender and Race in the United States, 1880–1917*. Chicago: University of Chicago Press, 1995.

Bellamy, Edward. *Looking Backward: 2000–1887*. New York: Signet Classic, 2000.

Belton, John. *American Cinema/American Culture*. New York: McGraw Hill, 1994.

Bernardi, Daniel, ed. *The Birth of Whiteness: Race and the Emergence of U.S. Cinema*. New Brunswick, NJ: Rutgers University Press, 1996.

Bernardi, Daniel, ed. *Classic Hollywood, Classic Whiteness*. Minneapolis: University of Minnesota Press, 2001.

Bernaerts, Lars. "*Fight Club* and the Embedding of Delirium in Narrative." *Style* 43, no. 3 (Fall 2009): 373–387.

Bingham, Dennis. *Acting Male: Masculinities in the Films of James Stewart,*

Jack Nicholson, and Clint Eastwood. New Brunswick, NJ: Rutgers University Press, 1994.

Biskind, Peter. "American Beauty or American Pie?" *Nation* 270, no. 13 (April 3 2000): 11–12.

_____. *Down and Dirty Pictures: Miramax, Sundance, and the Rise of Independent Film.* New York: Simon & Schuster Paperbacks, 2004.

_____. "Rebel Without A Cause: Nicholas Ray in the Fifties." *Film Quarterly* 28 (Fall 1974): 33–38.

_____. *Easy Riders, Raging Bulls: How the Sex-Drugs-and-Rock'n'Roll Generation Saved Hollywood.* New York: Simon & Schuster, 1998.

_____. *Seeing is Believing: How Hollywood Taught Us to Stop Worrying and Love the Fifties.* New York: Henry Holt and Company, Owl Edition, 2000.

The Blackboard Jungle. DVD. Directed by Richard Brooks. Metro-Goldwyn-Mayer, 1955.

Bodnar, John. *Blue-Collar Hollywood: Liberalism, Democracy, and Working People in American Film.* Baltimore: The Johns Hopkins University Press, 2003.

Bowser, Eileen. *The Transformation of Cinema, 1907–1915.* Vol. 2 of *History of the American Cinema.* Berkeley: University of California Press, 1994.

Brinckmann, Christine Noll. "The Politics of *Force of Evil*: An Analysis of Abraham Polonsky's Preblacklist Film." *Prospects* 6 (1981): 357–386.

Buhle, Paul. "Abraham Lincoln Polonsky's America." *American Quarterly* 49, no. 4 (December 1997): 874–881.

Bullshit Job.com, http://www.bullshitjob.com/officespace/.

Bush, Gregory W. "Like 'A Drop of Water in the Stream of Life': Moving Images of Mass Man from Griffith to Vidor." *Journal of American Studies* 25, no. 2 (August 1991): 213–234.

Byars, Jackie. *All That Hollywood Allows: Re-reading Gender in 1950s Melodrama.* Chapel Hill: University of North Carolina Press, 1991.

Cain, William E. "Presence and Power in *McTeague.*" In *American Realism: New Essays,* 199–214. Edited by Eric J. Sundquist. Baltimore: The Johns Hopkins University Press, 1982.

Capra, Frank. *The Name Above the Title: An Autobiography.* New York: MacMillan, 1971.

Carney, Raymond. *American Vision: The Films of Frank Capra.* Hanover, NH: University Press of New England, 1986.

Chafe, William H. *The Unfinished Journey: America Since World War II.* 3rd. ed. Oxford: Oxford University Press, 1995.

Chambers, John Whiteclay. *The Tyranny of Change: America in the Progressive Era, 1890–1920.* 2nd ed. New Brunswick, NJ: Rutgers University Press, 2004.

Christensen, Terry. *Reel Politics: American Political Movies from Birth of a Nation to Platoon.* New York: Basil Blackwell, Inc, 1987.

Citizen Kane. DVD. Directed by Orson Welles. RKO Pictures, 1941.

Cleveland, Grover. "Woman's Mission and Woman's Clubs." *Ladies Home Journal* 22 (May 1905).

Clockwatchers. DVD. Directed by Jill Sprecher. Goldcrest Films International, 1997.

Cohen, Lizabeth. *A Consumer's Republic: The Politics of Mass Consumption in Postwar America.* New York: Alfred A, Knopf, 2003.

Cook, David A. *Lost Illusions: American Cinema in the Shadow of Watergate and Vietnam, 1970–1979.* Vol. 9 of *History of the American Cinema.* Berkeley: University of California Press, 2002.

Coontz, Stephanie. *The Way We Never Were: American Families and the Nostalgia Trap.* New York: Basic Books, 1992.

Cooper, John Milton. *Pivotal Decades: The United States, 1900–1920.* New York: W. W. Norton & Company, 1990.

Costello, Donald P. "From Counterculture to Anticulture." *The Review of Politics* 34, no. 4 (October, 1972): 187–193.

Cott, Nancy. *The Bonds of Womanhood: "Woman's Sphere" in New England, 1780–1835.* 2nd ed. New Haven, CT: Yale University Press, 1997.

Crafton, Donald. *The Talkies: American Cinema's Transition to Sound, 1926–1931.* Vol. 4 of *History of the American Cinema.* Berkeley: University of California Press, 1999.

Crawford, Matthew B. *Shop Class as Soulcraft: an Inquiry into the Value of Work.* New York: The Penguin Press, 2009.

The Crowd. VHS. Directed by King Vidor. Metro-Goldwyn Mayer, 1928.

Cuordileone, K. A. "'Politics in an Age of Anxiety': Cold War Political Culture and the Crisis in American Masculinity, 1949–1960." *The Journal of American History* 87 (September 2000): 515–545.

Davidson, James W., and Mark H. Lytle. "Where Trouble Comes: History and Myth in the Films of Vietnam." In *After the Fact: The Art of Historical Detection,* 6th ed. Edited by James W. Davidson and Mark H. Lytle, 420–447. McGraw-Hill, 2009.

Deacy, Christopher. "Integration and Rebirth through Confrontation: *Fight Club* and *American Beauty* as Contemporary Religious Parables." *Journal of Contemporary Religion* 17, no. 1 (2002): 61–73.

Debs, Eugene V. "Capitalism and Socialism," 1912. *Eugene V. Debs Internet Archive.* http://www.marxists.org/archive/debs/ works/1912/ appeal.htm.

Deneen, Patrick J. "Awakening from the American Dream: The End of Escape in American Cinema?" *Perspectives on Political Science* 32, no. 2 (Spring 2002): 96–103.

Diggins, John Patrick. *Proud Decades: America in War and Peace, 1941–1960.* New York: W.W. Norton & Company, 1988.

Dirty Harry. DVD. Directed by Don Siegel. Warner Bros., 1971.

DuBois, Ellen Carol, and Lynn Dumenil. *Through Women's Eyes: An American History with Documents.* 2nd ed. Boston: Bedford/St. Martin's, 2009.

Eastwood, Clint. "Eastwood Talks Dirty Harry." *Playboy* interview. (February 1974). Available at http://www.thedirtiest.com/playboy.htm.

Easy Rider. DVD. Directed by Dennis Hopper. Columbia Pictures, 1969.

Edwards, Rebecca. *New Spirits: Americans in the Gilded Age, 1865–1905.* New York: Oxford University Press, 2006.

Engelhardt, Tom. *The End of Victory Culture: Cold War America and the Disillusioning of a Generation.* Amherst: University of Massachusetts Press, 1995.

Enstad, Nan. *Ladies of Labor, Girls of Adventure: Working Women, Popular Culture, and Labor Politics at the Turn of the Twentieth Century.* New York: Columbia University Press, 1999.

Falling Down. DVD. Directed by Joel Schumacher. Warner Bros., 1993.

Faludi, Susan. *Backlash: The Undeclared War against American Women.* New York: Crown Publishers, 1991.

_____. *Stiffed: The Betrayal of the American Man.* New York: Perennial Harper Collins, 2000.

Farber, David, ed. *The Sixties: from Memory to History.* Chapel Hill: University of North Carolina Press, 1994.

Fight Club. DVD. Directed by David Fincher. 20th Century–Fox, 1999.

Fink, Leon, ed. *Major Problems in the Gilded Age and the Progressive Era.* 2nd ed. New York: Houghton Mifflin Company, 2001.

_____. *Workingmen's Democracy: The Knights of Labor and American Democracy*. Urbana: University of Illinois Press, 1983.

Fitzhugh, George. *Cannibals All! Or, Slaves without Masters*. C. Vann Woodward, ed. Cambridge, MA: Belknap Press of Harvard University, 1960.

Force of Evil. DVD. Directed by Abraham Polonsky. Metro-Goldwyn-Mayer, 1948.

The Fountainhead. DVD. Directed by King Vidor. Warner Bros., 1949.

Friedan, Betty. *The Feminine Mystique*. New York: W.W. Norton, 1963.

Gilmore, David D. *Manhood in the Making: Cultural Concepts of Masculinity*. New Haven, CT: Yale University Press, 1990.

Gitlin, Todd. *The Sixties: Years of Hope, Days of Rage*. New York: Bantam Books, 1987.

Glenn, Susan A. *Female Spectacle: The Theatrical Roots of Modern Feminism*. Cambridge, MA: Harvard University Press, 2000.

Goldman, Eric F. *The Crucial Decade—And After: America, 1945–1960*. New York: Vintage Books, 1960.

Gomery, Douglas. "U.S. Film Exhibition: the Formation of a Big Business." In *The American Film Industry. Rev. ed.* Edited by Tino Balio, 218–228. Madison: University of Wisconsin Press, 1985.

Goodman, Paul. *Growing Up Absurd: Problems of Youth in the Organized System*. New York: Random House, 1956.

Gordon, Colin, ed. *Major Problems in American History, 1920–1945: Documents and Essays*. Boston: Houghton Mifflin Company, 1999.

The Graduate. DVD. Directed by Mike Nichols. Embassy Pictures, 1967.

The Great Depression. VHS. Episode one, "A Job at Ford's." Directed by Lyn Goldfarb and Stephen Stept. Boston: WGBH, Blackside Productions, 1993.

The Green Berets. DVD. Directed by John Wayne. Warner Bros., 1968.

Guide to the Records of the U.S. House of Representatives at the National Archives, 1789–1989. Record Group 233. Records of the Committees on Education and Labor. URL: http://www.archives.gov/legislative/guide/house/chapter-09-labor.html.

Haller, Max, and Markus Hadler. "How Social Relations and Structure Can Produce Happiness and Unhappiness: An International Comparative Analysis." *Social Indicators Research* 75, no. 2 (January 2006): 169–216.

Hausman, Vincent. "Envisioning the (W)hole 'Behind Things': Denying Otherness in *American Beauty*." *Camera Obscura* 19, no. 55 (January 2004): 112–149.

Hewison, David. "'Oh Rose, thou art sick!' Anti-individuation Forces in the Film *American Beauty*." *Journal of Analytical Psychology* 48 (2003): 683–704.

High Noon, DVD. Directed by Fred Zinneman. United Artists, 1952.

Hodgson, Godfrey. *America in our Time: from World War II to Nixon—What Happened and Why*. Princeton, NJ: Princeton University Press, 2005.

Hofstadter, Richard. *The Age of Reform: from Bryan to F.D.R.* New York: Vintage Books, 1954.

Howells, William Dean. *A Traveler from Altruria* New York: Sagamore Press, 1957.

Huston, Shaun. "Filming Postbourgeois Suburbia: *Office Space* and the New American Suburb." *The Journal of Popular Culture* 42, no. 3 (2009): 497–514.

It's a Wonderful Life. DVD. Directed by Frank Capra. Liberty Films, 1946.

Joe. DVD. Directed by John G. Avildsen. Cannon Films, 1970.

Johnny Guitar. DVD. Directed by Nicholas Ray. Republic Pictures, 1954.

Kaplan, Amy. *The Social Construction of*

American Realism. Chicago: University of Chicago Press, 1988.

Kapsis, Robert E., and Kathie Coblentz, eds. *Clint Eastwood Interviews.* Jackson: University Press of Mississippi, 1999.

Karlyn, Kathleen Rowe. "'Too Close for Comfort': *American Beauty* and the Incest Motif." *Cinema Journal* 44, no. 1 (Fall 2004): 69–93.

Kasson, John F. *Houdini, Tarzan, and the Perfect Man: The White Male Body and the Challenge of Modernity in America.* New York: Hill & Wang, 2001.

Kimmel, Michael S. *Manhood in America: A Cultural History,* 2nd ed. New York: Oxford University Press, 2006.

King, Jr., Dr. Martin Luther. "A Time to Break Silence." In *A Testament of Hope: The Essential Writings and Speeches of Martin Luther King, Jr.* Edited by James M. Washington. New York: HarperCollins Publishers, 1986.

Kolko, Gabriel. *The Triumph of Conservatism: A Reinterpretation of American History, 1900–1916.* New York: The Free Press, 1963.

Koszarski, Richard. *An Evening's Entertainment: The Age of the Silent Feature Picture, 1915–1928.* Vol. 3 of *History of the American Cinema.* Berkeley: University of California Press, 1994.

LaFeber, Walter. *America, Russia and the Cold War, 1945–1966.* New York: Wiley, 1967.

Lasch, Christopher. *The Culture of Narcissism: American Life in an Age of Diminishing Expectations.* New York: W. W. Norton & Company, 1979.

Law, Shirley. "Looking Closer: Structure, Style and Narrative in *American Beauty.*" *Screen Education* 43 (June 2006): 123–129.

Leuchtenburg, William. *The Perils of Prosperity, 1914–1932.* 2nd edition. Chicago: University of Chicago Press, 1993.

Lev, Peter. *The Fifties: Transforming the Screen, 1950–1959.* Vol. 7 of *History of the American Cinema.* Berkeley: University of California Press, 2003.

Leverenz, David. "Manhood, Humiliation and Public Life: Some Stories." *Southwest Review* 71 (Fall 1986): 442–462.

Lewis, Sinclair. *Babbitt.* New York: Harcourt, Brace and Company, 1922.

Licht, Walter. *Industrializing America: the Nineteenth Century.* Baltimore: Johns Hopkins University Press, 1995.

The Life and Times of Rosie the Riveter. DVD. Directed by Connie Field. Clarity Films, 2007.

Lipsitz, George. *Class and Culture in Cold War America: "A Rainbow at Midnight."* New York: Praeger, 1981.

_____. *Rainbow at Midnight: Labor and Culture in the 1940s.* Urbana: University of Illinois Press, 1994.

_____. *The Possessive Investment in Whiteness: How White People Profit from Identity Politics.* Philadelphia: Temple University Press, 1998.

Long, Elizabeth. *The American Dream and the Popular Novel.* Boston: Routledge & Kegan Paul, 1985.

Lost in America. DVD. Directed by Albert Brooks. Warner Bros., 1985.

Making Sense of the Sixties. "Seeds of the Sixties," episode 1. VHS. Directed by David Hoffman (WETA, 1991).

The Man in the Gray Flannel Suit. DVD. Directed by Nunnally Johnson. Twentieth Century–Fox, 1956.

May, Elaine Tyler. "Explosive Issues: Sex, Women, and the Bomb." In *Recasting America: Culture and Politics in the Age of Cold War.* Edited by Lary May, 154–170. Chicago: University of Chicago Press, 1988.

_____. *Homeward Bound: American Families in the Cold War Era.* New York: Basic Books, 1988.

May, Lary, ed. *Recasting America: Culture and Politics in the Age of Cold War.* Chicago: University of Chicago Press, 1989.

_____. *Screening Out the Past: the Birth of Mass Culture and the Motion Picture Industry.* Chicago: University of Chicago Press, 1980.

_____. *The Big Tomorrow: Hollywood and the Politics of the American Way.* Chicago: University of Chicago Press, 2000.

McElvaine, Robert S. *The Great Depression: America, 1929–1941.* New York: Times Books, 1993.

McKitrick, Casey. "'I Laughed and Cringed at the Same Time': Shaping Pedophilic Discourse Around *American Beauty* and Happiness." *Velvet Light Trap* 47, no. 2 (Spring 2003): 3–12.

Melville, Herman. "Bartleby, the Scrivener: A Story of Wall Street." In *Eight American Writers.* Edited by Norman Foerster and Robert P. Falk, 808–839. New York: W.W. Norton & Company, Inc., 1963.

Meyerowitz, Joanne, ed. *Not June Cleaver: Women and Gender in Postwar America, 1945–1960.* Philadelphia: Temple University Press, 1994.

Mills, C. Wright. *The Power Elite.* New York: Oxford University Press, 1956.

_____. *White Collar: The American Middle Classes.* New York: Oxford University Press, 1951.

Mintz, Steven, and Randy W. Roberts, eds. *Hollywood's America: Twentieth-Century America Through Film.* 4th ed. West Sussex, UK: Wiley-Blackwell, 2010.

Monaco, Paul. *The Sixties: 1960–1969.* Vol. 8 of *History of the American Cinema.* Berkeley: University of California Press, 2003.

Montgomery, David. *Workers Control in America: Studies in the History of Work, Technology, and Labor Struggles.* Cambridge: Cambridge University Press, 1979.

Montgomery, Maureen E. *Displaying Women: Spectacles of Leisure in Edith Wharton's New York.* New York: Routledge, 1998.

Morgenson, Gretchen, and Joshua Rosner. *Reckless Endangerment: How Outsized Ambition, Greed, and Corruption Led to Economic Armageddon.* New York: Times Books, 2011.

Munby, Jonathan. "'Manhattan Melodrama's'Art of the Weak': Telling History from the Other Side in the 1930s Talking Gangster Film." *Journal of American Studies* 30, no. 1 (April 1996): 101–118.

_____. *Public Enemies, Public Heroes: Screening the Gangster from Little Caesar to Touch of Evil.* Chicago: University of Chicago Press, 1999.

Musser, Charles. *The Emergence of Cinema: The American Screen to 1907.* Vol. 1 of *History of the American Cinema.* Berkeley: University of California Press, 1994.

National Film Preservation Board. http://www.loc.gov/film/filmnfr.html.

Navasky, Victor S. *Naming Names.* New York: Viking Press, 1980.

Nelson, Dana D. *National Manhood: Capitalist Citizenship and the Imagined Fraternity of White Men.* Durham, NC: Duke University Press, 1998.

Noble, David W. *Death of a Nation: American Culture and the End of Exceptionalism.* Minneapolis: University of Minnesota Press, 2002.

_____. *The End of American History: Democracy, Capitalism, and the Metaphor of Two Worlds in Anglo-American Historical Writing, 1880–1980.* Minneapolis: University of Minnesota Press, 1985.

Nystrom, Derek. "Hard Hats and Movie Brats: Auteurism and the Class Politics of the New Hollywood." *Cinema Journal* 43, no. 3 (spring 2004): 18–41.

Office Space. DVD. Directed by Mike Judge. 20th Century–Fox, 1999.

Our Daily Bread. VHS. Directed by King Vidor. King W. Vidor Productions, 1934.

Palahniuk, Chuck. *Fight Club.* New

York: Henry Holt and Company, LLC, 1996.

_____. Interactive on-line question and answer session with public via ABC News. URL: http://abcnews.go.com/onair/DailyNews/chatpalahniuk991116.html.

Parrish, Michael E. *Anxious Decades: America in Prosperity and Depression, 1920–1941*. New York: W. W. Norton & Company, 1992.

Patai, Daphne, ed. *Looking Backward, 1988–1888: Essays on Edward Bellamy*. Amherst: University of Massachusetts Press, 1988.

Patterns. DVD. Directed by Fielder Cook. United Artists, 1956.

Peis, Kathy. *Cheap Amusements: Working Women and Leisure in Turn-of-the-Century New York*. Philadelphia: Temple University Press, 1986.

Pfeil, Fred. *White Guys: Studies in Postmodern Domination and Difference*. New York: Verso, 1995.

Pizer, Donald, ed. *Documents of American Realism and Naturalism*. Carbondale: Southern Illinois University Press, 1998.

_____. *Twentieth-Century American Literary Naturalism: An Interpretation*. Carbondale: Southern Illinois University Press, 1982.

Polonsky, Abraham. Interview in *Tender Comrades: A Backstory of the Hollywood Blacklist*. Patrick McGilligan and Paul Buhle, eds., 481–494. New York: St. Martin's Press, 1997.

The Power and the Prize. Directed by Henry Koster. Metro-Goldwyn-Mayer, 1956.

Prince, Stephen. *A New Pot of Gold: Hollywood under the Electronic Rainbow, 1980–1989*. Vol. 10 of *History of the American Cinema*. Berkeley: University of California Press, 2002.

Rabin, Kathy. "American Beauty???" *Journal of Family Social Work* 6, no. 1 (2001): 97–99.

Reich, Robert B. *Supercapitalism: The Transformation of Business, Democracy, and Everyday Life*. New York: Vintage Books edition, 2008.

The Richest Man in the World: Andrew Carnegie. VHS. Directed by Austin Hoyt. WGBH Educational Foundation, 1997.

Riesman, David. *The Lonely Crowd: A Study of the Changing American Character*. New Haven, CT: Yale University Press, 1950.

Roberts, Randy, and David Welky. "Coming to Terms with the Vietnam War: A Sacred Mission: Oliver Stone and Vietnam." In *Hollywood's America: Twentieth-Century America Through Film*. 4th ed., 281–300.

Robinson, Sally. *Marked Men: White Masculinity in Crisis*. New York: Columbia University Press, 2000.

Roediger, David R. *The Wages of Whiteness: Race and the Making of the American Working Class*. New York: Verso, 1991.

Rogin, Michael Paul. *Ronald Reagan, The Movie: and Other Episodes in Political Demonology*. Berkeley: University of California Press, 1987.

Roosevelt, Theodore. New Nationalism Speech, 1910. *TeachingAmericanHistory.org*. http://teachingamericanhistory.org/library/index.asp?document=501.

Rosenbloom, Nancy J. "From Regulation to Censorship: Film and Political Culture in New York in the Early Twentieth Century." *The Journal of the Gilded Age and the Progressive Era* 3, no. 4 (October 2004): 369–406.

Ross, Steven J. *Working-Class Hollywood: Silent Film and the Shaping of Class in America*. Princeton, NJ: Princeton University Press, 1998.

Ryan, Michael, and Douglas Kelner. "Films of the Late 1960s and Early 1970s: from Counterculture to Counterrevolution, 1967–1971." In *Hollywood's America: Twentieth-Century*

America Through Film, 255–263. 4th ed. West Sussex, UK: Wiley-Blackwell, 2010, 255–263.

Schatz, Thomas. *Boom and Bust: American Cinema in the 1940s.* Vol. 6 of *History of the American Cinema.* Berkeley: University of California Press, 1999.

Schlesinger Jr., Arthur M. *The Vital Center: The Politics of Freedom.* Boston: Houghton Mifflin, 1949.

Schultz, Robert T. "Celluloid History: Postwar Society in Postwar Popular Culture." *American Studies* 31 (spring 1990): 41–63.

_____. "Illusions of Consensus and Conformity in Postwar America." *American History.* ABC-CLIO, 2011. Web.

_____. *Conflict and Change: Minneapolis Truck Drivers Make a Dent in the New Deal.* Prospect Heights, IL: Waveland Press, 2000.

_____. "White Guys Who Prefer Not To: From Passive Resistance ('Bartleby') to Terrorist Acts (*Fight Club*)." *The Journal of Popular Culture* 44, no. 3 (June 2011): 583–605.

The Searchers. DVD. Directed by John Ford. Warner Bros., 1956.

Sedgwick, John, and Michael Pokorny. "The Film Business in the United States and Britain During the 1930s." *Economic History Review* 58, no. 1 (February 2005): 79–112.

Seed, David. "The Flight from the Good Life: *Fahrenheit 451* in the Context of Postwar American Dystopias." *Journal of American Studies* 28, no. 2 (August 1994): 225–240.

Simon, Bryant. "Race Reactions: African American Organizing, Liberalism, and White Working-Class Politics in Postwar South Carolina. " In *Jumpin' Jim Crow: Southern Politics from Civil War to Civil Rights.* Edited by Jane Dailey, Glenda Elizabeth Gilmore and Bryant Simon, 239–259. Princeton, NJ: Princeton University Press, 2000.

Sklar, Kathryn Kish. *Catharine Beecher: A Study in American Domesticity.* New Haven, CT: Yale University Press, 1973.

Sklar, Martin J. *The Corporate Reconstruction of American Capitalism, 1890–1916: The Market, The Law, and Politics.* Cambridge: Cambridge University Press, 1988.

Sklar, Robert. *City Boys: Cagney, Bogart, Garfield.* Princeton, NJ: Princeton University Press, 1992.

_____. *Movie-Made America: A Cultural History of American Movies.* New York: Vintage Books, 1976.

Sloan, Kay. "Silent Cinema as Social Criticism: Front Page Movies." In *Hollywood's America: Twentieth-Century America Through Film.* 4th ed. Edited by Steven Mintz and Randy W. Roberts, 31–42. West Sussex, UK: Wiley-Blackwell, 2010.

Slotkin, Richard. *Gunfighter Nation: The Myth of the Frontier in Twentieth-Century America.* Norman: University of Oklahoma Press, 1998.

Smith College web site: http://www.smith.edu/about_smithtradition.php.

Spigner, Dr. Clarence. "Racist Cops on Screen: Cinema Imitates Life or Vise Versa?" http://www.blackpast.org/?q=blog/clarence/ racist-cops-on-screen-cinema-imitates-life-or-vice-versa.

Steinbeck, John. *The Grapes of Wrath.* New York: Penguin Books, 1976.

Stevenson, Adlai. "A Purpose for Modern Woman." *Woman's Home Companion* (September 1955): 29–31.

Streible, Dan. *The Birth of Whiteness: Race and the Emergence of U.S. Cinema.* New Brunswick, NJ: Rutgers University Press, 1996.

Sundquist, Eric J., ed. *American Realism: New Essays.* Baltimore: Johns Hopkins University Press, 1982.

Thoreau, Henry David. *Walden and Other Writings by Henry David Thoreau.* Edited by Joseph Wood Krutch. New York: Bantam Classics, 1981.

Time Magazine, December 26, 2011, vol. 178, No. 25.

To Kill a Mockingbird. DVD. Directed by Robert Mulligan, 1962. Universal Pictures.

Tocqueville, Alexis de. *Democracy in America*. Vol. II. Phillips Bradley edition. New York: Vintage Books, 1945.

Toth, Csaba. "The Transatlantic Dialogue: 19th-Century American Utopianism and Europe." PhD diss. University of Minnesota, 1992.

_____. "Utopianism as Americanism." *American Quarterly* 45, no. 4 (December 1993): 649–658.

Trachtenberg, Alan. *The Incorporation of America: Culture and Society in the Gilded Age*. New York: Hill and Wang, 1982.

Tripp, Daniel. "'Wake Up!': Narratives of Masculine Epiphany in Millennial Cinema." *Quarterly Review of Film and Video* 22, no. 2 (April-June 2005): 181–188.

Variety Film Reviews, 1907–1980. Vols. 1–16. New York: Garland Publishing, 1983.

Vasey, Ruth. *The World According to Hollywood, 1918–1939*. Exeter, UK: University of Exeter Press, 1997.

Vaughn, Stephen. "Morality and Entertainment: the Origins of the Motion Picture Production Code." *The Journal of American History* 77, no. 1 (June 1990): 39–65.

Vest, George G. "Remarks." *Congressional Record*. 49th Congress, 2nd Sess. January 25, 1887, 986.

Vineberg, Steve. "'American Beauty': No Joy in the Gilded Suburbs." *Chronicle of Higher Education* 46, no. 10 (October 29, 1999): B10.

Wall Street. DVD. Directed by Oliver Stone. 20th Century–Fox, 1987.

Welter, Barbara. "The Cult of True Womanhood, 1820–1860." *American Quarterly* 18 (1966): 151–174.

Whitfield, Steven J. *The Culture of the Cold War*. Baltimore: The Johns Hopkins University Press, 1991.

Whyte, Jr., William H. *The Organization Man*. New York: Simon & Schuster, 1956.

Will Success Spoil Rock Hunter. Directed by Frank Tashlin. 20th Century–Fox, 1957.

Williams, William Appleman. *The Contours of American History*. New York: New Viewpoints, 1973.

Wilmington, Michael. "Nicholas Ray's *Johnny Guitar*." *Velvet Light Trap* 12 (Spring 1974): 21.

Wilson, Christopher P. *White Collar Fictions: Class and Social Representation in American Literature, 1885–1925*. Athens: University of Georgia Press, 1992.

Wilson, Sloan. *The Man in the Gray Flannel Suit*. New York: Simon & Schuster, 1955.

Wilson, Woodrow. The New Freedom, 1913. *TeachingAmericanHistory.org*.

Wright, Will. *Sixguns and Society: A Structural Study of the Western*. Berkeley, University of California Press, 1975.

Index

Numbers in **bold italics** indicate pages with photographs.

225